iWoz

iWoz

Computer Geek to Cult Icon:
Getting to the Core of Apple's Inventor

Steve Wozniak
with
Gina Smith

headline
review

First published in 2006 by W.W. Norton

First published in 2006 in Great Britain
by Headline Review
An imprint of Headline Publishing Group

1

Cataloguing in Publication Data is available from the British Library

HB: ISBN 0 7553 1406 9 (10 digit)
ISBN 978 0 7553 1406 5 (13 digit)

TPB: ISBN 0 7553 1407 7 (10 digit)
ISBN 978 0 7553 1407 2 (13 digit)

Printed and bound in Australia by Griffin Press

Headline's policy is to use papers that are natural, renewable and recyclable products and
made from wood grown in sustainable forests. The logging and manufacturing processes are
expected to conform to the environmental regulations of the country of origin.

Headline Publishing Group
A division of Hodder Headline
338 Euston Road, London NW1 3BH

www.reviewbooks.co.uk
www.hodderheadline.com

TO OUR
mothers & fathers

Contents

iWoz

Chapter 1

Our Gang: The Electronics Kids

You usually start books like this by talking about your parents: who they were, or what they did for a living before you were born or while you were growing up. But the thing is, I never did know for sure what my dad did for a living. As early as I can remember, my brother, sister, and I all had to grow up with this secret. And as secrets go, oh man, this one was huge. We weren't even allowed to talk about his work or ask questions about it in the house. The conversation was strictly off-limits.

I did know Dad was an engineer, and I knew he worked in the missile program at Lockheed. That much he said, but that was pretty much it. Looking back, I figure that because this was in the late 1950s and early 1960s at the height of the Cold War, when the space program was so hot and top secret and all, probably that's why he couldn't tell me anything more about it. What he worked on, what he did every day at work, he'd say absolutely nothing about. Even up to the day he died, he didn't give so much as a hint.

I remember how in 1960, when I was ten, I finally understood why he'd never be able to. He said it was because he was a man of his word. Once, when he was explaining why you should never lie under oath in court, that's what he said: "I'm a man of my word."

Now, on my own, I managed to put together little bits and pieces. I remember seeing NASA-type pictures of rockets, and stuff related to the Polaris missile being shot from submarines or something, but he was just so closemouthed about it, the door slammed there.

I tell you this because I'm trying to point out that my dad believed in honesty. Extreme honesty. Extreme ethics, really. That's the biggest thing he taught me. He used to tell me it was worse to lie about doing something bad under oath than it was to actually do something bad, even like murdering someone. That really sunk in. I never lie, even to this day. Not even a little. Unless you count playing pranks on people, which I don't. That's comedy. Entertainment doesn't count. A joke is different from a lie, even if the difference is kind of subtle.

The other thing my dad taught me was a lot about electronics. Boy, do I owe a lot to him for this. He first started telling me things and explaining things about electronics when I was really, really young—before I was even four years old. This is before he had that top secret job at Lockheed, when he worked at Electronic Data Systems in the Los Angeles area. One of my first memories is his taking me to his workplace on a weekend and showing me a few electronic parts, putting them on a table with me so I got to play with them and look at them. I can still picture him standing there working on some kind of equipment. I don't know if he was soldering or what, but I do remember him hooking something up to something else that looked like a little TV set. I now know it was an oscilloscope. And he told me he was trying to get something done, trying to get the picture on the screen with a line (it was a waveform) stable-looking so he could show his boss that his design worked.

And I remember sitting there and being so little, and thinking: Wow, what a great, great world he's living in. I mean, that's all I thought: Wow. For people who know how to do this stuff—how to take these little parts and make them work together to do something—well, these people must be the smartest people in the world. That was really what went through my head, way back then.

Now, I was, of course, too young at that point to decide that I wanted to be an engineer. That came a few years later. I hadn't even been exposed to science fiction or books about inventors yet, but just then, at that moment, I could see right before my eyes that whatever my dad was doing, whatever it was, it was important and good.

●   ○   ●

A couple of years later—I was six, maybe seven—I remember Dad demonstrating another piece of equipment for a bunch of people at his company. A big group of people was there. These weren't just people he worked with, but also our whole family and other families, too. I think it was just a drilling machine he was demonstrating.

And my dad, even though I was just this little kid, told me I would be the one to get to throw the switch to turn it on. He said I had to do it at the exact right time.

I remember worrying about how I would know when the right time was and thinking: Now? Now? When should I do this? Now? My dad was busy talking and joking with the families of the guys who worked there, who were going to watch me do it. Then suddenly it felt like the right time. I can't explain why, but I just felt inside it was the right time. So I went ahead and threw the switch.

I heard a lot of laughter, and I didn't know why. Suddenly I realized I had thrown the switch too early. Now that I look back on this, I see this might be the beginning of my shyness, you know, getting butterflies in your stomach because you're afraid of failure when you have to talk or something.

Or maybe that was my first prank, but it was definitely unintentional!

• ○ •

But there were also lessons from my dad, serious lessons that got me an incredibly early start in engineering. These lessons would always start because I'd ask a question. And I had a lot of questions.

Because my dad was an engineer, there were all kinds of interesting things lying around my house. And when you're in a house and there are resistors lying around everywhere, you ask, "What's that? What's a resistor?" And my dad would always give me an answer, a really good answer even a seven-year-old could understand. He was just an extremely good teacher and communicator.

He never started out by trying to explain from the top down what a resistor is. He started from the beginning, going all the way back to atoms and electrons, neutrons, and protons. He explained what they were and how everything was made from those. I remember we actually spent weeks and weeks talking about different types of atoms and then I learned how electrons can actually flow through things—like wires. Then, finally, he explained to me how the resistors work—not by calculations, because who can do calculations when you're a second grader, but by real commonsense pictures and explanations. You see, he gave me classical electronics training from the beginning. For engineers, there's a point in life when you understand things like how a resistor works. Usually it comes much later for people than it did for me. By the fourth grade, I really did understand things like that.

And my dad was always around to help me understand still more things. Like light. How does a lightbulb work? I wanted to know. Not many people my age knew—probably most people who are grown up still don't. But he explained it to me: first how lights are made, then how electrons went through wires, and how those were what made a lightbulb glow. And I wanted to know how, how did it glow? So he went back to the beginning, explaining to me how Thomas Edison invented lightbulbs and what he had to figure out to do it. He realized that basically you had to create a vacuum—it had to be a vacuum because if there were oxygen in it, the wire would just burn up when it got hot. So this vacuum (remember, a vacuum has no air in it) is in this little bulb, and the point was to get heat—by moving a lot of electrons through a wire—into it.

And the more electrons that go through the wire—that is, the higher the current—the brighter the lightbulb will glow. Cool! I was eight or even younger when I understood this, and knowing it made me feel different from everyone else, different from all the kids I knew. I started to feel as if I knew secrets no one else knew.

I have to point out here that at no time did my dad make a big deal about my progress in electronics. He taught me stuff, sure, but he always acted as if it was just normal for me. By the sixth grade, I was really advanced in math and science, everyone knew it, and I'd been tested for IQ and they told us it was 200-plus. But my dad never acted like this was something he should push me along with. He pulled out a blackboard from time to time, a tiny little blackboard we had in our house on Edmonton Avenue, and when I asked, he would answer anything and make diagrams for it. I remember how he showed me what happened if you put a plus voltage into a transistor and got a minus voltage out the other end of the transistor. There must have been an inverter, a type of logic gate. And he even physically taught me how to make an AND gate and an OR gate out of parts he got—parts called diodes and resistors. And he showed me how they needed a transistor in between to amplify the signal and connect the output of one gate to the input of the other.

To this very moment, that is the way every single digital device on the planet works at its most basic level.

He took the time—a lot of time—to show me those few little things. They were little things to him, even though Fairchild and Texas Instruments had just developed the transistor only a decade earlier.

It's amazing, really, to think that my dad taught me about transistors back when almost no one saw anything but vacuum tubes. So he was at the top of the state of the art, probably because his secret job put him in touch with such advanced technology. So I ended up being at the state of the art, too.

The way my dad taught me, though, was not to rote-memorize how parts are connected to form a gate, but to learn where the electrons flowed to make the gate do its job. To truly internalize and understand what is going on, not just read stuff off some blueprint or out of some book.

Those lessons he taught me still drive my intelligence and my methods for all the computer designs I do today.

•   ○   •

But even with all of this—all the lessons and explanations a kid could understand—I want to tell you about the single most important lesson he taught me. Because this is what I have always hung on to, more than even the honesty thing. He drilled into me what it means to be an engineer. What I am talking about is what it means to be an engineer's engineer. A serious engineer. I so clearly remember him telling me that engineering was the highest level of importance you could reach in the world, that someone who could make electrical devices that do something good for people takes society to a new level. He told me that as an engineer, you can change your world and change the way of life for lots and lots of people.

To this day, I still believe engineers are among the key people in the world. And I believe that I will be one forever, and I have dedicated my whole life to engineering. I realize that when engineers create something there is often an argument that the creation could be used for bad or good. Like the atomic bomb. My dad had the opinion that change is what moves the world forward and that's the path we're on and basically all change is good. That any device people want is good and should be made and not get stopped by governments or anyone else. And I came to that same view when I was very young, ten or maybe younger. Inside my head—and this is what has really stayed with me—I came to the view that basically, yes, technology is good and not bad.

People argue about this all the time, but I have no doubts about it at all. I believe technology moves us forward. Always.

●　○　●

Now, you've got to realize that, electronics-wise, 1950s Northern California was another world compared to what things are like now. For example, where I was growing up, everybody who owned TVs and radios literally had to replace the bad vacuum tubes inside them themselves. Grocery stores had these giant tube testers that everyone in the family—kids, parents, everyone—knew how to use. I mean, we knew that when the TV went bad you opened it up and then took all the tubes to the grocery store, where you'd insert them in that machine. There was a meter on it that would tell you if the tube was good, weak, or bad. You could buy replacements for the bad tubes right there in the grocery store and take them home to reinsert in your TV.

In case you're too young to remember, this was a clunky solution, but it worked pretty well. The only bad part was the human effort this required—taking out the tubes, testing each of them, putting them back in. So much work! I used to look at those tubes, trying to take apart what they were made of. They were just little filaments—they ran hot and could burn out like a lightbulb. It was as simple as that. I remember wondering what it would take to build a tube that wouldn't burn out, or a TV that didn't need tubes to work at all. How much easier they would be for people.

That's how I was, how I've always been—and still am, it seems. I've always had this technical side and then this human side. For instance, I remember telling my dad when I was ten that when I grew up, I wanted to be an engineer like him, but I also remember saying I wanted to be a fifth-grade teacher, like Miss Skrak at my school. Combining the human and the technical turned out to be the main thing for me later on. I mean, even when it came down to something like building a computer, I remember watching all those geeks who just wanted to do the technical side, to just put some chips together so the design worked.

But I wanted to put chips together like an artist, better than anyone else could and in a way that would be the absolute most usable by humans. That was my goal when I built the first computer, the one that later became the Apple I. It was the first computer to use a keyboard so you could type onto it, and the first to use a screen you could look at. The idea of usable technology was something that was kind of born in my head as a kid, when I had this fantasy that I could someday build machines people could use. And it happened!

Anyway, anyone you meet who knows me will tell you that that is exactly me—an engineer, but an engineer who worries about people a lot.

● ○ ●

According to my birth certificate, my full name is Stephan Gary Wozniak, born in 1950 to my dad, Francis Jacob Wozniak (everyone called him Jerry), and to my mom, Margaret Louise Wozniak. My mother said she meant to name me Stephen with an *e*, but the birth certificate was wrong. So Stephen with an e is what I go by now.

My dad was from Michigan; Mom was from Washington State. My dad and his brother, who later became a Catholic priest, were raised in a strict and pious Catholic household. But by the time my parents had me—I'm the oldest of three—my dad had rebelled against that: the Catholicism, I mean. So I never got any exposure to religion. Church, mass, communion. What is that? Seriously, I couldn't tell you.

But from the earliest age, I had a lot of conversations with my parents about social policies and how things work. As for religion, if I asked, my dad would say, no, no, he was scientific. Science was the religion. We had discussions about science and truth and honesty, the first discussions of many that formed my values. And what he told me was, he just wanted things to be testable. He thought that to see if something is true, the most important thing is to run experiments, to see what the truth is, and then you call it real. You don't just read something in a book or hear someone saying something and just believe it, not ever.

I eventually came to conclude that, yes, I believed the same thing. And at a super young age, I knew I would do something scientific when I grew up, too.

• ○ •

I forgot to mention before that my dad was kind of famous, in his own way. He was a really successful football player at Caltech. People used to tell me all the time that they used to go to the games just to see Jerry Wozniak play. And my mom, she was great to me and my younger brother and sister. She'd be home when we came home from school, and she was always really pleasant and funny and interesting and gave us stuff to eat that was special to us. And was she ever funny! I think it was from her—definitely not my dad—that I got this sense of humor of mine. The pranks I like to play, and the jokes. I have been playing pranks on people for years and years. And my mom, well, I guess you could thank her for that. She just has this wonderful sense of humor.

When I was in the sixth grade in 1962, my mother was big into Republican politics. She was a huge supporter of Richard Nixon, who was running for governor of California, and there was some event in San Jose where Nixon was speaking and she said, "Oh, Steve, why don't you come along?" And she had a plan, a joke I would do. She wanted me to meet him and tell him, opening up a piece of paper, that I represented the Ham Radio Operators of Serra School, and that our group unanimously supported Richard Nixon's election for governor. The joke was, I was the only sixth-grade ham radio operator in the school, probably in the whole state. But I did it. I walked up to Nixon and presented the paper, which we literally wrote with a crayon just before leaving home.

I said, "I have something for you." Nixon was really gracious, I thought. He seemed kind, and he smiled at me. He signed one of my schoolbooks I had with me, and even gave me the pen he signed it with. About twenty flashbulbs went off, and I ended up on the front page of the *San Jose Mercury News* for this. Me! The only ham radio operator at Serra School and probably the youngest one in the whole state, representing a club made up of nobody but me, presenting a fake certificate like it was the real thing. And everyone believed it. Wow!

So it was funny and everything, but something bugged me, and I'm going to tell you that it still bugs me to this day. Why did nobody get the joke? Doesn't anybody check facts? The newspaper cutline said something like, "Sixth grader Steve Wozniak represents a school group that's for Nixon." They didn't get that there was no school group, that it was all a joke my mom made up. It made me think that you could tell a newspaperperson or a politician anything, and they would just believe you. That shocked me—this was a joke they took for a fact without even thinking twice about it. I learned then that you can tell people things—crazy jokes and stories—and people will usually believe them.

● ○ ●

We spent most of my early years in Southern California, where my dad worked as an engineer at various companies before the secret job at Lockheed.

But where I really grew up was Sunnyvale, right in the heart of what everyone now calls Silicon Valley. Back then, it was called Santa Clara Valley. I moved there when I was seven. It was all just really agricultural. It was totally different from the way it is now. There were fruit orchards everywhere. Our street, Edmonton Avenue, was just a short one-block street bordered by fruit orchards on three of four sides. So pretty much anywhere you drove on your bike you'd end up in an apricot, cherry, or plum orchard. And I especially remember the apricots. Every house on my block had a bunch of apricot trees in their yard—our house had seven of them—and in the fall the apricots would get all soft and kind of splatter wherever they landed. You can imagine what great projectile weapons they made.

When I think of that street, looking back, I think it was the most beautiful place you could imagine growing up. It wasn't as crowded back then, and boy, was it easy to get around. It was as moderate of temperature as anywhere else you could find. In fact, right around the time I moved there—this was 1958—I remember my mother showing me national articles declaring it to be the best climate in America. And as I said, since the whole place had barely been developed, there were huge orchards every which way you went.

Edmonton Avenue was actually a small Eichler subdivision—Eichler homes of that period were kind of famous for being architecturally interesting homes in middle price ranges. They stand out as special homes to this day. And the families in them were a lot like mine—middle class, with dads commuting to work at the new electronics and engineering companies starting up, and moms at home. Because of that, and the fact that a bunch of my friends could pretty easily get electronics parts and all kinds of wires from our dads' garages or company warehouses, I thought of us as the Electronics Kids. We grew up playing with radios and walkie-talkies and weird-looking antennas on our roofs. We played baseball and ran around, too. A lot.

I remember when I was in the fifth grade I was really athletic. I was always being told I was the best runner, the top athlete in school, the best baseball player, and I was really popular because of all that. But electronics was really my life, and I loved devising all kinds of projects with the Electronics Kids.

In fourth grade for Christmas, I got the most amazing gift from my parents. It was an electronics hobby kit, and it had all these great switches and wires and lights. I learned so much playing with that stuff. And it was because of that kit that I was able to do the neatest things with the Electronics Kids. I was the key kid in designing a house-to-house intercom connecting about six of our houses.

The first thing to do was to get the equipment we needed. The main thing was wire. But where were a bunch of kids supposed to get yards and yards of wire? And how we got it—it was just unbelievable. One of the guys in my group, Bill Werner, literally walked up to a phone guy and asked him if he could have some telephone wire. He'd seen long spools of it in the guy's truck, so he just asked him for one of them. I don't know why, but the telephone guy just gave it to him, saying, "Here's a cord, kid."

What Bill got was a spool of wire about a foot in diameter. It was a lot, a whole lot, of wire. It was two-wire cable, solid copper wire inside of plastic insulation in the colors white and brown, twisted every inch or so to keep the two wires together and to minimize electrical noise from being picked up. Think of it as a plus wire and a minus wire. If some electrical interference is strong, it gets picked up equally by the plus and minus wires due to their being twisted. The point is that there is never a single wire that is always slightly closer to the interference signal. The plus and minus wires serve to cancel out the interference. You get as much minus as plus. That's how telephone cords work, as I found out from this. It is also where the term "twisted-pair" comes from.

And so then I figured out what to do with all this cord, designing on paper really careful lines with my different-colored pens. And I figured out where the switches would be, and how we would connect carbon microphones (that's how microphones were back then) and buzzers and lights so we kids wouldn't be waking our parents up with loud noises that would let them know what was up. We had to make sure we could do this in absolute secrecy, and that we kids could turn the buzzers off at night so we could wake ourselves up just by the light.

Once we finished the design, the bunch of us rode our bikes down to Sunnyvale Electronics, the local store and hangout for kids like us. We bought all this neat stuff, the microphones and the buzzers and the switches, you name it.

The next thing we did was connect the wire between all the houses. There were these wooden fences that separated all the houses on our short little street, and we just went along the fence in broad daylight, stringing this wire along and stapling it in. You know, it's possible that putting staples into wire would short it out. We were so lucky that didn't happen. And we stapled that wire all the way up the block—from one of my friends' houses to mine, and then I set up my switch box, drilled some holes in it, mounted some switches, and you know what? It worked! So then we had a house-to-house secret intercom system so we could talk to each other in the middle of the night.

We were about eleven or twelve then, so I'm not trying to convince you this was a professional modern engineering system, but it really worked. It was just a tremendous success for me.

In the beginning, we used it to call each other, I guess it was just so cool to be able to talk to each other. We'd call each other up and say things like, "Hey, this is cool! Can you hear me?" Or, "Hey, press your call button, let's see if it works." Or, "Try my buzzer out, give me a call." That was about the first week or two, and after that we started using it as a way to sneak out at night.

It didn't ring in this case, it had to quietly buzz, and it had to work on lights. So Bill Werner or one of the other guys would signal me, or I would signal one of them, and we had a code that would mean different things. I can't tell you how many nights I woke up to that buzzer or a light thinking: Oh boy, we're going out tonight!

We were a group of kids who loved climbing out our windows and sneaking out at night. Maybe it was just to talk, or go out and ride bikes, or sometimes it was to toilet-paper people's houses. Usually girls' houses. Ha. We'd go out in the middle of the night and say things to each other like, "Does anyone know anyone who has a house we should toilet-paper tonight?" To tell you the truth, I never had any idea who we should toilet-paper—I never thought like that—but the other guys usually had someone in mind.

And then we would go to the all-night store and try to buy, like, twenty-five rolls of toilet paper. I remember the clerk saying, "Hey, why do I get the feeling that this isn't to be used for its intended purpose?" I laughed and told him that we all had diarrhea. And he sold it to us.

Chapter 2

The Logic Game

I did a lot of reading at night when I was a kid, and one of my absolute favorites was the Tom Swift Jr. series. I would just eat up those books so quickly; new issues would come out a couple of times a month and I'd devour them. I don't think it would be exaggerating at all to say he was truly my hero.

Now, Tom Swift Jr. was this kid—a teenager, actually—older than me but still a kid like me. So I looked up to him. And he was also a scientist/engineer who got to build things in a laboratory. Anything Tom wanted he could build, and he had his dad to help him with things. He'd go in and hook wires together and make contraptions at a company he and his dad owned. So Tom had his own company, he had his own modes of travel, and he had his best friend named Bud Barclay. Anyway, in my opinion, Tom Swift Jr. had the perfect life. And whenever there was a crisis on Earth, any kind of conflict that needed handling, he sprang into action. Say the authorities on Earth had detected some alien energy source and the only way to hold it back would be with a plasma field. Well, Tom Swift Jr. would build a plasma field. He could build a submarine if he wanted to. There was no limit to what he could build. I remember once he built a spaceship to win a race around the Earth to get the money to do something good—you know, something good for the planet and all the people on it.

That was the kind of thing I wanted to do—build something that would end up allowing me to do something really good for people. I wanted to be a do-gooder from the start, just like Tom Swift Jr. was.

Well, my mom set a curfew at 9 p.m. every night. But after she turned the lights out, I used the light from this little streetlight outside my window to read. It hit my floor in one certain space. I would put the Tom Swift Jr. book down there on the floor where the light shone in, then put my head over the edge of the bed so I could read it late, late into the night. I wanted to be just like Tom Swift Jr.

And like Tom Swift Jr., I did work with my dad a lot on projects. In fact, my very first project—the crystal radio I built when I was six—was really all because of my dad. It took me a very long

My Hero

Tom Swift Jr. was the hero of a whole series of children's adventure novels published by the same people (Stratemeyer Publishing) that did the Nancy Drew and Hardy Boys titles.

James Lawrence, who said he had a deep interest in science and technology, was the author of most of the titles. I mentioned Bud Barclay already, Tom Swift Jr.'s best friend, but the stories had other elements in common. Anyone who's read them may remember dastardly spies from Eastern European countries like "Brungaria," and an amazingly capable element called "Tomasite," which could make anything atomic-powered.

One famous plot—I believe it was in book 22—involved scientifically regenerated dinosaurs. That was decades before *Jurassic Park*.

time in my life to appreciate the influence he had on me. He started when I was really young, helping me with these kinds of projects.

•   ◦   •

My dad's and my relationship was always pretty much about electronics. Later, it became about what I did as an engineer working at Hewlett-Packard on calculators, or on the first computers I built at Apple. But first, for years and years, it was all about what Dad did in engineering. I watched, listened, and worked with him. It was about how fast he could show me things and how fast I could learn them.

Dad was always helping me put science projects together, as far back as I can remember. When I was six, he gave me that crystal radio kit I mentioned. It was just a little project where you take a penny, scrape it off a little, put a wire on the penny, and touch it with some earphones. Sure enough, we did that and heard a radio station. Which one, I couldn't tell you, but we heard voices, real voices, and it was just so darned exciting. I distinctly remember feeling something big had happened, that suddenly I was way ahead—accelerated—above any of the other little kids my age. And you know what? That was the same way I felt years later when I figured out how resistors and lightbulbs worked.

But now I had actually built something, something they didn't have, a little electronics thing I had done and none of them were able to do. I told other kids in the first grade, "I built a crystal radio," but no one knew what I was talking about. None of them. I felt at that moment a kind of glimmer that I might have a lead in things like this from then on. Does that sound crazy? But after building that little crystal radio and telling everyone about it, I knew I had done something most people would think was hard and few kids my age had done. And I was only six. I thought: Okay. That's done. What else can I do?

It's funny, because ever since that crystal radio project when I was six, I've spent a lot of time trying to explain my designs and inventions to people who didn't know what I was talking about. So this has happened and keeps happening to me over and over. Even now.

• ○ •

All through elementary school and through eighth grade, I was building project after electronic project. There were lots of things I worked on with Dad; he was my single greatest influence.

In the fifth grade, I read a book called *SOS at Midnight*. The hero of the book was a ham radio operator, and all his friends were ham radio operators. I remember how they sent each other messages with the ham radio and when, after the main guy got kidnapped, he was able to beat the kidnappers by cleverly rewiring the TV a little and sending out a signal to his friends. The story was okay—it was just a story. But what really got me was the fact that there were people who used these ham radios to speak to each other long distance—city to city, even state to state. Now, this was a time when it was hard for me to imagine even making a long-distance phone call you could actually afford. Ham radio was the most effective way to reach out to people in faraway places without leaving home—and cheaply. This was something that much later led to my phone phreaking (using special tones to make free long-distance calls) and then to my use of the ARPANET, which later evolved into the Internet we have today.

The other thing—the special thing—was on the last page of *SOS at Midnight*. It said how to become a ham radio operator. It said you can become a ham radio operator at any age. All you had to do was contact the American Radio Relay League (ARRL) for more information.

I went to school the next day and told my buddy on safety patrol, "I'm going to get a ham radio license!" I was really boasting, because no one back then knew what I was talking about.

Ham Radio Making a Difference

To this day, ham radio is popular all around the world. It's a hobby. Ham radio amateurs use their two-way radios to talk to each other, share information, and just have fun.

But it's more than a hobby. From the start, ham radio operators performed a public service in protecting the airwaves from radio pirates, and being extremely ethical about how they used public airways.

Many ham radio operators from the early days have gone on to make significant contributions to society. There is a lot of practical applicability in the building and use of ham radio. I'm a good example.

Ham radios were pretty obscure. But this kid I told, he said, "Oh, you know, there's this guy down the street, Mr. Giles, and he's teaching a class on this. Are you in it?" So this was really lucky. I remember being astounded. It turned out that on Wednesday nights Mr. Giles—who actually was a ham radio operator—had these classes I could take. I learned Morse code there, I learned some of the electronics calculations I needed, I learned what frequencies ham radio operators were allowed to use. Basically, I got to learn all the stuff that was going to be on the test you had to take to be a licensed ham radio operator. My dad saw what I was doing, and he got his license with me. We both took the test and passed when I was in the sixth grade. And for that Christmas, I got kits to build a Hallicrafters transmitter and a Hallicrafters receiver. In today's money, it probably cost a couple thousand dollars. That's a lot of money to spend on a sixth grader. And building the radio transmitter and receiver was a lot of work! You had to unpackage hundreds of parts. I had to learn to solder for that, too. In fact, I soldered together the whole

A Little More About the Transistor

The transistor will likely go down as one of the greatest inventions in modern history, ranking right up there with the car, the telephone, and Gutenberg's printing press. William Shockley and his team at Bell Labs invented the transistor in 1947.

Put most simply, a transistor is a tiny electronic device to control the flow of electricity. But a transistor is more than that. It has two key abilities: the first is to amplify an electric signal, and the other is to switch on or off (1 or 0), letting current through or blocking it as necessary.

Transistors are in practically all modern electronics these days, from musical birthday cards, to your car, to your personal computer. Since 1947—and this is what has made the computer revolution possible—it has become cheaper and cheaper to pack more transistors onto a computer chip every year. (This is known as Moore's Law, which Intel founder Gordon Moore defined in the 1960s. He said that every year manufacturing would get so good that double the number of transistors would be able to fit on a chip for the same price.)

A simple logic gate comprises about twenty transistors, compared to an advanced computer chip in a modern (circa 2006) computer, which can include as many as a billion transistors.

thing. We also had to go up on the roof and string antennas of a certain length, to be right for the signals I needed. This was the beginning of learning the kinds of things I would need later to design and assemble computer boards like the one that later became the Apple I.

I loved my transmitter and receiver. They were such standouts in ham radio quality—these days, I even see these models featured in radio museums and collectors' magazines. I didn't really get into talking to the other ham radio operators—they were so much older than me and we really didn't have anything except for the ham radios in common. So after building it, I have to admit the whole thing got a little boring. But this experience was a major one. For one thing, I'm fairly sure I was one of the youngest ham radio operators in the country. That was huge for me. But even more importantly, I learned all about the process of getting a ham radio license—what I needed to know, what I needed to build the equipment—and then I built the radio. It gave me a lot of confidence for doing all kinds of other projects later on.

So my dad ended up being a key influence here, too. I mean, he even got his ham radio license with me—studying with me and taking and passing the test! The thing is, he never really tried to lead me in any direction or push me into electrical engineering. But whenever I got interested in something he was right there, always ready to show me on his blackboard how something worked. He was always ready to teach me something.

• ○ •

My mom really pushed me along, too. In the third grade, when I started doing math flash cards at school, my mom practiced multiplication with me the night before we'd have to do them in school. And as a result, in school I was the only boy who could beat the girls at them. I remember a teacher said, "Wow, that's incredible. I never had a boy before who could beat the girls at flash cards." And again, that was high praise. Girls always seemed to get better grades than boys, I thought. And then I thought: Whoa. My gosh, I'm good at something—math— and I'm going to work harder at it. And I worked harder and harder to try to always be the best, to try to always be ahead. That's what really put me ahead at such a young age, this drive to keep my lead.

I had a teacher in both the fourth and fifth grades, Miss Skrak, who really praised my science projects, like I was the smartest kid in the class because I knew science so well. As you'd predict,

I accelerated even more later on. In sixth grade I was doing electronics projects most kids never figure out how to do even in high
school-level electronics. So I was very lucky with all my teachers,
especially Miss Skrak. She came along at just the right time in my
life.

•   ○   •

At about this time, there was another lucky accident. I found
this article about computers in one of the old engineering journals my dad had hanging around. Back then, back in 1960, writing about computers wasn't common at all. But what I saw was
an article about the ENIAC and a picture of it. The ENIAC—
which stood for Electronic Numerical Integrator And Computer—was the first true computer by most people's definition.
It was designed to calculate bomb trajectories for the military
during World War II. So it was designed back in the 1940s.

This journal had all kinds of pictures of huge computers and
articles describing them. These computers were unlike anything
I'd ever seen. One picture showed a big round tube that looked
like a TV tube. And the article explained that the round tube was
where these huge computers stored data. It used phosphor lights
and then it could read if the phosphors (lights) were on or off—
just like the digits 1 and 0 on today's computers can be interpreted as On or Off—and then it could reset them quickly. This,
the article explained, was actually a way to store data, and I was
just intrigued by that idea. I was about eleven years old at the
time.

Suddenly I realized that some incredible things were just starting to happen with computers at these very early stages. Of
course, they were nowhere near the point of making computers
affordable or usable for the world. They weren't even talking
about a point where anyone could buy a computer and put it in
your house and learn how to use it yourself. I thought that would
be just the best thing, and that was the dream—The Dream, I

have to put that in capital letters—because it was the single force that drove me for years afterward. How to make The Dream come true. I thought about that constantly.

There were so many incredible things happening with computers at that time, and I would never have known about them if I hadn't been too shy to do anything but read magazines at my house. The amazing thing was that at this early stage in my life, I'd managed to find this journal Dad had with this stuff in it. This was a magazine most people were never supposed to see or even be interested in because it was targeted to high-level government engineers.

After that, I was addicted. I started reading and rereading this journal and others my dad had. I remember one day finding an article on Boolean algebra. That's the type of mathematics computers use. And I learned about De Morgan's Theorem, which is what Boolean algebra is based on. And that's how logic became the heart of my existence, there in the fifth grade. I was learning that formula and figuring out how to use it so I could swap ANDs and ORs in logic equations. In logic, for instance, you might ask if a word starts and ends with vowel. Well, then the formula would be an AND—there's a vowel at the beginning and a vowel at the end. That's AND in Boolean algebra. But what about a word that starts with a vowel but doesn't end with one, or the other way around, but not both? That's an OR statement in Boolean algebra.

And in this journal they had diagrams of AND gates and OR gates and I copied them, learning to draw them the standard way.

For instance, a half-moon shape with a dot in the middle represents an AND gate. If it has a plus sign in the middle instead of a dot, it's an OR gate. Then I learned how to draw a picture that represented an inverter—it's a triangle pointing to the right with a little tiny circle at the very end of its tip. What's funny is, I use these very same symbols when I design electronics to this day, and I learned all this in my room with these journals in front of me on my bed in fifth grade.

Here's what was amazing to me back then. I thought to myself: Hey, at my current level of fifth-grade math, I am able to learn the math used by a computer—De Morgan's Theorem, Boolean algebra. I mean, anyone could learn Boolean algebra and they wouldn't even need a higher level of math than I already had in fifth grade. Computers were kind of simple, I discovered. And that blew me away. Computers—which in my opinion were the most incredible things in the world, the most advanced technology there was, way above the head, above the understanding, of almost everyone— were so simple a fifth grader like me could understand them! I loved that. I decided then that I wanted to do logic and computers for fun. I wasn't sure if that was even possible.

To say you wanted to play with computers in those days, well, that was so remote. It was like saying you wanted to be an astronaut. It was 1961; there weren't even real astronauts yet! The odds of being one seemed really slim. But logic was different. I could see that it just came so easily for me. And it always would.

So that's how computers became the heart of my life straight through. As a matter of fact, computer logic was something I eventually became better at than probably any other human alive. (I can't be sure of that, of course. Maybe there were really high-up people in colleges who were as good at applying De Morgan's Theorem in their heads.) But by the time I designed the first Apple computer, logic was my life. I know it sounds unbelievable, but I just loved logic and everything about it, even back then.

● ○ ●

I was in elementary school and junior high at a time when science projects were cool—when you weren't strange if you did one, and you got celebrated if you won an award. So I got celebrated a lot. My science fair projects are some of the things I am still proudest of. We're talking third, fourth, fifth, sixth, and eighth grades here. (For some reason, I didn't enter a project in the seventh grade.) And these projects were hard, harder than kids many grades ahead of me could ever pull off, and I knew it even then. I put some science projects together that, for that audience of kids and judges, just blew their minds. I was like a hero, and I won all kinds of awards, including top honors at the Bay Area Science Fair.

The science fairs gave me the feeling of what I was and could be in the world, just by entering something good in a science fair. The teachers recognized something different about me immediately; some of them even started calling me Science Whiz because I had all these great projects in the science fairs. And probably as a result of that, by sixth grade I was doing electronics projects few people in high school could even understand yet. Those kinds of acknowledgments and those kinds of achievements made me want to keep working at those things until they would be my things in the world.

• ○ •

My first science competition was in third grade, and I won. But the project was pretty simple, really. Basically I put together this little contraption with a light and a couple of batteries and a little wire—all mounted on a piece of wood. It was a working flashlight! A lot of people were surprised by that, and I won. No big deal, it turns out, because I felt inside it wasn't really that impressive, and I knew I would do even better the next time.

It was in the fourth grade that I did the first project that really taught me about things I would need later—physics, electronics, and the project materials. It was an experiment to see what would happen if you dipped these two carbon rods into any liquid of your choice. The carbon rods were connected by a wire to a lightbulb and an AC plug. By dipping the carbon rods into the liquid, the liquid in effect became one of the "wires." It could either act as a good wire or a bad wire—that is, it could conduct electricity well or it could conduct electricity poorly. If the light-bulb glowed, brightly or dimly, you could see how well the liquid could conduct electricity.

I used every liquid I could get my hands on—water, Coca-Cola, iced tea, juice, beer. Which liquid conducts electricity best? (The answer turned out to be salt water.) This is an extremely important thing to know if you want to understand, for instance, hydroelectric machinery or even just plain old batteries.

●　○　●

But the next experiment, man, that was a big one. What I did was build this giant real-life electronic model representing what each of the ninety-two atoms in the periodic table looks like in terms of its electrons.

In case you don't remember, electrons orbit the center of an atom in much the same way planets orbit the sun. The Earth, for instance, has a different orbit than, say, Neptune.

My project aimed to demonstrate, with the click of a switch, how many electrons orbit each atom in the periodic table, and which orbit around the nucleus they should be in. For instance, if I hit the switch for hydrogen, one light would turn on, in the orbit nearest the center of the hole, which represented the nucleus.

To pull off this project, I had to drill ninety-two holes in a big aluminum sheet. The holes were located toward the bottom; each one would hold one switch corresponding to each element. One switch would be for hydrogen, one for gold, one for helium, and so on.

Now, I painted a very large picture resembling a bull's-eye target—concentric circles in different colors, with a tiny target in the middle to represent the center of the atom, which is the nucleus. And I had to drill ninety-two holes into the big orbit picture, several in each orbit, corresponding to where the electrons could be in an atom.

The end result was this. Ask me to show you the electrons for any of the ninety-two natural elements. Let's say oxygen. I would hit the oxygen switch, and the eight lights representing the eight electrons that rotate around the oxygen atom would turn on, all in the proper orbits.

I knew what the proper orbits were because I'd used this big reference book called *The Handbook for Chemistry and Physics*.

This project ended up getting terribly complicated, because by the time I was dealing with all ninety-two elements I was stuck with dealing with ninety-two different sets of switches.

That got so tough I finally had to use the information my dad taught me about the diode, which is the first electronics part I ever learned about, really. Unlike a resistor, a diode is a one-way street. You can send electrons—that is, electricity—just one way. Electricity can go through, but it can't come back through. If you try, it will short everything out. And this was a problem because I'd gotten to the point where if I tried to turn on some middle-level element and its electrons, I wound up with a feedback path that ended up turning on a bunch of lower elements and extra electrons that really didn't belong there. Anyway, I needed a solution, and that's how I learned all about diodes.

Along with this huge display, I also displayed a large collection of elements. You know, jars of beryllium, pieces of copper, even a bottle of mercury. I got a lot of these samples just by asking a professor at San Jose State to donate them to me.

And yes, I won. First place. Blue ribbon. And that was cool.

But it wasn't the most important thing. Looking back on it now, I see this was an amazing learning experience, just classic. My dad guided me, but I did the work. And my dad, to his credit, never tried to teach me formulas about gravitational power and electric power between protons, or stuff like what the force is between protons and electrons. That would have been way beyond what I could understand at that point. He never tried to force me to try and jump ahead because I wouldn't have learned it. I wasn't ready for that level of knowledge.

● ○ ●

In sixth grade, small step by small step, I learned how to build AND and OR gates, the basic building blocks of computer technology. Digital circuits figure everything out—and I mean everything—based on what is on (1s) and what is off (0s).

I was really getting into logic. My dad had helped me understand the concept of logic earlier by using the classic paper-and-pen tic-tac-toe game. This game, if you understand the logic, you will never, ever lose. That's what I based my next project on: the tic-tac-toe machine. The machine I built would never, ever lose. It is so totally a logic game, but it is also a psychological game because you can beat someone who thinks they can never be beaten. If the X is here and the other X is over there, what should the outcome be? This plywood was covered with parts and it was a huge project. And having a huge project is a huge part of learning engineering—learning anything, probably.

Doing long, long jobs that aren't just some real simple quick thing like a flashlight, but things that take weeks to build, really demonstrates that you've mastered something great. Like, for instance, creating a computerized tic-tac-toe machine that really works by logic.

Unfortunately, though, the system didn't win. It blew up. What I mean by blew up is, the night before the competition, some of the transistors started to put out smoke. Obviously something was wrong. I knew it was going to take forever to find out what piece of equipment had blown and there was no way I was going to be able to do this in time for the contest. What a disappointment, because I like to win. I always, as early as I can remember, wanted to be the best at things. And I often was, as luck had it.

But I also thought at the time that it didn't mean as much to me at that point, just winning the science fair, because I knew, and my dad knew, that I had actually built this fairly complicated logic machine and it worked.

I mean, even as a kid it was obvious to me what the important thing really was. I said to myself, Look, showing someone an award from a science fair is not as important as knowing you already have the award somewhere at home. And that's not as important as having earned it, even if you don't have the award at home at all. And that's not as important as the most important thing: that you've done the learning on your own to figure out how to do it. I did that learning on my tic-tac-toe machine, and it was very, very close to being done and complete. I'm still proud of it. For me it's the engineering, not the glory, that's really important.

● ○ ●

Okay, so I'd built that tic-tac-toe system basically by putting together electronic gates. The idea was to put the gates together into a system of transistor circuits that would never let you beat it. And as I said, I came up with the rules by playing all possible games.

But in the eighth grade I did something altogether different. I came up with a machine I called the Adder/Subtractor. This would be the closest thing to an actual computer I'd ever designed. I can say this because I designed it so it would do something—you could add or subtract numbers, and the result would show up on an electric display—but also because it wasn't made up of just a set of logic gates like the tic-tac-toe machine. Addition and subtraction are logic, just like tic-tac-toe; based on inputting 1s and 0s, you can calculate what 1s and 0s come out.

The Adder/Subtractor wasn't more complicated in terms of size or construction time than the tic-tac-toe machine, but this project actually had a goal that was closer to real computing. A more important purpose than tic-tac-toe. We're taught to add and subtract in school, but nobody teaches you tic-tac-toe. It's not that important. Adding numbers could put a man on the moon; tic-tac-toe couldn't.

My project had a function, a real function that was useful. You could input numbers, add or subtract one, and see your answer.

This Adder/Subtractor was about a foot square. I had a plastic board filled with holes and store-bought connectors I could plug down into the holes to form connection points. I plugged the connectors in where needed and soldered transistors and other parts to them.

I had ten little switches to represent 0s and 1s, and another set of switches to represent more than 0s and 1s. So if you wanted to add 3 plus 2, on one row you would have to toggle the rightmost two switches (which is equivalent to 0000000011, the binary number representing 3) on the top row. Then, to represent 2, I had to toggle the next to last switch to the right on the bottom row. In binary, that is 0000000010. The answer would show up in lights, the lights I had attached. In this example, two lights would be on—representing 0000000101, which represents 5. This would all be assuming that you had the Adder/Subtractor in "add" mode instead of "subtract" mode.

What was impressive about this was that I knew so many levels of electronics, logic, binary number theory, soldering, and all the experiences of my life so far just added up. I could explain to judges how binary numbers worked, how you added and subtracted them, and then I could explain how gates were made of diodes and transistors. I would then show the right combination of gates that made a one-bit adder (something that could only add 0 and 1). I could show them a simple modification I did that could do subtraction as well. I also told the judges how I'd solved a nonworking problem in the electronics of a gate, switching from resistors to diodes. That's real electronics know-how.

On the one board were ten Adder/Subtractor circuits side by

side handling carries and borrows (remember arithmetic) so you could add or subtract larger numbers—any number up to 1,023.

But here's the thing. I took it down to the Bay Area Science Fair one night, to set it up before the day of judging. Some people showed me where to put it and asked me if I'd like to tell them about it. I told them no, figuring that I'd just tell them the story on judging day. By then I'd gotten kind of shy. Looking back, I think I may have turned down the judges without knowing it.

When I showed up on judging day, all the projects already had their awards. The judging had already happened somehow! I had an honorable mention, and there were three exhibits that had higher awards than mine. I saw them and remember thinking they were trivial compared to mine, so what happened? I then looked in the fair brochure and those three were all from the school district that was putting on the fair.

I thought, Hey, I've been cheated. But that night, I showed the machine and talked to lots of people—including, I'm sure, the real judges—and it seemed like they really understood how big my project was. I mean, it was great and I knew it and everyone knew it. I was able to explain how I'd used logic equations and gates and how I'd combined gates and transistors with binary number (1s and 0s) arithmetic to get the whole thing working.

After that, the Air Force gave me its top award for an electronics project for the Bay Area Science Fair, even though I was only in eighth grade and the fair went up to twelfth grade. As part of the award, they gave me a tour of the U.S. Strategic Air Command Facility at Travis Air Force Base. And they gave me a flight in a noncommercial jet, my first-ever flight in any plane. I think I might have caught my love for flying then.

When I look back, that Adder/Subtractor was such a key project in my getting to be the engineer who ended up building the first personal computer. This project was a first step to that. It was a large project, for one thing, involving more than one hundred transistors, two hundred diodes, and two hundred resistors, plus relays and switches. And it performed a function that was useful: addition and subtraction.

And thanks to all those science projects, I acquired a central ability that was to help me through my entire career: patience. I'm serious. Patience is usually so underrated. I mean, for all those projects, from third grade all the way to eighth grade, I just learned things gradually, figuring out how to put electronic devices together without so much as cracking a book. Sometimes I think, Man, I lucked out. It seems like I was just pointed in such a lucky direction in life, this early learning of how to do things one tiny little step at a time. I learned to not worry so much about the outcome, but to concentrate on the step I was on and to try to do it as perfectly as I could when I was doing it.

Not everyone gets this in today's engineering community, you know. Throughout my career at Apple and other places, you always find a lot of geeks who try to reach levels without doing the in-between ones first, and it won't work. It never does. That's just cognitive development, plain and simple. You can't teach somebody two cognitive steps above from where you are—and knowing that helped me with my own children as well as with the fifth graders I taught later on. I kept telling them, like a mantra: One step at a time.

Chapter 3

Learning by Accident

Throughout most of elementary school, I was a little shy, but at least I had a lot of friends and was really athletic. I was the de facto leader of the Electronics Kids because I already knew so much of the stuff we needed to build the things we wanted to build. This was a close group in the neighborhood, and that was great. I loved being able to excel at things, and having people recognize me for that. Not out of ego, really, just a drive to be the best.

I was good at swimming and football and made the All-Stars in Little League, where the other kids told me I was the best pitcher and runner and hitter on my teams. In fifth grade I was the smartest student in my class, according to my teachers at least, and I was elected school student body vice president. Do I sound like I'm bragging? I know I do, but I don't mean to. I was just so proud of all that. All these activities built up my self-esteem, and that was an important part of my internal development.

But things changed in sixth grade. I wasn't so popular anymore. In fact, suddenly it was like I was invisible. All of a sudden, other kids didn't recognize me as much for my math and science skills, which really bothered me. I mean, that's what I was best at. This was a time when a lot of students start flirting and engaging in all kinds of small talk that I didn't relate to. So I wasn't included. My natural shyness just made me bottom out in sixth grade. I really stopped enjoying school so much. Socially, I went straight to the bottom.

I think of the years after that, seventh and eighth grades especially, as terrible years. Where before I was popular and riding bikes and everything, suddenly I was socially shut out and not popular at all. It seemed like nobody spoke to me for the longest time. I was in the advanced classes and got good grades, but I didn't have much enjoyment doing it.

As an example, I remember few teachers from those bad years.

The only way I can explain it is that when kids that age start getting social, your position in the group starts getting important to a lot of people. I've watched this happen with my own kids and the kids I've taught. Who are the talkers? Who makes the decisions? Who rises to the top? And because I became so shy when I hit adolescence—well, I just went to the bottom. It was a tremendous shock for me. Except for the science projects, which still got me recognized by my teachers and grown-ups, I felt terribly awkward. I couldn't identify with other kids my age anymore. The way they spoke—I felt like I didn't know their language anymore. And I'd feel too scared to talk because I thought I'd say the wrong thing.

At the same time I was starting to feel advanced, science- and electronics-wise, I felt shunned by all these kids who suddenly, and for no reason I could understand, just couldn't accept me anymore. I did electronics when a lot of others started hanging out and partying and drinking and going to, well, I guess you would call them make-out parties.

This started in sixth grade, and in many ways, that shyness is still with me. Even today. I have friends who can just go up and talk to anybody. They're suave and make friends so easily. Small talk, they can do that. I can't possibly do that. I can give speeches because I've had something like thirty years of experience doing it, and I have techniques I use to make it easier, techniques I gained gradually from having to do public speaking for many years. I just make lots of jokes to get everyone laughing. Or I build and show off some electronic device to get people talking to me about it.

Or—and maybe you know this about me—I break the ice and make people laugh by pulling pranks on them. I could write a whole book on those pranks alone, that's for sure.

• ○ •

I did a ton of pranks in junior high and high school. I got caught many times in junior high. The main thing I learned was that if you told a few others about a prank, the word spread and you got caught quickly. In high school I was careful in this regard. I made sure to keep my pranks quiet.

Once, for the benefit of everyone in my twelfth-grade driver's education class, I built an electronic siren—it sounded just like a real police siren—that I could start and stop, holding it under my chair in the dark during the movie that played as we drove in our simulators. I wanted to see if anyone braked and pulled over. I'd make it with tons of batteries so it would last a month or more and place it on top of the TVs that were in every classroom. (The TVs were up high, supported from and attached to the ceiling, so the teachers couldn't see my sirens.) The teachers would think the TV had a problem. It's hard to isolate where a very high pitch is coming from; I'd read that somewhere.

But later in the twelfth grade, I got caught again. Big-time.

I got the idea to build a little electronic metronome—you know, the thing that goes tick, tick, tick, to keep time when people take piano lessons. I built it, heard the ticking, and thought: Hey, this kind of sounds like a bomb. So I took some batteries, took the labels off the batteries so they looked like plain metal canisters, and I taped them together. And then I wrote in big letters on it: CONTACT EXPLOSIVE.

I thought: Oh, this will be funny. I'll stick it in Bill Werner's locker. I just happened to know his locker code. Bill's locker was near mine so I put my so-called electronic metronome in. Now, this was in the morning before school, and after I put it in there, I could barely hear it ticking. Nobody was going to be tricked by this if they couldn't even hear it! I'm thinking: What a bummer and what a waste if this thing isn't going to work. But when I came out of my last final that day, my counselor walked up to me and said: "Steve, the vice principal wants to see you in his office." This was a bad sign. Then again, I thought maybe there was a chance I was getting the math award for a math contest I had recently competed in and that's why he wanted to see me. So I didn't know for sure if I was in trouble or not.

Well, I sat in the chair in the office waiting for the vice principal to come in, and all of a sudden this police officer walks in the door carrying a box with wires coming out of it. And I just thought, Oh my god, they called the bomb demolition squad! Then they called me into a room and a cop said, "Look, your buddy told us everything." I figured the guy who told them was this guy I knew, Jerry, who was the only friend I'd told about the plan. But no, I later found out it was a mistake on my own part that got me caught. I realized many years later that they meant they had actually heard it from Bill Werner, whose locker they found it in. Turns out they'd hauled him out of a final—he looked at the design and said, "Oh, I know those components. Woz did it." Well, that's what I get for using some of the same parts Mr. Taylor, who lived next door to me, paid Electronics Kids like me and Bill Werner with when we worked in his yard.

So I could've denied it at that point, when I still thought it was Jerry who told them, and in fact, we all had an agreement that none of us involved in a prank would ever tell on the other ones. But anyway, I knew I was in big trouble, and finally they sat me down with the principal, and the vice principal, the counselor, the dean, and two police officers. And the principal starts telling me how the English teacher, Mr. Stottlemeier, had heard a ticking sound in the locker. The principal, Mr. Bryld, told me how he opened the locker, clutched the device to his chest, and then ran all the way out to the football field and dismantled it!

I started laughing, even though I was trying not to, so then I tried to cough to cover it up. But I couldn't even do that, because I knew I had rigged the metronome with a switched resistor to start ticking faster when someone opened up the locker door.

I'll tell you, laughing about that—and how could I not laugh—well, it didn't fix the problem any. They debated for a while what to do with me, and decided to send me to juvenile hall—that's right, juvie!—for a night. Just one night.

The principal was terribly upset because there had been some actual bomb threats at the school a few weeks earlier. This wasn't a bomb. It was a metronome, a joke. But I still had to go to juvie that one night, and I did make some good use of my time while I was there. I thought: Well, what do they always say about prisoners in prisons? That they teach each other crimes. So I did my fair share. I pointed out to all these big tough guys in juvie how to remove the electrical wires on the ceiling fan. I said, "Take those wires off and touch them to the bars when the jailer comes to open the bars and he'll get shocked!" I sure had a fun time there. All those guys in there treated me really nice. This is way, way before it was cool to be a nerd, of course.

● ○ ●

Later, much later, I found a group where being a nerd was cooler. In the mid-1970s, a couple of years before we started Apple, I joined a club called the Homebrew Computer Club. I loved this group and attended almost every meeting from the time they started meeting in Gordon French's garage in Menlo Park every other Wednesday from 1975 up until 1977, the year we incorporated Apple. These people had the same dream I had—to learn how to build a computer everyone could afford and use. These were my kind of people. Their prime focus was a build-it-yourself device called the Altair (which could be expanded into a usable computer with a huge amount of money) and the things you could do with it. And they used to have an hour or more of random announcements (called the "random-access period") where anyone who had anything to say could say it if they just raised their hand.

I had a lot to say, but I was unable to raise my hand or say a thing. I used to just sit on the edge of my chair listening to them tell every rumor in the industry about what technologies were coming out next. I was that shy. I was in the back row just like I had been in junior high school.

I finally ended up having to get up and show everybody two real computers I'd built. (One of these became the foundation for the Apple I designs.) And as soon as people saw what I had done, and that it was really impressive, suddenly we all had something to talk about.

From elementary school on, even up to starting Apple and beyond, I used my clever designs as an easier, more comfortable way to communicate with others. I believe all of us humans have an internal need to socialize. In my case it came out mainly by doing impressive things like electronics and incredibly showy and clever things like pranks.

It was probably the shyness thing that in the sixth grade and afterward put me on the hunt for electronics journals. That way, I could read about electronics stuff without having to actually walk up to someone and ask questions. I was too shy to even go to a library and ask for a book on computers called *Computers*. And because I was way too shy to learn the ordinary way, I ended up getting what was to me the most important knowledge in the world accidentally.

• ◦ •

Then, in high school, a lot changed again. Most of it had to do with an electronics teacher I had named Mr. McCollum. He had a huge, huge influence on me.

Now, Mr. McCollum was an interesting guy. For one thing, he was a military guy before he was a teacher, which meant he could tell a lot of jokes, even off-color jokes. So he related well to his students. Keep in mind that back then, the students in an electronics class were mostly low-performing students. Electronics was like a vocational course. There were only a few electronics students who, like me, were taking top classes in other areas. And remember that I was a math whiz. I won the math award from my junior high graduation and had won some yearly math awards from my high school, too.

Combine math and electronics and you know what you get? It's called engineering.

Mr. McCollum would stand there in front of us doing calculations on this big yellow slide rule. He would do more calculations on that slide rule than we even did in chemistry; the course was that intensive. And Mr. McCollum wrote that course himself. He wrote handouts that went in a logical order—you know, step by step, going up the electronics ladder. You learn one thing about resistors, then a more complicated thing, then you learn faster, then you put them together. It was such a good way to teach electronics that I used it later when I taught my own computer classes in later life.

And Mr. McCollum had the most amazing collection of electronics equipment, really advanced stuff. It was all test equipment I could never afford on my own, and it was better than what even most college-level labs had then. Mr. McCollum had been resourceful and had gotten the school to buy less expensive electronics kits in the few first years of Homestead High School. As his students learned electronics, they built the kits of equipment to take them further. Now, by my senior year, we had pretty complete labs.

So we had a lot of equipment. And what a fun class that was. You build something and it works. You don't stop finding things you forgot or did wrong until it works. And you learn about what happens when things go wrong, which is the number one thing former electronics students always remember about their classes. We all got zapped with accidental shocks now and then. Like the time I got hit with 22,000 volts from a TV set and flew back about five feet. Whoa. But that, I swear, is what hardware guys like me get used to. We grow up not fearing shocks as much as other people.

I now have a roulette shocker—four people stick in their thumbs and, to the accompaniment of music and flashing lights, it gradually slows down cycling until one person gets a shock. Hardware guys will play this game but software guys are always way too chicken.

Mr. McCollum let me do as much as I wanted—he even prevented me from getting bored by letting me go to work at a company during school hours on Fridays. It was Sylvania, in Sunnyvale, and I got to learn how to program a computer. Mr. McCollum said that I knew everything in his course and I'd just play pranks on the others in class. Well, we had no computer in our school, so that was the first time I really got face to face with a computer I could program, and after that there was no turning back.

I never thought I'd be near a computer in my life. I thought, Oh my god! Computers! I bought a FORTRAN book and told myself, I'm going to learn how to program. An engineer down there at Sylvania taught me how to use a keypunch. I remember typing out my first little program and his helping me put it into the computer and running it.

The first real program I tried to write was called the Knight's Tour. You jump a knight piece around the chessboard, only in valid moves for a knight, in a pattern so that it hits every one of the sixty-four squares on the board exactly once. This is not easy to do. I wrote my program to go up two squares, then over one again and again, to try all the moves until you can't move again. And if it didn't hit all the squares by the time it got stuck, the program would back up and change a move and try again from there. It would keep backtracking as far as it needed and then kept going. That computer could calculate instructions a million times a second, so I figured it would be a cinch and would solve this problem quickly.

So here I am with my program and I'm planning how this is just the beginning of my solving all the sophisticated problems of the world, but guess what? The computer doesn't spit out anything. The lights on the computer flickered, and then the lights just stayed the same. Nothing was happening. My engineer friend let it run a while longer and said, "Well, probably it's in a loop." And he showed me what an infinite loop is—when a program gets stuck and does the same thing over and over and never ends. (Just as an aside, Infinite Loop is today the name of the street where the current Apple headquarters is located.) Anyway, the next week I went back and I wrote my program so that I could flip a switch in order to get printouts of whatever chessboard arrangement it was working on. I remember pulling the printouts out and studying them that very day and realizing something. The program was in fact working the way it was supposed to. I hadn't done anything wrong. It just wasn't going to come up with a solution for 10^{25} years. That's a lot longer than the universe has even been around.

That made me realize that a million times a second didn't solve everything. Raw speed isn't always the solution. Many understandable problems need an insightful, well-thought-out approach to succeed. The approach a program uses to solve something, the rules and steps and procedures it follows, by the way, is called an algorithm.

What Is the Knight's Tour?

The Knight's Tour is more than just a mathematical problem where you have to get a knight around a chessboard. It's an ancient puzzle, and people have been trying and failing at it for centuries. The goal is to move the knight sixty-four times so it lands on each and every chess square only once.

I found two sites you might like if you're interested in this. http://www.borderschess.org/KnightTour.htm is a Knight's Tour puzzle you can do without a chessboard. You do it online. Another page on the same site—http://www.borders chess.org/KTsimple.htm—is an actual instruction guide so you can learn how to do it and blow other people's minds! Good luck.

• o •

I had this tremendous respect for teachers back then, I really did. I thought they were just the smartest people in the world, right up there with engineers. They were able to stand up there and talk so naturally, just teach us like that. I mean, I knew I was real smart, but because teachers had the ability to read up on topics and then talk about them with so much confidence, I figured they had to be much smarter than I was. I thought at the time that all my high school teachers were smart thinkers.

Now I'm a bit more cynical after seeing too many cases where intelligence in students is defined as everyone reading the same thing, including the same newspaper and magazine articles, and having the same answer, and agreeing with the way the matter is presented.

If you read the same things as others and say the same things they say, then you're perceived as intelligent. I'm a bit more independent and radical and consider intelligence the ability to think about matters on your own and ask a lot of skeptical questions to get at the real truth, not just what you're told it is.

I had a really long walk to and from Homestead High School every day, and I started using that time to really think. It was a walk of a few miles, and I started to analyze my own intelligence. I was struggling in my head with the fact that I had been extremely smart in math and science and weaker in English and history. Why was that? Well, I figured those were more subjective categories, and I watched as nice, sweet-talking girls went up to the teacher and got their grades raised right there on the spot. And I thought: Well, gosh, when you're just writing words down, they're just words—it's all subjective and it's hard to tell what the real answer is. What I loved most about math was that you had to have an answer that was either correct or incorrect. You know what I mean? No gray areas—your answer was correct or incorrect and that was it. (Once I found I did have an answer that the teacher marked incorrect but I knew was right. And it turned out the book was wrong. Books do that sometimes.) Compare this to a book report or an essay you're supposed to write where there are so many interpretations and so many ways to write it. Who's to say which version the teacher will like? Who's to say who really understood the book, or who got more out of it?

And so somewhere on those long, long walks, I decided that logic was superior. This confirmed what I already thought, but I remember these walks really cementing the idea. I realized that I probably was not in the mainstream of people and social goings-on. I realized I thought differently than most other kids I knew. I thought: Hey, things are facts or things are lies. Mathematics is a truth because two plus two equals four, and if someday somebody finds out two plus two equals five, well, then we just have to come up with a new truth to deal with that. And to me, the very closest thing to truth—the main ethic I'd gotten from my dad and the ethic he'd ingrained in me—was logic. Logic was the thing. I decided that the most important measure of a person was truth, and that the calculations engineers made were the mark of people who lived truthfully.

● ○ ●

One day at Sylvania I saw a manual entitled *The Small Computer Handbook*. I had this interest in computers but I only found out about them and how they worked by lucky accidents. This was one of my life's luckiest accidents.

The Sylvania engineers let me take this handbook home. Inside, it described the guts of the Digital Equipment PDP-8 minicomputer. This computer sat in a tall rack of equipment and had switches and lights and looked like it belonged on a factory floor or somewhere. I couldn't say exactly because I'd never seen a real computer anywhere other than Sylvania. This one handbook finally solved a search I'd been on since fourth grade to discover what a real computer was inside.

I had a good knowledge of logic design, combining parts to make logic circuits. Now I had a description of what a real computer was. On my own I sat down for many nights figuring out ways to combine logic parts to make one of these PDP-8 computers. That first computer design of mine on paper was huge and unfinished and probably full of errors. But it was just a start.

Over the next few years, beginning with my senior year in high school, I found ways to obtain manuals for almost every minicomputer being made. There was a flood of these minicomputers introduced in this time frame. They were taking computing to a smaller level than the huge machines that filled rooms. A typical minicomputer with enough memory to program (in a friendly programming language) was about the size of a microwave oven.

I got manuals for minicomputers from Varian, Hewlett-Packard, Digital Equipment, Data General, and many more companies. Whenever I had a free weekend, I'd take catalogs of logic components, chips, from which computers are made, and a particular existing computer description from its handbook, and I'd design my own version of it. Many times I'd redesign the same computer a second or third time, using newer and better components. I developed a private little game of trying to design these minicomputers with the minimum number of chips. I have no idea why this became the pastime of my life. I did it all alone in my room with my door shut. It was like a private hobby. I didn't share this activity with my parents, friends, teachers, or anyone over the years. It was that private.

Because I could never afford the parts to build any of my computer designs, all I could do was design them on paper. Typically, once I started a design, I'd stay up very late one or more nights in a row, sprawled on my bedroom floor with papers all around and a Coke can nearby. Since I could never build my designs, all I could do was to try and beat my own designs by redesigning them even better, using fewer parts. I was competing with myself and developed tricks that certainly would never be describable or put in books. I had a hunch after a year or so that nobody else could do the sorts of design tricks I'd come up with to save parts. I was now designing computers with half the number of chips the actual company had in their own design, but only on paper.

Chapter 4

The "Ethical" TV Jammer

A guy named Rich Zenkere was selected class clown of
Homestead High Class of 1968. He was a funny guy who sat next
to me in a lot of classes because in most of our classes we had to
sit in alphabetical order. And Wozniak is pretty close to Zenkere
in the alphabet. So Rich, some other guy who sat near us, Scott
Sampson, and I agreed that the three of us should look for colleges together.

We planned to visit Caltech. We planned to fly down to
Pomona, California, where Scripps, Pomona College, and California Polytechnic are located.

And then we got this great idea to visit the University of Colorado at Boulder. It was where Rich's dad had gone.

What an exciting time this was for me. I had never been out of
California in my life. I remember we got on the plane in San Jose
Airport, back when it had only two gates, and took a 707 to Denver. We drove from Denver to Boulder by taxi and arrived when
it was too dark to see anything. We passed out from exhaustion
in the hotel room. And then, in the morning, we turned on the TV
to find that it had snowed something like a foot and a half the
night before. So we pulled the drapes, and sure enough there
were inches and inches of snow outside. We were all excited.

I had never been around real snow in my life. Where I lived, it might snow a little some years, but never enough to stick on the ground and definitely never enough to make a snowball with. So this was amazing! All of a sudden we were outside throwing snowballs at each other. This was a whole new adventure for me.

For some weird reason, we had shown up over Thanksgiving weekend. I guess we thought they'd have tours on a holiday, but of course they didn't. So we just kind of walked around the empty campus for a couple of days. At one point we actually found an engineering building and there was a student inside. He walked us around the halls and showed us where the different departments were. He showed us all the engineering stuff and talked to us about the kinds of engineering projects going on at Colorado.

Walking through the snow those two days, I was just so enamored of the place. The brick buildings were beautiful. Their reddish color looked so impressive up against the backdrop of the Flatiron Mountains. It was a college out in the middle of nowhere—it was about a mile walk to the city.

I thought, This is just so beautiful. It's so wonderful to walk around this campus in the snow. And it was that snow that made me decide this was the college I was going to be attending. Its entrance requirements were low compared to my grades and SAT scores—I had perfect 800 scores on all my science and math entrance tests except for chemistry, where I only got a 770. But this was the college I was going to go to. The snow made me decide. I made the final decision right then and there.

• ○ •

The only problem was, my dad said Colorado would be too expensive. Next to some state university in New England, it charged the second-highest tuition in the country for out-of-state students.

But we finally worked out a deal. He said I could go to Colorado for my freshman year and then to De Anza Community

College, which was close to home, for my sophomore year. After that, I would transfer to the University of California at Berkeley for my junior year, where tuition would be much, much cheaper. I also applied to Berkeley—my parents forced me to—and I sent in my application on the very last day you could.

I was accepted at Colorado and my parents paid everything in advance that summer, including the dorm fees and the tuition fees. But then my dad kept imploring me to go to De Anza, it was so much closer to home and cheaper. And he could afford, then, to give me a car.

So I went down to register at De Anza and saw that the classes for chemistry, physics, and calculus were all full. What? I couldn't believe it. Here I was—the star science and math student at my high school and all set to be an engineer—and the three most important courses I needed were locked out.

It was horrible. I called the chemistry teacher on the phone, who said if I showed up I could probably get in, but I couldn't shake this terrible feeling that my future was shutting down. I could see it shutting down right in front of me. I felt my whole academic life was going to be messed up right from the start. And it was right then that I changed my mind, and decided to see if it was still possible to go to Colorado.

School had already started there, but after a couple of calls I found out I could still go. I had everything set up, airplane flight schedule and everything. I bought the tickets, went down to San Jose Airport, and flew into Colorado the next day. Just in time for the third day of classes.

I remember arriving on campus that fall and thinking it was so beautiful, early September in Colorado. The leaves were yellow and orange and gold, and I felt like I was just so lucky.

My roommate was Mike. The first thing I noticed when I walked into the dorm room with my bags was that he'd posted up about twenty foldout *Playboy* centerfolds on the walls.

Wow, that was different! But I thought Mike was a neat guy, and I used to like listening to his stories of life as a military brat, about his high school in Germany and all the experiences he had. He was very sexually advanced, I thought. Sometimes he'd tell me he wanted the room alone on certain nights, and I knew why. I'd say, Well, okay. I'd take this tape recorder I had and a bunch of reel-to-reel tapes—Simon & Garfunkel was my big group then—and I'd go over to Rich Zenkere's room and come back much later. I remember one time I was sleeping and he brought in this Mormon girl in the middle of the night. He was really something.

Meanwhile, I'd hang around with other friends I'd made in the dorm. I went to football games. Our mascot was a buffalo named Ralphie (a humiliating name for anyone!), and a bunch of students dressed like cowboys would race him around on the field before the game. Ralphie was a real buffalo. I remember how my friend Rich Zenkere told us that, twenty years earlier, Colorado's main rival back then, the Air Force Academy, managed to kidnap him. And when the Air Force Academy players showed up for the big game they cooked and ate poor Ralphie.

I believed the story at the time, but you never knew about Rich. He took things so lightly and easily, always smiling and joking about the most serious things. He was a little bit dishonest, though. We worked together washing dishes at a girls' dorm, and he ended up getting fired for faking time cards and stuff.

I spent a lot of time in Rich's room with him and his two roommates, Randy and Bud, playing hearts, poker, and bridge. Randy was interesting to me because he was a serious Christian—a born-again Christian—and the other two guys would denigrate him for it. Like he was dumb because of it. But I used to spend a lot of time talking to him about his beliefs. I had never had any kind of religious training whatsoever, so I was impressed when he told me about Christian things like "turning the other cheek" and forgiveness. I definitely became his friend. So anyway, we'd usually play cards late into the night, and I remember thinking, This is just the best year of my life. It was the first time in my life I could decide what to do with my time—what to eat, what to wear, what to say, what classes to take and how many.

And I was meeting all kinds of interesting people. The bridge thing ended up getting huge for me. We started playing it right around finals week, and then it stuck. The four of us played bridge right off the seat of our pants. We didn't have any books or tables in front of us, or anything that normal bridge players use. We just sort of figured out for ourselves what bridge bids worked and which ones didn't. I mean, in my mind, bridge is more sophisticated than other games.

A lot of card games are based on "tricks" where one person puts a card down and the other players follow with their own cards, and the highest-ranking card of the suit of the first card down wins. That's a trick. Now, in hearts, you try to avoid taking certain cards: for example, every heart you win in a trick counts against you. In spades, you have a round of bidding first, betting how many tricks you and your partner—the person across the table from you in a game of four players—will take. If you bet five tricks and get that many, you get fifty points. But if you overbid and don't get as many tricks as you thought you would, you lose that many points. In spades, all of the spades have the special ability to trump the other cards.

But bridge is at the top end. You not only bet how many tricks you can take with your partner, whose hand you cannot see, but you also have to bet which suit will be the trump suit that beats all other suits.

Bridge is such a good balance of strategy and offense and defense. And at the same time, you're looking at your hand and trying to guess what others might have and passing signals for the bidding. You have to play on so many levels at once. We really started out, like I said, knowing nothing. So we all had fun, since we were all playing at the same level.

But it's funny, we thought we were real bridge players, but we never could've gotten around and competed with real bridge players. A few years later when I was working at Hewlett-Packard, I tried to join a bridge club in my apartment building and I couldn't even begin to play with those women. You see, I'd never really memorized all those rules of how much you bid when you have which hands. So all I'd end up doing is messing up my partner.

These days, I can play bridge pretty well, but it's only because I read the bridge column in the newspaper every single day for years until I could figure out the formulas in my head.

● ○ ●

During college, I worked on one of my favorite projects ever. I called it the TV Jammer.

The TV Jammer came out of this thing I'd seen my old friend Allen Baum's father, Elmer, do over the summer. Mr. Baum was an engineer, and he'd worked out this little circuit on a piece of paper. It included a transistor, a couple of resistors, a capacitor, and a coil that could put out a signal in the TV frequency range. I looked at it, thinking how cool it would be if you could tune it, the same way you could tune your transistor radio, just by turning a dial. So I built a few of these—devices that let you jam a TV if you just dialed into the right frequency. They were cool.

Well, at some point during my freshman year at Colorado, I thought it was time to have fun with the TV Jammer. I walked over to Radio Shack and looked at all their transistors. I saw they had only one transistor rated for 50 MHz up toward the TV frequencies. I brought that one home. I also bought a little transistor radio so I could use parts of it, like resistors of certain values and the tuning capacitor, the part the tuning knob connects to. That would give me a big wide tuning range.

I hand-wrapped a coil out of some thick wire I had—about three turns—and I soldered on a little tap halfway down one of the turns and put a capacitor there. The whole thing was as small as my little finger, just tiny. I built it on top of the case of a 9-volt battery in a neat way. You know that little clip on top of the 9-volt? I stripped it out, hand-soldered it to the connectors on my little TV Jammer circuit, and then I could plug another 9-volt battery in as my power source. So I was able to carry this 9-volt battery case with the TV Jammer on it totally concealed. Except for a little six-inch wire that acted as an antenna, which I had to hang out the side to transmit. I put it up my sleeve to hide it.

I went over to a friend's to try it out on his TV—he had a little black-and-white TV in his dorm room—and sure enough, I was able to jam his TV black.

I walked into the main lounge of our dorm where everybody was watching a big black-and-white TV. I tuned the TV Jammer and, whack, it blacks out. Wow, I thought, that's a funny joke.

I showed it one day to Randy Adair, my Christian friend, and he said, "You should try it on the color TV that's in the basement of Libby Hall," the girls' dorm.

I walked in there and saw a lot of guys and girls. They were in there watching that TV all the time, it turned out. I walked in back where I was in the dark enough, and I turned the TV Jammer on, expecting it would kill the picture. All it did was fuzz it up, though.

Well, without any planning whatsoever, my friend Randy, sat in the front row of chairs, leaned over the TV, and whacked it really hard. I caught on quickly. I instantly made the TV picture go clear, which of course made everyone think that the whacking worked on the TV. I waited for a couple of minutes and jammed it again. It fuzzed up the picture again and Randy hit it again. And I made it go clear again. A couple of minutes later I jammed it again, but this time I let Randy hit it three or four times before his whacking "worked."

So anyone watching would think that, okay, hitting harder works better. They all thought something was loose inside the TV and that by hitting it hard with your hand you could fix it. It was almost like a psychology experiment—except, I noticed, humans learn better than rats. Only the rats learn it quicker.

Then, later that night, Randy didn't get up to whack the TV. So someone else did. I was hoping that would happen! Someone else whacked it, and I made it so the TV worked. Ha! A whole audience of guinea pigs. I couldn't have wished for more. Over a period of about two weeks, I went there every night to watch people whack the TV. When that didn't work, they'd start to fine-tune it—in those days, TVs came with tuning controls—and I would quietly work the TV Jammer so that if they tuned it just right, the TV worked again.

After a while, I made it so that if someone touched the tuner and adjusted it to fix the picture, it would work. But then when they pulled their hand away, the screen would go bad again. Until they put their hand back on the tuning control, that is. I was like an entertainer. A puppeteer—with live puppets under my control.

Then the people got this superstition about how it mattered where your body was. I remember one time there were three people trying to fix the TV. By this time I would wait for some interesting thing they would do to fix the picture so I could trick them into thinking they had done it. One of the three guys had his hand in the middle of the TV screen. He was standing with one foot up on a chair. Seeing his hand accidentally rest in the middle of the TV screen, I took my cue and fixed the picture. One of the three guys announced, Hey, the picture's good. They relaxed. When the guy in front pulled his hand back, I made the picture go bad again.

The guy in back of the TV turning the dials on the back of the

TV said, "Let's all try to get our bodies where they were and maybe it will work again!"

A few seconds later, the guy in front rested his hand back on the middle of the screen and I did it again, fixed the picture. He tested it by pulling his hand away—I made the picture go bad— and then putting it back on the screen—and I made it go good again.

Then I noticed him take his foot off the chair and put it down on the floor. Again, I ruined the picture. When he put his foot back on the chair, he looked so startled when the picture went clear again. God, was I good to pull this off without ever getting caught.

He turned to the other students in the room and loudly announced, "Grounding effect." He had to have been an engineering student to have known a word like that back then.

The dozen or so students stayed for the second half hour of *Mission Impossible* with the guy's hand over the middle of the TV! And TVs were pretty small back then.

The only trouble is, I'd gone too far. For the next few weeks, virtually no one showed up in that TV room. They had had enough.

• ○ •

Later in the year, they all came back again. So again I would play with this game, and just have so much fun. Sometimes people would have to pound the TV as hard as they could on top. Other times, there had to be three people on the TV at once— one pounding, one tuning, and one turning the color dial on the back that adjusted how much red, green, and blue the picture had. After that, they needed more than me to get the picture back! So a repairman had to be called.

After the repairman came, I heard someone at the TV mention that he'd said it was an antenna problem. I jammed the TV again, so what did they do? Of course, someone picked up the twin-lead antenna wire and lifted it up over his head. I made the screen go good. He put it down and I made the screen go bad again. Up, good . . . down, bad. And after a while, I made it so he had to hold up the antenna higher and higher. This guy's trying to watch the last five minutes of some show, and he's stretched out to the ceiling, it was hilarious.

Except for Randy, I never told anyone else about it the whole year. I found it just amazing that at no time did anyone suspect that a human was toying with them. They never caught on! It was so funny. I couldn't make up a story this good. The only time I regretted using the TV Jammer in the TV room was during a daytime watching of the Kentucky Derby. Of course, I timed it down to the last stretch, and then I jammed the TV. Those kids erupted like animals, throwing chairs at the TV and everything. If it had been a human being, they would have beaten him to a pulp, they were that upset. And I felt horrible because I knew that if they had found me out on that day, it would've been hospital time.

There's a point where a joke crosses to a point where it is beyond funny—not funny anymore but scary—and this was it.

● ○ ●

I had a computer class at Colorado where I took the TV jamming concept a little further.

Just the fact that I was able to take a computer class was amazing. Back then, there were only a few colleges that had computer courses. Undergraduate computer classes were virtually unheard of, so this was a graduate class. Being enrolled in engineering at Colorado, even as a freshman, meant I could take any engineering class, even graduate classes, as long as I met the prerequisites. And luckily there weren't any for this course. This class was just amazing—in it, they taught everything about computers, their architecture, their programming languages, their operating systems, everything. It was such a thorough course.

The only problem was, it was held in the engineering building, where the classrooms were really small. So only a third of our class got to see the professor in person in one room. The other two-thirds had to watch on TV, on closed circuit, in a room that had four TV sets on the wall.

So I thought, Okay. What a great opportunity for the TV Jammer. But first I had to make an even smaller TV Jammer, a version that would be even harder to detect. So I built one inside of a Magic Marker, including the battery and everything. (I'd taken the pen apart and put in a AA battery. At the very end of the pen I put in this little thumbscrew for tuning.)

I took it to computer class one day. I went to my usual seat over to the left rear of the class, and I took my little TV Jammer pen, turned it on, and tried to jam the TVs. I didn't know if I was going to be able to do this—I wasn't sure if it was even possible to jam TVs where the antennas came in on a coax. After all, coaxial cable was unusual in those days. The normal thing was to have twin-feed antennas.

But, sure enough, all the TV sets jammed. The one real near me didn't jam up that bad, but the other ones did. Well, almost instantly these three teaching assistants started looking at us. One of them said, "Okay. Whoever's got the transmitter, turn it off."

Wow. I didn't even know there were TAs in the class. So while they're looking right at us, saying "turn it off," do you think I'm going to reach my hand down and turn it off in plain sight? No way.

My plan had been to just jam it for a few seconds, but now I couldn't turn it off without getting caught.

So I'm sitting there kind of scared, afraid to move because they're watching us so closely. I couldn't even put my hand near it for fear that it might make the images on-screen wobble. I didn't even want to reach over to my Magic Marker and click the Jammer off because the guy next to me would hear me click something. He'd know I did it.

Eventually the TAs sat down, but they kept watching us. There was nothing they could do. And you know, the TVs weren't jammed so bad that we couldn't watch the professor or take notes. So our class just went on, with all of us watching the jammed TVs.

So I've got my Magic Marker TV Jammer sitting there between the two rings of my binder when suddenly the guy who's sitting the closest to the TV jammed the worst, in the right rear of the classroom, decides to gather his books and leave early. I decided to make the TVs waver as he was walking out. I felt like I could get away with it. I couldn't resist.

As he was leaving, the picture back there on the right rear TV went perfect. One of the TAs pointed at him. The TA said, "There he goes."

Pranks are entertainment, comedy. Not only did I manage to pull off this prank, but I managed to make it look as if someone else had done it. That's a step beyond the old rule "Don't get caught." I learned how to use that technique many times throughout my prank career. And if you're shocked that I can trick people with my pranks and not feel dishonest about it, remember that the basic form of entertainment is to make up stories. That's comedy.

I don't know if they ever did anything to that guy, but I doubt it. I hope not. It's not like they could catch him with a TV Jammer. As far as I knew, I had the only one.

● ○ ●

But I did end up getting in some trouble that year.

You see, I started writing programs that could kick paper out of the computer over at the computer printers everyone had to use at the Computer Center of the University of Colorado. That wasn't a big deal. But then I thought, Okay, what are computers for? They're for calculating numbers. Calculation has always been central to my association with computers, you know. So I tried to think up something really clever.

I wrote seven programs—they were all real simple but extremely interesting in a math sense. One of them dealt with what I called "magic computer numbers." That would be the powers of two. So 2^1 equals 2, 2^2 is 4, 2^3 is 8, 2^4 is 16. These are the binary numbers all computers work with, so they are the most special of all the computer numbers.

I made it so the printer would print out the results formatted in a way that was readable. For instance, one line might say: 1, 2. That meant 2 to the first power is 2. The next would say 2, 4: 2 to the second power is 4. You will see that the numbers get really big really fast. For example, 2 to the eighth power is 256; 2 to the sixteenth power is 65,536. So pretty soon I am filling up pages with these really long numbers! After enough pages, the powers of 2 would be almost a line long. Then they would expand to two or three lines. Eventually it got to where each number might be a whole page or more!

Another program worked with Fibonacci numbers. These are numbers that go in a sequence like 1, 2, 3, 5, 8, 13, 21, 34 . . . Each Fibonacci number is the sum of the two numbers preceding it. So it's a never-ending sequence. All of my seven programs did this— calculated numbers in these long, ridiculously long, sequences.

Some programs have loops and don't stop running because there is a bug, or a problem, with a program. That is called an infinite loop, which I told you about in connection with the chess game I did back in high school. Anyway, the Computer Center automatically kicked off any program that ran more than 64 seconds. So I figured out that all my computers could print out 60 pages in under 64 seconds, and that's why I wrote each program to print out only 60 pages all numbered page 1, page 2, etc. The next time I ran the program, it would print the next 60 pages (beginning at 61), and so on. I wrote all my programs so they would punch some cards I could use the next time so the programs could pick up where they left off.

I would walk over to the Computer Center every morning and drop my seven programs off. Then, around noon, I would pick up my outputs and resubmit the programs. Then I would come back in the evening and resubmit them. I would get three runs a day times 60 pages times seven programs piling up in my dorm room. Mike, my roommate, started getting a little upset at all the space it was taking up. It was really piling up: reams and reams, feet and feet of computer paper, all stacking up in my dorm room.

Then, one afternoon, I got to the Computer Center for an afternoon run and they didn't have my programs there. There was a note there saying I should see my professor right away.

I went to see him in his office. He said, "Okay, sit down." He started a tape recorder—he punched a button and started recording us. I remember I got a bit scared.

"You've been running these programs on your own," he said.

And I said, "Yes. We were in a programming class. I was learning programming. I ran them under my own student number. I didn't try to hide the fact I was running them."

"This had nothing to do with our class," he said.

"It was FORTRAN," I told him.

"This is not the FORTRAN we teach," he said. And he was right. Because I had gone way into the manuals to find little

What Is FORTRAN?

FORTRAN is a computer language developed in the 1950s and still heavily used for scientific computing and numerical computation half a century later. The name comes from the words "Formula Translation." As a compiled language, it is typically faster and more powerful than an interpreted language such as BASIC.

tricks of mathematical symbols. I had gone way beyond simple programming, and we both knew it.

He said it took him a long time studying my programs to figure out what they did, but he finally figured them out. He said: "Are you trying to get me?"

Get him? I didn't know what he meant by that. I guess he felt threatened by the unrest happening in relation to the Vietnam War. The Students for a Democratic Society (SDS) was big on that campus. But I was totally apolitical except for registering once to be in the University Republicans Club! I mean, I was just a mild, meek engineering student and would never be involved in anything politically subversive.

"Out to get you?" I said. I had no idea what he was talking about.

Well, he picked up the phone and called someone at the Computer Center. "These programs . . . Mr. Wozniak should be billed for this computer time."

Then I found out what I'd done. I'd run my class five times over its annual budget for computer time. I didn't even realize there were budgets. I thought if you're in a computer class, you get computer time. That was logical to assume. But now I realized I ran up a whole lot of money on his account, and my best guess is he was using me to get out of it. I didn't think they would actually charge me, a student. A freshman. But I was scared because the amount he was talking about was in the thousands of dollars—many times the out-of-state tuition money.

So that's how it became very clear to me, at the end of that school year, that I was not going to make it an issue with my parents and try to go back to Colorado. I was on probation for computer abuse. I wouldn't let my parents find out. I didn't want them to get billed this huge amount of money. So that's how I decided to go to De Anza Community College the next year, instead of going back to Colorado like all my friends.

What really bothers me when I think of this now is, they shouldn't have charged me. They should've praised me for doing these brilliant programs all on my own.

And I did get an A-plus in that class.

• ○ •

Now I was back home and attending De Anza Community College. I spent a lot of time designing and redesigning computers on paper, which is what I'd been doing in high school. Like when I took the manuals of popular minicomputers at the time (the pizza-box-sized, rack-mounted computers from Varian, Hewlett-Packard, Digital Equipment, and other companies in 1969 and 1970) and redesigned them, over and over, on paper so they would take fewer chips and run more efficiently.

By the time I finished at De Anza, I had literally designed and redesigned some of the best-known computers in the world. I'd become an expert on designing them, no question, because I'd redesigned their prototypes so many dozens of times. I'd done everything but build them. There was no doubt in my mind that if I ever did build them, I could get them to work. I was this virtual expert—and yes, I mean that in the software sense of the word "virtual." I never built those computers, but I was so entranced by and familiar with their innards that I easily could have taken any one of them apart and rebuilt it so that the computer would be cheaper, better, and more efficient.

I never had the courage to ask chip companies for free samples of what were then expensive chips. A year later I would meet Steve Jobs, who showed me how brave he was by scoring free chips just by calling sales reps. I could never do that. Our introverted and extroverted personalities (guess who's which) really helped us in those days. What one of us found difficult, the other often accomplished pretty handily. Examples of that teamwork are all over this story.

• ○ •

Once, at De Anza, my quantum physics teacher said, "Wozniak. That's an unusual name. I knew a Wozniak once. There was a Wozniak who went to Caltech."

"My father," I said, "he went to Caltech."

"Well, this one was a great football player."

That was my father, I told him. He was the team's quarterback.

"Yes," the teacher said. "We would never go to football games, but at Caltech, you had to go just to watch Jerry Wozniak. He was famous."

You know, I think my dad was the one good quarterback Caltech ever had. He even got scouted by the Los Angeles Rams, though I don't think he was good enough to play pro. Still, it was neat to hear from a physics teacher that he remembered my dad for his football. It made me feel like I shared a history with him. The teacher once even brought me a Caltech paper from back in those days with a picture of my dad in his uniform.

I didn't get along with all the teachers, though. I was taking an advanced-level math class, and the teacher caught me not paying attention. (I was trying to figure out how to write a FORTRAN compiler in machine language for the Data General Nova.)

I was just at the first line where you have to enter something and store it in memory when he said: "You've got so much potential, Wozniak. If only you'd just put yourself into this material."

It stung me the way he said that in front of the whole class. That wasn't necessary. I just wanted to sit in class and do whatever it was I felt like doing. Maybe I was bored, I don't know. I was the sort of person who read the book, took the test, and got good grades in subjects like math.

•   ○   •

It was also at De Anza that I got this mental turnaround on politics. I started seriously thinking about whether the Vietnam War was right or wrong. Who was it helping, and did we have any place there?

Back in high school, I was for the war. My father told me our country was the greatest in the world, and my thinking was like his: that we had to stand up for democracy versus communism; and the reasons why, stemming from our Constitution. I had never thought deeply about political issues aside from that, and I was really for my country, right or wrong. I mean, I was for my country the same way you root for your school's team, right or wrong. At the University of Colorado, the University Republicans Club was one of the only two clubs I joined (the other was the Amateur Radio Club).

But I started to wonder why so many people were protesting the war so visibly. A lot of academics and journalists were talking about the history of the Vietnamese people and had explanations for why the U.S. position was wrong. It was a civil war, involving treaties, agreements, and a history that didn't affect the United States one whit. The trouble is, I could find no intelligent academic reasoning coming from the pro-war side, just the constant refrain that we were doing good. They could only say that we were there protecting democracy.

One of my biggest problems was that South Vietnam, which we were supposedly protecting, wasn't even close to a democracy. It was more like a corrupt dictatorship. How could we ever stand up for a dictatorship? I started seeing that there was a lot more truth on the side of the people against the war.

The people against the war were also talking about how good peace was compared to war. Sure, the world can't live in perfect peace and harmony, but it's a good ideal. I had come to learn of Jesus, from my friend Randy Adair in college, that he always tried to find ways toward peace. Although I'm not a Christian per se, and don't belong to any religion, what Jesus the historical figure stood for were things I stood for, and those stories Randy told me about him struck a chord with me emotionally. I didn't believe in violence or hurting people.

At De Anza, I thought deeply about the war. I considered myself to be athletic and brave. But would I shoot a bullet at another human being? I remember sitting alone at the white Formica table in my bedroom, coming to the conclusion that I could let someone shoot at me, but I couldn't shoot back.

I thought, What if I'm in Vietnam and I'm shooting at some guy? He's just like me, that guy. He sits down just like I do. He plays cards and he eats pizza, or the equivalent of it, just like normal people I know. He has a family. Why would I want to hurt this person? He might have his reasons for being where he is in the world—and Vietnam had its reason—but none of these reasons ever touched me in California.

From that standpoint, I could see how this war could be a pretty dangerous one for me. Because I was morally and truthfully a conscientious objector in every sense. But the military only counted you as one if you were in a church (which made you exempt from conflict duties), and I had no church. I had no religion. I just had my own logic.

So I wasn't a conscientious objector, I just objected to my personally having to kill or hurt anyone.

Chapter 5

Cream Soda Days

When I was about nineteen, I read the Pentagon Papers and learned what was really going on in Vietnam. As a result, I started to have some major conflicting feelings and some nasty fights with my dad.

By then he was drinking heavily, and he wasn't the greatest opponent to argue with. But I had a new truth that replaced the old one even more strongly. I started to believe in peace. And I began to realize how far governments would go in order to get people to believe them.

For one thing, the Pentagon Papers showed what the CIA and the Pentagon people truly knew, and that the president was being carefully coached to put words together and lie to the American people. He was saying the opposite of the truth to trick the American people into thinking they should actually support the war. For instance, the papers got right down to the Gulf of Tonkin incident—which never happened the way the government said it did. The papers also said how, in every battle, the public was always told that ten times as many Viet Cong as Americans died, despite the fact that we had no way to count them. And most Americans believed this crap. The Pentagon Papers documented this deliberate deception.

Learning about that was one of the hardest things I had to deal with in my life. You see, I just wasn't raised to believe that a democracy like ours would spread these kinds of lies. Why was the United States government treating the American people as the enemy and purposely duping them? It made no sense to me.

And the worst thing that came after that, for me, wasn't the Vietnam War itself, but the pain and stress it caused people. That's because, as I was becoming an adult, I started gaining a new ethic—a profound care for the happiness and welfare of people. I was just starting to figure out that the secret to life— and this is still true for me—is to find a way to be happy and sat- isfied with your life and also to make other people happy and satisfied with their lives.

Even in high school, where I believed in truth with a capital T, I was willing to change my beliefs if someone came along to show

The Gulf of Tonkin

Not everyone reading this is going to remember this incident, but finding out about it was instrumental in changing my own feelings about the Vietnam War.

The Gulf of Tonkin incident was an alleged attack on two American destroyers (the USS *Maddox* and the USS *C. Turner Joy*) in August of 1964 in the Gulf of Tonkin by North Viet- namese gunboats. Later research indicates that most of the attacks did not actually occur.

According to the Pentagon Papers and various reports, the attacks were pretty much made up by President Lyndon B. John- son's administration. The U.S.-supported South Vietnamese regime had been attacking oil-processing facilities in North Viet- nam, but it was the CIA that helped plan and support it in order to give the administration a good reason to involve the U.S. in the conflict.

me something better. That's what the Pentagon Papers did for me. They pointed out that even the president was subject to the pressures of the military-industrial complex, the major institution of our land. And after reading this, I decided not to vote, that it wouldn't matter either way. I figured that pretty much I'd get the same life no matter who was elected. I thought it was better not even to go into the voting booth.

But I did vote a couple of times. I voted for a guy named George McGovern, who promised he'd find a way to stop the war. I voted for Jimmy Carter, because the words he spoke seemed to come from the same philosophical point of view as my own. He believed, as I did, that war was a last resort and not a first.

I voted for George W. Bush in 2000, because I thought it would be nice to have an average Joe kind of person in the White House instead of a smart, well-educated one. Someone who could only speak in very small words. Okay, I'm joking. The fact is I voted for Ralph Nader. But since all the pundits said that a vote for Nader was a vote for Bush, I now tell people I voted for Bush just to watch their jaws drop.

Seriously, though, I still think about this whole era with a lot of pain. Being brought up by my dad, who'd taught me that we had the best government in the world and that our government was the best one there ever could be even with its flaws, well, that kind of fell apart. He told me the purpose of the government was to take care of its people and make things better for them.

During the Vietnam War, of course, there was a mandatory draft. When you turned eighteen, you had to register. If you were a college student, you would get what was called a 2S deferment; otherwise you would be classified as 1A. That meant that any day the military could draft you and send you off to boot camp.

Once you were 1A, the government had a year to draft you. After that, you would be exempt. That's why not everyone who was 1A wound up serving.

I submitted a report card to the San Jose draft board in order to get my 2S deferment, but I didn't submit one of the proper forms the government required to show you were a college student. By mistake I only sent in my report card.

A couple of months later, a big delay, I received notice that the San Jose draft board had voted five to three to make me 1A. What? But I was a student.

This is when I decided that I would go to prison or Canada or, more likely, try to get let off by a judge rather than go to Vietnam. In fact, a judge in San Jose—his name was Judge Peckham—had let a couple of guys off as conscientious objectors despite their lack of membership in a church.

One of those people let off had been one of the brightest math stars at my high school, Allen Stein. Quite a coincidence. So I had good reason to expect the same in my situation.

So since I was 1A anyway, I took a year off from school to program computers and earn money to pay for my third year of college and buy a car.

Then an amazing thing happened. The U.S. Congress created a draft lottery. That meant that those of us who were 1A would know the likelihood of our being called up. This was so it wouldn't be random. That way, you would know your chances—and I thought it was great. It helped me plan my life.

The way the draft lottery worked was your birthday determined what order you got called in. They would assign everyone's birth date to a number from 1 to 366. So January 1 might be 66, January 2 might be 12, it was totally random.

Well, during the week before they announced the results of the lottery, I got a feeling I have never had before or since. A feeling of physical warmth, like I was going to be protected and get a high number in this lottery. I had a stronger level of certainty than I would ever have let myself feel about the unknown. I can't explain it. I'm not a superstitious person in any way. I have always believed in reality, the truth, and the provable. But this was so certain in my head. I rode my bike around, just smiling and smiling and smiling about it. I couldn't stop. It was a wonderful, positive feeling, and I couldn't ignore it and pretend it wasn't there.

And sure enough, I read in the newspaper the day of the draft lottery that I got number 325. A great number! That meant it was virtually certain I wouldn't be drafted. It's so weird. I got such a great number, but I wasn't even surprised or elated. I felt like I'd known it all along. The feeling I'd had was that strong.

But then something terrible and unexpected happened.

About a week after I got my draft lottery number, I got a letter from the San Jose draft board. It said—in one sentence—that they were granting me a student deferment after all.

This, after taking months to notify me that they'd voted five to three not to grant my student deferment when I deserved it, was bad enough. But worse, it also meant that in a later year they could make me 1A a second time.

I stood there with the letter in my hand, stunned. They were playing tricks with my life. Dirty tricks. They used the application I'd made for a student deferment as an excuse to grant it to me now, knowing that I already had a great 1A number.

• ○ •

From that point on, I saw that the government would do whatever it could to beat a citizen, that it was just a game. And this was the exact opposite of the way I had thought of government my whole life. That episode taught me an important lesson about government, authority, even the police. You couldn't trust them to do the right thing.

Now I had to go back to the draft board and request to keep my 1A—which was what I'd had anyway—and keep the same number. Luckily, they agreed.

I can't even describe to you the shock and disgust I felt at our government: that they would play this kind of game with my life, that they didn't care about people the way my dad had taught me. I'd thought the government was here to protect us, but that turned out to be wrong. I now believed the government was just out to do what was good for the government and would lie about anything they could get away with. They were not there to do sensible things, and they played with my life in the worst possible way.

From then on, my dad and I were at complete odds. I never trusted authority after that. That's too bad, because since founding Apple and all, I've met lots of good people in the government. But still, this hangs over me. I can hardly trust anything I read.

So between the time I was a kid, when my dad taught me extreme ethics, and the time I realized what was going on with the Vietnam War, I changed profoundly, a full 180 degrees. I became skeptical. I stopped believing blindly in things. It was a major turning point. I lost the trust I'd always had in institutions of all kinds and it has never really returned.

I swore to myself I would put up my own life before letting something like the Vietnam War ever happen again to young kids.

• ◦ •

Maybe you've seen pictures of me from the early days and thought I looked like a hippie. I guess I did, a little. But let me tell you, I was never a hippie.

I tried to be a hippie, but I could never be what they were— not in high school or even in college when all that protest stuff was going on. I'd try to hang out with hippies because I stood with them politically, but they'd usually ask me to leave because I wouldn't use drugs. I still wanted to hang around them because I felt my mind was so open—as open as theirs were—and I got what they were saying. I wanted them to be open with me, but their drugs got in the way. They didn't trust me because I wouldn't do drugs with them.

But I believed in almost everything they were trying to do. Everything I was reading about hippies and hippie beliefs in the late 1960s—the free love movement, things like putting flowers in guns—I knew that was me and what I wanted to be. I agreed with every bit of it. I believed, like hippies did, that everybody should be able to get along and help each other out and live out whatever kind of existence they wanted. And I believed it could be an existence without structure and without laws and without organization and without politics.

People should just agree to live together and be good people, I really believed that. I was tremendously influenced by these kinds of hippie thoughts, these kinds of philosophies.

I would wear this little Indian headband, and I wore my hair really long and grew a beard. From the neck up, I looked like Jesus Christ. But from the neck down, I still wore the clothes of a regular kid, a kid engineer. Pants. Collared shirt. I never did have the weird hippie clothes. I was still middle ground; I was still the way I'd grown up. No matter how hard I tried, it was like I couldn't get outside of normal. Hippie is a way of life, not just a matter of clothes and hair, and I didn't lead that kind of life. I didn't live in weird little places with no money with weird curtains hanging in my windows. And I didn't do drugs. I wouldn't.

At the time, not doing drugs or drinking made me real different. I mean, at the time, especially during my second year at De Anza and for years and years after, people would say things like: "Oh, using LSD can really expand your mind." I remember a guy—John was his name—who claimed that all the A's he got were when he was on acid.

But I thought to myself: Well, if drugs are really better for your mind and can make you think better, then wait a minute. When you take a drug, it's you plus the drug that's working, right? It's not just you. And I really, really wanted to be successful in my life just based on me and my mind alone. I knew that I was bright and that my brain was going to take me places. I didn't ever want it to be an equation that amounted to a result coming from my brain plus something else. I wanted to be judged on my own abilities, on what I did and what I thought, and that alone. So that was pretty much my view on drugs, and I never did any of them.

As for drinking, I didn't even get drunk until I was thirty, in 1980. It was on my first flight out of the United States to Sri Lanka. I was extremely scared on the plane so I was drinking. I wasn't sure they'd let you off a plane if you were drunk. I managed to walk off the plane without assistance, and I ended up telling a really awful joke to a customs official:

A lady who'd never seen an elephant before saw an escaped one in her garden. Shrieking, she called the police. "There's a huge animal in my garden!" she said. "Pulling up the vegetables with his tail! And you wouldn't believe where he's putting them!"

I don't remember if he laughed or not. I don't think so. It's not a joke I normally would have told. It's sort of dumb and hard to get.

Anyway, I never liked alcohol. It made people act noisy and out of control. My dad, for instance, he used to drink martinis. I always noticed how he reasoned differently when he was drunk. Especially as he and I got older, I thought it got really out of hand, the way he would get drunk and yell at my mother. That's not the way he was when he wasn't drinking.

So I didn't drink or do drugs, and as I said, that usually made it kind of weird for the hippie people I wanted to be friends with, people who thought like me in every other way. What a sad thing. During that second year at De Anza, I remember driving my first car down to Santa Cruz. This was back when there were hitchhikers all over the place. (The car I was driving was this purple convertible I'd named Hubbs after a weird chemistry professor I had, but it wasn't that funny a joke because neither the car nor the professor was really that weird.)

Anyway, I stopped and picked up a group of people. They were definitely hippies. And I took them down to Santa Cruz. We're hanging out on the boardwalk and I notice that one of them, a young girl sitting on a bench, was breast-feeding. Breast-feeding! I'd never seen anything like that before in my life! I just turned my head away really quickly, but it made such an impression on me. I started talking to her, and immediately fell in love with her and her baby. It turned out that she and her baby and a bunch of people all lived together in this commune near me in Sunnyvale. Later I would ride my bike out there a lot and stop at a park near their house and read books. I would go over and hang out with them. We'd eat and do the ohm chanting and all of that. And they would take me with them to meet all these Eastern philosophy-type teachers, really getting me exposed to Eastern thoughts of peace and quietness. I listened to these principles of meditation, and I would just sit down and try to get my head into a quiet place by myself.

The sad thing was, eventually even these hippies didn't want to hang around me anymore. It made them uncomfortable that I didn't do drugs.

So this was a hard social time for me. I remember that at one point I was taking some night classes at San Jose State and this pretty girl comes up to my table in the cafeteria and says, "Oh, hi." She just starts talking to me, and I'm so nervous all I can think to ask her is what her major is. She says, "Scientology." I'd never heard of this, but she assured me it was actually a major and I believed it.

She invited me to a Scientology meeting, and of course I went. I ended up in the audience watching this guy make this incredible presentation about how you can basically be in better control of yourself and that you could get really happy from that.

After the meeting, the girl I met sat with me in some little office for an hour, trying to sell me these courses to become a better person. I was going to have to pay money for them.

I said to her, "I've already got my happiness. I've got my keys to happiness. I don't need anything. I'm not looking for any of this stuff." And I meant it. The only thing I might've wanted was a girlfriend, that's for sure, but the rest of the stuff I already had. I had a sense of humor, and I had this attitude about life that let me choose to be happy. I knew that whether to be happy was always going to be my choice, and only my choice.

Plus I had these values, values I'd grown up with. I already had this peaceful feeling inside my head. To this day, I'm one of those people whose head just floats. I really did feel happy most of the time. I still do.

So the bottom line, of course, is she never sold me any courses or anything. In fact, she just walked out and never came back. When I wasn't interested in buying her courses, she left and just let me sit there. I sat and sat, waiting for her to come back. Finally I walked out the door and left, too. I thought, Man, that's too bad. She was just about sales, that's all she was.

• ○ •

After my year at De Anza, I decided the thing to do was to take a job where I could actually program computers. I thought I'd skip a year of school so I could earn enough money to go for a third one, at Berkeley maybe.

Now, for a while I'd been telling my dad that I definitely was going to own a 4K-byte Data General Nova someday. That was just enough kilobytes needed to program in. It was this huge, powerful computer at the time. I loved its internal architecture and everything about it. I even had a poster of it up in my room. So I heard there was a place in Sunnyvale that sold these Data General computers. My friend Allen Baum and I drove down to the place.

Well, the office was beautiful, and right in the middle of the lobby was this big glass display with a large computer in it. It wasn't a room-sized computer like a mainframe, but a midsized computer. It was about as large as a refrigerator, with other things like large printers and disk drives the size of dishwashers attached to it. There were some wires hanging loose with engineers working on them. And I thought, Wow, here's a computer actually being designed and built. That was a shock for me to see.

Another shock turned out to be that I had walked in the wrong door, that I wasn't at the Data General company at all, but at a smaller company called Tenet. Allen and I both filled out applications for jobs as programmers—and you know what? We got them.

We got to program in the language FORTRAN, and also in machine language, which is nearest to the lowest-level language (1s and 0s) a computer can understand. We got to know that computer so deeply that summer. We really got into the depths of its architecture. Personally, I didn't think much of the architecture inside, although they ended up building something pretty good—a working computer, a fast computer, a low-cost computer for what it was. I mean, it cost more than $100,000, and those were 1970 dollars. I was impressed by that. It had an operating system that worked well and several programming languages.

Now, of course, in no way was that Tenet computer like our computers today. It had no screen for a display and no keyboard to type into. It had lights you had to read off a front panel, and it took information from punch cards. But for the time being, yeah, I guess it was pretty cool.

● ○ ●

Tenet actually went out of business the next summer—I stayed for the duration, having decided not to return to school that year after all—but my time there turned out to be really fortunate.

You see, during the summer, I remember telling one Tenet executive how I had spent the last few years designing and redesigning existing computers on paper but could never build one because I didn't have the parts.

One time, at my old friend Bill Werner's house, I got Bill to call up a chip company, but he could never get them to give us free parts, never. But I asked this Tenet executive, and he said, "Sure, I can get you the parts." I guess he had access to sample parts, and that was what I needed.

To help him avoid having to get me tons and tons of parts—parts I would need to build some kind of existing minicomputer—I decided I would build a computer that was just a little one with very few chips.

I'm talking about, like, about twenty chips—which is very, very few chips compared to the hundreds it would have taken to build a normal computer at the time.

Now, I had this other friend, Bill Fernandez, who lived down the block. I started hanging around at his house, and we just started putting together this little computer I designed (first on paper, of course) piece by piece, bit by bit. He helped me by doing all kinds of things—like soldering, for instance.

Anyway, we would do this in his garage, and then we'd ride our bikes down to the Sunnyvale Safeway, where we would buy Craigmont cream soda, and then drink it while we worked on this machine. That's how we started referring to it as the Cream Soda Computer. All the Cream Soda Computer was, really, was a little circuit board that allowed you to plug in connectors and solder the chips I had to the connectors. This board was tiny—I would say it was no larger than four to six inches.

Like all the computers at the time, there wasn't a screen or a keyboard. No one had thought of that yet. Instead you'd write a program, punch it into a punch card, slide it in, and then you'd get your answer by reading the flashing lights on the front panel. Or, for instance, you could write a program that would tell the computer to beep every three seconds. And if it did, then you would know it was working. It turned out just as I had designed it, with few chips because I didn't want to ask that executive for too many free samples. So it was just the most minimum thing you could even call a computer. What I mean by that is, it could run a program. It could give you results.

The other significant thing about it was the fact that it had 256 bytes of RAM. (That's about the size in memory a word processor would take today to store this very sentence.)

RAM chips were almost unheard of at this time. Back then, almost all computers had a type of memory called "magnetic core memories." When you dealt with them, you had to deal with messy voltages to spike the right currents down the wires, the wires that had to go into these little round magnetic cores that looked like tiny donuts you needed a magnifying glass even to see. This was definitely not the type of electronics I had in mind. With RAM chips, though, you just plug them in and connect them to the CPU, the brain of the computer. You connect them to the processor with wires and that's that. So, as you can see, I was extremely lucky to get those eight chips that added up to 256 bytes. And as I said, even then you couldn't do much of anything in that small a space.

● ○ ●

What Is RAM?

RAM, short for random-access memory, was a new type of computer storage back in 1970. These are chips whose contents can be accessed in any (i.e., random) order. All computers today have RAM chips inside to store data—not permanently, but while your computer is on and you're working. When the computer shuts down, the contents of RAM goes away. That's why you need to save your programs to disk.

One day my mom called the *Peninsula Times* newspaper and told them about the Cream Soda Computer. A reporter came over and asked some questions about it and took some pictures. But just as he was finishing, he accidentally stepped on the power supply cable and blew out the computer. The Cream Soda actually smoked! But the article ran anyway, and that was pretty cool.

But you know what? I knew deep inside that it didn't matter that I had built this computer. It didn't matter because the computer couldn't do anything useful. It couldn't play games, it couldn't solve math problems. It had way too little memory. The only important thing was that finally, finally, I'd been able to actually build a computer. My very first one. It was an extraordinary milestone in that sense.

Five years later, companies would be building and selling computer kits that were just about at this level—they had the same amount of memory and the same awkward front panel of lights and switches.

Looking back, I see the Cream Soda Computer as kind of a jumping-off point for me. And I got there early.

●   ○   ●

One other thing: the Cream Soda Computer turned out to be the way I first met Steve Jobs. I was four years ahead of him in school so I didn't know him; he was closer to Bill Fernandez's age. But one day Bill told me, "Hey, there's someone you should meet. His name is Steve. He likes to do pranks like you do, and he's also into building electronics like you are."

So one day—it was daytime, I remember—Bill called Steve and had him come over to his house. I remember Steve and I just sat on the sidewalk in front of Bill's house for the longest time, just sharing stories—mostly about pranks we'd pulled, and also what kind of electronic designs we'd done. It felt like we had so much in common. Typically, it was really hard for me to explain to people the kind of design stuff I worked on, but Steve got it right away. And I liked him. He was kind of skinny and wiry and full of energy.

So Steve came into the garage and saw the computer (this was before it blew up) and listened to our description of it. I could tell he was impressed. I mean, we'd actually built a computer from scratch and proved that it was possible—or going to be possible—for people to have computers in a really small space.

Steve and I got close right away, even though he was still in high school, remember, and lived about a mile away in Los Altos. I lived in Sunnyvale. Bill was right—we two Steves did have a lot in common. We talked electronics, we talked about music we liked, and we traded stories about pranks we'd pulled. We even pulled a few together.

●   ○   ●

When I met Steve Jobs I was still hanging out with this other guy I'd known since high school, Allen Baum.

Allen was kind of a nerdy, skinny guy with glasses when I first met him back in high school. We were both in the super-elite of students, not just the ones in top classes but students who outperformed pretty much everybody else. We'd be selected out by teachers to compete in math contests or go to speeches and lectures, that kind of thing. So we all knew each other. Most of us were considered by other kids to be kind of weird outsiders, and Allen was even smaller, scrawnier, and more outside than I was. He was even nerdier.

Later he came to be very into hippie things and San Francisco-type music like the Grateful Dead and Jefferson Airplane, but he started out just completely way, way on the outside.

From high school on, I used to like to go visit Allen and his parents. They were Jewish with relatives who'd died in concentration camps; it was shocking and all so new to me. Allen's father, Elmer, was an engineer who loved humor—he was incredibly funny—and he was really active in civil rights causes. His mom, Charlotte, was like that, too. I thought of Elmer and Charlotte Baum as being so much like me—just kind of casual and fun.

So, as I said, I was hanging out with Allen a lot when Steve Jobs, who by now was a junior at Homestead High, had an idea. He wanted to create a huge sign on a giant bedsheet with a flip-off sign—you know, the middle-finger salute—right during graduation. He thought the sign should say "Best Wishes." We started calling it the "Brazilian Best Wishes" sign.

So we went right to work. We got this big sheet—it had been tie-dyed because Allen and his brothers were always tie-dying everything back then—and spread it out in Allen's backyard. Anyway, we started sketching out our drawing with chalk—a big hand with its finger sticking up. And Allen's mother even helped us draw it—she showed us how to shade it so it looked more like a real hand, less like a cartoon. I remember how she sort of realized what the hand was doing partway through, but she just snickered at us and smiled, saying, "I know what that is." But she didn't stop us. I guess she didn't know what we planned to do with it, exactly.

On the sheet, we signed it "SWAB JOB. The S and W stood for Steve Wozniak, the A and B stood for Allen Baum, and JOB stood for Steve Jobs. We finished the sheet and rolled it up. Late that night, we climbed onto the top of the C building, where we planned to drop it. The idea was that we would attach it to this forty-pound fishing line and kind of pull it down when the graduating Homestead High seniors walked past.

Well, we practiced it and found out that you just can't pull a sheet down off a roof and have it roll down nicely. It doesn't come down off the roof easily, and it will pull other junk off the roof, and it can come down all weird in different shapes.

So the next night we tried to make this little cart thing with an axle and two wheels that we could pull. The idea was that it would let the sheet down gradually. The axle was nearly eight inches wide. But we found that one of the wheels would always get stuck on its little track. We just couldn't get it right.

By the fourth night of trying to do this, Allen and I were working alone. Steve just didn't have the stamina to stay up and work all night. And by then we'd come up with another idea. Don't use the axle, but keep the wheels. We rigged up this little hookup on the building, higher than the sheet would be, and attached the fishing line and a couple of skates to it. We then tested it out. We stood on the roof, let go of the fishing line, and watched the little skates roll down their ramps until they pulled the sheet down so it scrolled down, pulling down the left side and the right side together. Left to right. It worked perfectly.

We almost got caught that night, by the way. We tried to test it again, but a janitor came along. We just ducked on that roof and were lying down as low as we could. I remember the janitor moving his flashlight around and the light landing on my hand. But before he could call anyone, we ran out of there like crazy.

A couple of days later was graduation day. I woke up that morning to the phone ringing. It was Steve calling from school with bad news. It turned out someone, probably another student, had cut the fishing line and pulled the sign down that morning. So Steve got in trouble—I guess the "SWAB JOB" gave it away, and we never got to play our prank.

Afterward I thought about this a lot. I finally came to the conclusion that even though our "Brazilian Best Wishes" sign didn't come off, it wasn't a failure. Some projects are worth the energy and worth spending a lot of time on, even if they don't come out perfectly.

I learned about teamwork and patience and hard work from that prank—and I learned never to brag about my pranks. Because I found out a year later that Steve Jobs had shown some of the students our prank, showing off. And the guy who told me that—that Steve Jobs had shown him the sign—said he was the guy who cut it down.

• ○ •

Steve and I were into listening to Bob Dylan and his lyrics, trying to figure out who was better, Dylan or the Beatles. We both favored Dylan because the songs were about life and living and values in life and what was really important. The Beatles mostly made these nice little happy songs—you know, nice-to-know-you, nice-to-be-with-you, nice-to-be-in-love-with-you songs. They were simple—even after albums like *Rubber Soul* came out. The songs the Beatles did were not as deep down and affecting your soul and emotions as Dylan's were. They were more like pop songs. To us, Dylan's songs struck a moral chord. They kind of made you think about what was right and wrong in the world, and how you're going to live and be.

At any rate, this first introduction we never forgot, and later on Steve and I were really linked. Linked forever.

Chapter 6

Phreaking for Real

In 1971, the day before I headed off to my third year of college at Berkeley, I was sitting at my mother's kitchen table and there happened to be a copy of *Esquire* sitting there. Even though I never usually read this magazine, for some reason I started flipping through it that day.

I came upon an article called "Secrets of the Little Blue Box." Those were interesting enough words to make me stop skimming and read that article all the way through.

Now, it was labeled as a fiction article, and I had no idea what a Blue Box was until I started reading the article. But as soon as I did, it just grabbed me. Wow! You know how some articles just grab you from the first paragraph? Well, it was one of those articles, probably because this story was about tech people like me. Back then, there were never articles about tech people—really, never—so once I started reading this article, about people like me, I couldn't stop. It basically was a story about how a bunch of technical kids and young engineers around the country had figured out how to crack codes on the phone system. The article called them "phone phreaks." These people were able to figure out that by just whistling certain tones into a phone handset, they could make telephone calls within the Bell phone system for free.

Essentially, they first would dial an 800 or 555 number, any free exchange, then they would make this tone sound to seize the line. If this certain tone worked, they'd get a chirp that meant they were now in control of a piece of phone circuit equipment called a tandem. (A tandem just waits for special tones to direct calls throughout the phone system.) The phone phreak could then give the system the tones it needed to dial any seven- or ten-digit number just by making a bunch of certain sounds that were equal to the numbers on a phone from Ma Bell's perspective.

That sounded plausible in a way. I already had a basic idea about how the tone system worked on telephones. And the people in the article—in this story labeled "fiction"—were claiming that by doing this, they were finding out things about the phone system no one knew about. I'm talking about things like its inherent bugs and holes and weaknesses and, of course, all the ways to take advantage of them. So, as I said, they were doing things by whistling tones into the phone lines, by tricking operators, by bouncing calls off satellites and back to other countries. They were doing all this stuff. And though it was supposed to be a fictional story, I kept reading it over and over, and the more I read it, the more possible and real it sounded.

The other thing that intrigued me about the article was the fact that it described a whole web of people who were doing this: the phone phreaks. They were anonymous technical people who went by fake names and lived all over the place. Some were in the Northeast, some in the Southeast, some were in the West. Just all over. The story told a tale about some guys who drove out to Arizona, clamped a wire to a pay phone, and were somehow able to literally take over the whole country's phone networks. It said they were able to set themselves up into ten-way conference calls.

The characters the author made up, well, they just sounded too perfectly described to be fake. I remember how it spoke about some blind kids who just wanted someone to talk to. Somehow they'd gotten the phone company people to tell them some of the secrets of the phone company and were using them to talk to each other. That made sense to me, too.

The article also talked about the ethics these guys supposedly had. That it wasn't just about free calls. One of the guys said he was basically trying to do a good thing by finding flaws in the system and letting the phone company know what they were. That appealed to me.

The article also talked about one of the secrets these guys had discovered. Well, I already knew this secret, so I guess it was kind of a rediscovery. I'm talking about the technique of taking any phone—you can do it with any phone to this day—and tapping out phone numbers with the hook switch. What I mean is the actual switch on the phone that tells the phone company if the phone is on or off the hook. What you do is pick up the phone. You hear a dial tone, right? Then if you click that hook switch once, it's like dialing a "1." Click it twice really quickly and that is the same as dialing a "2." Clicking it ten times in a row would be the same as dialing a "0." (The reason this works goes back to the old days of rotary phones when you dialed a "5," and the dial would swing back five times—click click click click click.) And like I said, the system still works like that to this day. Try it.

But this was a trick only a very few people knew back then. So I could tell that the so-called fictional people being described were tech people too, much like me, people who liked to design things just to see what was possible, and for no other reason, really. And because I knew the hook switch thing, too, I immediately got suspicious.

● ○ ●

In the *Esquire* article, there was a phone phreak named Joe. He was blind. According to the article, he'd discovered this cool thing: that if you play a really high E—two octaves above the high E on the guitar, for example, which is 2,600 hertz (Hz) exactly—it was the exact tone that seized the tandem and gave you control of the phone system. It probably still works to this day, and you can try that, too. Anyway, Joe was able to actually make this whistle sound with his mouth!

Now, Joe had perfect pitch—probably because he was blind, I don't know. His first whistle seized the line, and then he could make a bunch of short whistles to dial numbers. I couldn't believe this was possible, but there it was and, wow, it just made my imagination run wild. Because just by whistling this high E, he could from there dial a long-distance call that would then be free. To the phone company, it would look like a free 800 or 555 long-distance phone call. And he was doing it all with his mouth!

The *Esquire* article also described someone who went by the name of Captain Crunch, after the cereal (Cap'n Crunch), which used to have a whistle toy in it. Captain Crunch used the whistle and discovered the same thing the blind phone phreak did: that if you plugged the right hole in the whistle and hit that high E, that 2,600 Hz sound—it blew just the right note that basically seized the phone line for anything you wanted to do.

To make a call after seizing the line, Captain Crunch used a device the article called a "Blue Box." It put pairs of tones into the phone, similar to the way touch-tone phones work. This method worked everywhere on the multifrequency (MF) system in the United States, where Joe's and the cereal box whistle only worked in a few places with old single-frequency equipment.

In the story, the guy who built the Blue Box supposedly stole or had loaned to him a standard phone company manual that listed all the frequencies he would need to build it. The article said the phone company figured it out and started to withdraw all those manuals from every library in the country. They made it secret, in other words. They wouldn't let it out anymore. But you

Here I am getting ready to work on the book with Gina in 2006.
(Photograph courtesy of Dan Sokol)

People used to go to Caltech games just to see my dad play. Here he is in uniform. *(Photograph courtesy of Margaret Wozniak)*

Here's my mom and dad's wedding picture. *(Photograph courtesy of Margaret Wozniak)*

They tell me I was reading at three. *(Photograph courtesy of Margaret Wozniak)*

My dad and the three of us siblings. From left: me, Mark, and Leslie. *(Photograph courtesy of Margaret Wozniak)*

Here I am at eleven, in Little League. *(Photograph courtesy of Margaret Wozniak)*

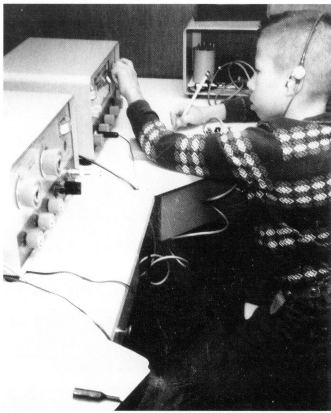

At eleven, I was one of the youngest ham radio operators in the world. But I got bored. No one my age to talk to! *(Photograph courtesy of Margaret Wozniak)*

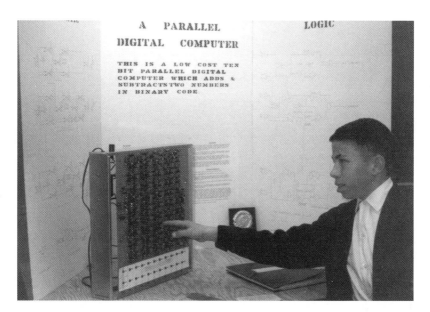

Here I am at thirteen showing off my science-fair-winning Adder/Subtractor. *(Photograph courtesy of Margaret Wozniak)*

Here I am at thirteen in 1963, graduating from junior high. *(Photograph courtesy of Margaret Wozniak)*

Here's Allen Baum and me (left) showing off our "Brazilian Best Wishes" banner, to shake things up at our old high school—then Steve Jobs's. Allen and I had graduated four years earlier. *(Photograph courtesy of Margaret Wozniak)*

Young Steve Jobs and me in 1974 with the Blue Box I designed. *(Photograph courtesy of Margaret Wozniak)*

In 1978, Apple got a real office. Here I am testing some new hardware. *(Photograph courtesy of Dan Sokol)*

Oh, how times have changed! Apple's headquarters at 1 Infinite Loop in Cupertino are pictured here. *(Photograph courtesy of Wikipedia)*

know what? The secret was already out. Way out. Too late for the phone company, or so the article said.

This idea of the Blue Box just amazed me. With it, you could just hook into some 800 number and use that line to make one call after another, all over the world. It didn't plug into the handset or anything. It was very simple. You just put its speaker up to the mouthpiece of the phone. Although it was incredibly easy, only something like a thousand people in the country, technical people like me, could ever have figured it out and used it.

• ○ •

One of the first things I did after reading the article was to call up my friend Steve Jobs. He was just about to start twelfth grade at Homestead High School, the same high school I'd gone to. I started telling him about this amazing article, and how it made sense, really made sense, in a technical way. I told him that, according to the fictional story, the whole system was grabbable. Attackable. And I told him how these smart engineers portrayed in the story overtook and used it. They apparently knew more about the phone system than even the phone company's engineers. If the article was real, and I thought it could be, that meant all the secrets of the phone company were out. It meant people like us were starting to create little networks in order to exploit them.

This was just the most exciting thing for us two young guys to be talking about. I was twenty; Steve was probably about seventeen at the time.

And while I was on the phone with Steve that afternoon, I remember I just stopped mid-sentence and remarked, "Wait, Steve, this article is just too real. They put in real frequencies like 700 Hz and 900 Hz. Fiction articles don't do that. They even gave the way to dial a '1,' a '2,' and a '3.' And they even gave the codes for dialing a call all the way to England."

Real fiction articles don't give things that can be checked and known like that, I said. So we came up with a plan to find out what was really the truth.

• ○ •

An hour later I picked Steve up and we drove down to SLAC, which is pronounced "slack" and is short for the Stanford Linear Accelerator Center. It had a great technical library, just tremendous. It had the kinds of technical books and computer books and magazines you wouldn't encounter in normal libraries or any other place I knew. If there was any place that had a phone manual that listed tone frequencies—the manual the phone company was trying to pull out of circulation—this would be it.

Anyway, I snuck into this library on many Sundays during my high school and early college computer design days. I never felt like it was sneaking, exactly, because they always left the doors open. In my experience, I've found that smart people often leave doors open. Maybe it's because they have other things on their minds.

So Steve Jobs and I snuck in that day, that Sunday in 1971, and started searching for books with telephone information. Like I said, that *Esquire* article sounded just a bit too realistic to be fiction. A fictional article might say that tones are used to dial numbers, but this article explained how the tones were in pairs. For instance, it said that the 700 Hz and 900 Hz tones together stood for a "1," that 700 Hz and 1,100 Hz meant a "2," that 700 Hz and 1,300 Hz together meant "3," and so on. There was even more detail than this, details I figured we could check right there at the SLAC library. So Steve and I sat in there looking for confirmation that this Blue Box thing was for real—we wanted the complete list of tones that could theoretically make all the digits. Because that would mean we could build one.

We were individually flipping through various books and I had a blue one in my hand, maybe two inches thick, with some phone system reference like the CCITT Handbook. In case you're wondering, CCITT is a long-forgotten acronym that stands for the Comité Consultatif International de Télégraphique et Téléphonique. It's the French name for an international standards-setting group for telegraph and, later, telephone systems.

I was flipping around and suddenly stopped on a page. There it was: a complete frequency list for MF (multifrequency) telephone switching equipment.

Sure enough, just as the *Esquire* article said, a "1" was composed of 700 Hz and 900 Hz tones together. A "2" was composed of 700 Hz and 1,100 Hz together. A "3" was 700 Hz and 1,300 Hz.

I froze and grabbed Steve and nearly screamed in excitement that I'd found it. We both stared at the list, rushing with adrenaline. We kept saying things like, "Oh, shit!" and "Wow, this thing is for real!" I was practically shaking, with goose bumps and everything. It was such a Eureka moment. We couldn't stop talking all the way home. We were so excited. We knew we could build this thing. We now had the formula we needed! And definitely that article was for real.

That evening I went to Sunnyvale Electronics and bought some standard parts to build tone generators like the ones in the article. Immediately I found a tone generator kit and brought it back to Steve's house. Right there I soldered together two tone generators. Luckily, Steve had built a frequency counter before this, so we were able to put them together, plus a device that let you turn a dial and measure the tone it produced. For example, I could turn one dial and measure until I got the tone to approximately 700 Hz frequency. Then I could turn the other dial until it got to 900 Hz. Finally I'd play both tones at once and record the sound for about a second on a regular cassette tape recorder. Remember, those tones together meant a "1." Then I did the right combinations for the other digits. Eventually we had a seven-digit phone number and even a ten-digit number recorded.

Finally we set a tone to 2,600 Hz, which is the high E note that supposedly seized the free line mentioned in the article. It worked!

After dialing a free 555 long-distance information number, we heard that chirp the article had talked about. Then we presumed that the phone system was waiting for tones to tell it where to connect to. But uh-oh. We played the tones from our tape record-ing but we weren't able to get the call to go through.

Man, it was so frustrating. No matter how hard we tried to get the frequencies right, they wavered. I just couldn't make them accurate. I kept trying, but I just couldn't perfect this thing. I realized I didn't have a good enough tone generator to prove the article true or false one way or the other.

But I was not about to give up.

• ○ •

The next day was my first day at Berkeley. I was involved with my classes—I thought they were great classes—but I kept think-ing about the Blue Box design. I took that *Esquire* article with me and started collecting every article from Sunday papers I could find about phone phreaks. I started posting articles I found about them on my dorm room wall. I started telling my friends what these phone phreaks were all about, how intelligent they must be, and how I was sure they were starting to take over the phone system all over the country.

So there I was at Berkeley, living in my little dorm room on the first floor of Norton Hall, my best school year ever. I could mes-merize an audience of kids with tales from this article and what Steve Jobs and I had been trying to do. I started gaining a repu-tation as the dorm's "phone phreak," which was fitting. Because one day I explored our dorm and found an unlocked telephone wire access box for our floor. I saw enough phone wires going up to the higher floors—there were a total of eight floors of dorm rooms, including my own above the common area—and I tapped pairs of wire and connected handsets to them. The idea was to determine for a fact which lines were the ones going to which dorm rooms. So I ended up being able to play around and find any particular phone line I wanted to.

Even though I was usually shy and went unnoticed, suddenly this phone phreaking stuff brought me out to a position of prominence in my dorm, where everyone was seeking some sort of partying and fun.

It was around this time that I discovered another kind of phone phreak box, called a "Black Box." Instead of letting you dial free numbers, like the Blue Box did, the Black Box meant anyone who called you wouldn't be billed for the call.

I found the schematics for the Black Box in Abbie Hoffman's *Steal This Book*, an underground book I somehow managed to get at a regular bookstore. (They kept it under the counter so no one would follow the order in its title!)

That same year, an issue of *Ramparts* magazine came out with a really well-explained and completely illustrated article on how to build a Black Box with about two dollars' worth of parts from Radio Shack. All you needed were a capacitor, a resistor, and a switch or push button.

Here's how it worked: when someone called you long-distance you pushed the button to briefly tell the local phone company that you were answering. This connected the faraway line to your own. Because you didn't answer for two seconds minimum, the local phone company didn't send back a billing signal. Yet you were still connected to the caller, and the capacitor of the Black Box allowed their voice to reach your phone (and vice versa) without the phone company sensing any sort of connection. This device worked very well. In fact, one pole-vaulter in my dorm got a letter one day from his parents wondering why they hadn't been billed for two calls from Florida.

By the way, the phone company sued *Ramparts* after the article ran and drove it out of business by 1975.

• ○ •

So while I'm playing with Black Boxes and spreading the word about the Blue Boxes, I started to seriously go to work on my own design. Only this time I tried a digital Blue Box design, which I knew would be able to produce precise, reliable tones. Looking back, I see that it was just a radical idea to do a digital Blue Box. In fact, I never saw or heard about another digital Blue Box. Making it digital meant I could make it extremely small and it was always going to work because it was based on a crystal clock to keep it accurate. That's the same way, by the way, watch crystals keep your watch running correctly.

I already had really good design skills by this point. I mean, I'd been designing and redesigning computers on paper all the way through high school and my last two years of college. I knew so much about circuit design, probably more than anyone I knew.

And then one day I did it. I designed my own digital Blue Box.

It was great. I swear to this day—the day I'm telling you this and the day you're reading it—I have never designed a circuit I was prouder of: a set of parts that could do three jobs at once instead of two. I still think it was incredible.

You see, the circuit, which generated codes corresponding to which button you pushed, used the chips in a very unusual way.

The way all electronics works, including chips, is that some signals are sent to the electronics, to their inputs. And the resulting signals come out of the chip on connections called outputs. Now, because I was familiar with the internal circuitry of the chips, I knew that tiny signals were actually being emitted by the inputs. After those tiny signals went through my button coding circuit, I directed them to a transistor amplifier, which supplied power to turn the chips on. So you can see the amazing thing. (At least, you can see it if you're an engineer.) The chips had to supply a signal to turn them on, and they did. That signal came from one side of the battery being connected, but not the other side.

I never have been able to do anything this out-of-the-box in any of my designs in my career at Hewlett-Packard or at Apple. That's saying a lot, because my designs have always been noted for being out-of-the-box. But this was cleverer than anything.

• ○ •

Now, I won't say that getting a Blue Box working was just an instant thing. That's not what happens in engineering. I was in school, taking classes, and it was probably a couple of months before I did this design. But once I designed it, building it took a day.

I brought it to Steve's house, and we tried it on his phone there. It actually worked. Our first Blue Box call was to a number in Orange County, California—to a random stranger.

And Steve kept yelling, "We're calling from California! From California! With a Blue Box." He didn't realize that the 714 area code *was* California!

Instantly we got in my car and drove up from Steve's house to the dorm at Berkeley. We had promised our parents, who all knew about the project, that we would never do it from home. That one call to Orange County would be the only illegal one from either of our parents' houses.

I wanted to do the right thing. I didn't want to steal from the phone company—I wanted to do what the *Esquire* article said phone phreaks did: use their system to exploit flaws in the system. These days, phone phreaks shun those who do it to steal.

Also, I would've died to meet Captain Crunch, who was really the center of it all. Or any phone phreak; it just seemed so impossible that I'd ever meet anyone else with a Blue Box.

• ○ •

One day Steve Jobs called me and said that Captain Crunch had actually done an interview on the Los Gatos radio station KTAO.

I said, "Oh my god, I wonder if there's any way to get in touch with him." Steve said he'd already left a message at the station but Captain Crunch hadn't called back.

We knew we just had to get in touch with this most famous— infamous, really—and brilliant engineering character in the world. After all, he was the guy we'd been obsessed with for months; he was the guy we'd been reading about and telling stories about. We left messages at KTAO but never heard back from Captain Crunch. It looked like a dead end.

But then, the most coincidental thing happened. A friend of mine from high school, David Hurd, called me and wanted to catch up. When he came up to visit, I started to tell him all these incredible Captain Crunch stories and about the Blue Box and he said, "Well, don't tell anyone, but I know who Captain Crunch is." And I looked at him, floored. How could some random friend from high school know who Captain Crunch was?

I said, "What?"

"Oh yeah," he said, "I know who he is. His real name is John Draper and he works at a radio station, KKUP in Cupertino."

The next weekend, I was sitting with Steve at his house and told him what I'd found out. Steve immediately called the station and asked the guy who answered, "Is John Draper there?" He didn't even say Captain Crunch.

But the guy said, "No, he dropped out of sight after the *Esquire* article."

Hearing that, we knew we'd found the real Captain Crunch. We left our phone number with the guy just on the off chance that Captain Crunch might call us back. And in about five minutes, Captain Crunch actually called!

We picked up the phone, and he immediately told us who he was. But he said he didn't want to say much on the phone. (I remember how, in the *Esquire* article, he had seemed pretty paranoid, sure that the phone line he was talking to the reporter on was bugged.)

Then we told him what kind of equipment we had, what we'd built. I told him it was a Blue Box that I myself had designed, and that it was digital. And he said, again, "Well, I can't talk on the phone about this, but I will come meet you in your dorm."

Man, I drove back to Berkeley just shaking the whole way. When I got there, I was telling everyone who'd listen, "Wow! Captain Crunch is coming here!" This guy I had made into a superhero—the hero of technology bandits or whatever you'd call him—the head guy, the best-known guy, was coming to my dorm room! And everybody was saying, "Can I come?"

But I said, no, no, I knew Captain Crunch wouldn't like that. So it was just my roommate, John Gott, Steve Jobs, and I who sat there in my dorm room, waiting and waiting.

Now, for some reason I was expecting this suave ladies' man to come through the door. I think it was because I'd read in the *Esquire* article that he'd tapped his girlfriend's phone line once and heard her talking to another guy, and then he called her up and said, "We're done." Just having a girlfriend, I guess, made him a ladies' man to me. I still had never even had a girlfriend.

But no. Captain Crunch comes to our door, and it turns out he's just this really weird-looking guy. Here, I thought, would be a guy who would look and act just far away and above any engineer in the world, but there he was: sloppy-looking, with his hair kind of hanging down one side. And he smelled like he hadn't taken a shower in two weeks, which turned out to be true. He was also missing a bunch of teeth. (Over the years, the joke I made up about him was that the reason he had no teeth was that he was stripping phone lines with them when the phone rang. Engineers know that the phone ringing signal is a high enough voltage to shock you really hard.)

So anyway, I saw him, and he didn't match my expectations. So I asked, "Are you Captain Crunch?" And he said, "I am he," and he walked in just majestically. What a line that was. "I am he." And there he was.

He turned out to be this really strange, fun guy, just bubbling over with energy. And he's sitting on the bed, looking at all my phone phreak articles taped to my wall, and all the circuits and magazines, and also weird things like the twenty pounds of saltines I'd swiped from the cafeteria by stuffing a few packets in my pockets at every meal.

And he looked around and saw wires coming out of the telephones; I could tell he was surprised. I was sitting there thinking: Wow, this is the most amazing night of my life of all time, and it's just beginning!

He started talking to us. I noticed he was kind of like one of these very hyper people who keep changing topics and jumping around, talking about different times in his life and different stuff he did. I kept trying to impress him with my Blue Box. I boasted about how small it was, how few parts it took, and how it was digital—that was the main thing. I told him there was just one thing, I hadn't figured out how to make international calls yet. And he showed me the procedure right away. Strangely enough, it was the same procedure we'd read about in the *Esquire* article, but it didn't work then, don't ask me why.

Then suddenly Captain Crunch said, "Wait, wait a minute. I am going to go out to my car now and get my *automatic* Blue Box."

We knew right away that this was going to be some incredible piece of equipment that's going to be something special, like the digital Blue Box I'd designed. The way he said it—automatic. It was sort of a competitive thing.

I had this image of what this van must look like—with everything he needed to seize phone systems and other stuff in it. I imagined racks of engineering equipment and telephone equipment based on what I'd read in *Esquire*.

So I asked him, "Can I come?" I just had to see it. It was as if

I'd be seeing history, like one of the Seven Wonders of the World.

Well, I followed him out to the parking lot where his VW van was parked. It was completely empty. It was a totally empty van. All it had in it was this little Blue Box device on the floor, and a strange kind of crossbow-shaped thing, like a cross. It turned out that was the antenna he used to run San Jose Free Radio, a pirate radio station. He said the reason he ran it out of his van was so that no one from the FCC could ever pinpoint his location. Brilliant!

So that was to his credit, but still, all this equipment I expected to see wasn't there, and then there were his looks, and the strangely empty van. Everything was starting to not add up all of a sudden. I started to feel queasy and uncomfortable standing there. My previous ideas about what phone phreaks were supposed to be like were not meshing with the person I was looking at. This was a technical scallywag.

Then we went back to my dorm room and he took out this automatic box and showed me a few of its special abilities. The box had sliding switches—ten of them—to let you set up each of ten possible digits in a phone number. You could just push a button on the box—beep beep beep—and dial the whole number from there, no whistling or tone signals required! I was totally impressed by this, it was just really great.

•   ○   •

Later on, four of us—Steve Jobs, Captain Crunch, a guy named Alan McKittrick (who we called Groucho), and I—headed to Kips pizza parlor. We kept trading codes for dialing into various places and techniques like using Blue Boxes from pay phones.

At around midnight, we said our goodbyes. Captain Crunch wanted to go over to Groucho's house first and then drive his van home to where he lived in Los Gatos. So Steve Jobs and I took Steve's car back to his house in Los Altos, where my Pinto was parked.

Steve mentioned that his car had been having generator prob-lems. When I asked what that meant, he said, "Pretty much the whole car can just suddenly shut down at some point."

About halfway down, in Hayward on what was then Highway 17, as I recall, it actually happened. The car lost all lights and power. Steve was able to pull over to the right near an exit and we walked to a gas station where there was a pay phone. We thought we'd call Groucho—a long-distance number from Hay-ward—and ask Draper to pick us up on his way down south.

Steve put a dime in the pay phone and dialed the operator. He told her he was about to make a "data call," to keep her from thinking that our line was going off the hook for the brief period while we used the Blue Box. He asked her to connect us to a free 800 number or long-distance directory assistance, some free call. Then we "blew it off" (seized the line with a 2,600 hertz tone) and Steve proceeded to use the Blue Box to call Groucho. But the operator came back on the line, so Steve hung up the phone quickly. This was not good!

We tried it again, telling the next operator that it was a data call and to ignore any weird light she might see. But the same thing happened. The operator came back on the line just before we made the connection. Again, Steve hung up instantly. We thought we were getting in deep trouble, that somehow our Blue Box had been detected.

Finally we decided to use coins and just call Groucho the legal way. We did and asked Captain Crunch to pick us up. All of a sud-den, a cop pulled into the gas station and jumped out real fast. Steve was still holding the Blue Box when he jumped out, that's how fast it happened. We didn't even have time to hide it. We were sure that the operator had called the cops on us, and that this was the end for sure.

The cop was kind of heavyset and walked past me for some reason, shining his flashlight on the plants about eight feet in front of me. I had long hair and a headband back then, so I guess he was looking for drugs we'd stashed. Then the cop started examining the bushes, rifling through them with his hands in the dark.

In the meantime, trembling with fear, Steve passed the Blue Box to me. He didn't have a jacket on, but I did. I slid it into my pocket.

But then the cop turned back to us and patted us down. He felt my Blue Box and I pulled it out of my pocket and showed it to him. We knew we were caught. The cop asked me what it was. I was not about to say, "Oh, this is a Blue Box for making free telephone calls." So for some reason I said it was an electronic music synthesizer. The Moog synthesizer actually had just come out, so this was a good phrase to use. I pushed a couple of the Blue Box buttons to demonstrate the tones. This was pretty rare, as even touch-tone phones were still kind of rare in this part of the country then.

The cop then asked what the orange button was for. (It was actually the button that sounded the nice pure 2,600 Hz tone to seize a phone line.) Steve told the cop that the orange button was for "calibration." Ha!

A second cop approached. I guess he had stayed back in the police car at first. He took the Blue Box from the first cop. This device was clearly their point of interest, and surely they knew what it was, having been called by the phone operator. The second cop asked what it was. I said it was an electronic music synthesizer. He also asked what the orange button was for, and Steve again said that it was for calibration. We were two scared young cold and shivering boys by this time. Well, at least Steve was shivering. I had a coat.

The second cop was looking at the Blue Box from all angles. He asked how it worked and Steve said that it was computer-controlled. He looked at it some more, from every angle, and asked where the computer plugged in. Steve said that "it con-nected inside."

We both knew the cops were playing with us.

The cops asked what we were doing and we told them our car had broken down on the freeway. They asked where it was and we pointed. The cops, still holding the Blue Box, told us to get in the backseat of their car to go check out the car story. In the

How Ma Bell Helped Us Build the Blue Box

In 1955, the *Bell System Technical Journal* published an article entitled "In Band Signal Frequency Signaling" which described the process used for routing telephone calls over trunk lines with the signaling system at the time. It included all the infor-mation you'd need to build an interoffice telephone system, but it didn't include the MF (multifrequency) tones you needed for accessing the system and dialing.

But nine years later, in 1964, Bell revealed the other half of the equation, publishing the frequencies used for the digits needed for the actual routing codes.

Now, anybody who wanted to get around Ma Bell was set. The formula was there for the taking. All you needed were these two bits of information found in these two articles. If you could build the equipment to emit the frequencies needed, you could make your own free calls, skipping Ma Bell's billing and monitoring system completely.

Famous "phone phreaks" of the early 1970s include Joe Engressia (a.k.a. Joybubbles), who was able to whistle (with his mouth) the high E tone needed to take over the line. John Draper (a.k.a. Captain Crunch) did the same with the free whistle that came inside boxes of Cap'n Crunch. A whole subculture was born. Eventually Steve Jobs (a.k.a. Oaf Tobar) and I (a.k.a. Berkeley Blue) joined the group, making and selling our own versions of the Blue Boxes. We actually made some good money at this.

backseat of a cop car you know where you are going eventually: to jail.

The cops got in the front. I was seated behind the driver. The cop in the passenger seat had the Blue Box. Just before the car started moving, or maybe just after, he turned to me and passed me the Blue Box, commenting, "A guy named Moog beat you to it."

Chapter 7

Escapades with Steve

The internal joy I felt when the cop believed our story about the Blue Box being the Moog synthesizer is almost indescribable.

Not only were we not being arrested for making illegal calls with or owning a Blue Box, but these supposedly intelligent cops had totally bought our B.S. God, I wanted to laugh out loud. Our moods changed instantly.

I mean, one second we thought we were being driven off to jail, and the next we realized we had bamboozled the police. Bamboozled up the yazoo! This was such an important lesson to learn in life, and such a continuing theme for me. Some people will just believe the strangest stuff, stuff that doesn't bear any semblance to reality.

After the cops dropped us off, we waited at the gas station until finally Captain Crunch showed up in his van. That van sure was scary to ride in as a passenger. It felt like it was going to fall over, it was so rickety. It didn't feel solid at all. It was probably about 2 a.m. by the time we got back to Steve's house all the way down in Los Altos. I picked up my car—I had an ochre-colored Pinto at this time—and drove it back to Berkeley.

I was tired. I shouldn't have been on the road. Because you know what happened? Somewhere near Oakland on Highway 17,

I fell asleep at the wheel. I don't know how long my eyes were closed, but suddenly I opened my eyes and it looked to me like the guardrail was jumping onto my windshield. It looked so strange, like a dream. I grabbed the steering wheel, yanked it as hard as I could to the right, and the car just started spinning around and around.

The only thing holding me in that car was the seat belt.

As the car was spinning, I was thinking, This is it. I might die. I could really die. But then the car slid to a stop up against the center guardrail, and it turned out that only the side of the Pinto that hit the guardrail was damaged. But it totaled my car.

• ○ •

Losing my Pinto changed my life completely. One of the major parts of my life at Berkeley was taking groups of people down to Southern California or even as far south as Tijuana, Mexico, on weekends. Actually, my first thought after the crash wasn't, Oh, thank god I'm alive, but Man, now I'm not going to be able to take my friends on wild adventures anymore.

The car crash was the main reason that, after this school year, my third year at Berkeley, I went back to work instead of coming back to school. I needed to earn money, not just for the fourth year of college but also for a new car.

If I hadn't gotten in the car accident that year, I wouldn't have quit school and I might never have started Apple. It's weird how things happen.

• ○ •

But for the rest of the year at Berkeley, I kept playing with my Blue Box. Captain Crunch's design had given me an idea: to add a single little button where I could preprogram a ten-digit number.

The number I chose to dial was this weird joke line in Los Angeles. It was called Happy Ben. When you called it, this cranky old guy—he sounded like a real old guy—would answer in this old voice like gravel: "Hey," he'd say, "it's me, Happy Ben." And then he'd sing, off-key, and with no music: "Happy days are here again / happy days are here again / happy days are here again / happy days are here again." And then, "Yep, it's me again. It's Ben."

Don't ask me why, but of all the joke lines in the world I now had free access to with my Blue Box, that one number always cheered me up and made me smile. It was just the fact that this grumpy-sounding old guy would sing that song in such a truly happy way. Somehow that style of humor made me laugh. I hope to do the same thing myself someday. Maybe I can sing the national anthem on a joke line. I still might.

• ○ •

Now that I had a Blue Box that could call anywhere, even internationally, I had a lot of fun calling joke lines all over the world. I'd walk up to a pay phone, dial some 800 number, seize the line with the Blue Box, push the automatic button—beep beep beep—and there he was again. Happy Ben singing "Happy Days Are Here Again." It was my favorite thing.

But I hadn't forgotten what was supposed to be the real mission of phone phreaking: not to mess up the system, but to find flaws and curious things and secrets the phone company never told anyone about. And I really did stick with the honesty thing. Even when I made my calls to friends, relatives, to people I normally would've called anyway, I made a point of paying for those calls. I didn't use the Blue Box. To me, that would have been stealing, and that wasn't what I was about.

But I did like to use the Blue Box to see how far it could get me. For instance, I would make a call to an operator and pretend I was a New York operator trying to extend the lines for phase measurements, and she would connect me to London. Then I'd talk that operator into connecting me to Tokyo. I would go around the world like this sometimes three times or more.

And by this time I got great at sounding official, or doing accents, all to fool operators around the world. I remember one very, very late night in the dorm when I decided to call the pope. Why the pope? I don't know. Why not? So I started by using the Blue Box to call Italy Inward (country code 121), then I asked for Rome Inward, and then I got to the Vatican and in this heavy accent I announced I was Henry Kissinger calling on behalf of President Nixon. I said, "Ve are at de summit meeting in Moscow, and ve need to talk to de pope."

And a woman said, "It's five-thirty here. The pope is sleeping." She put me on hold then for a while, and then told me they were sending someone to wake him and asked if I could call back. I said yes, in an hour.

Well, an hour later I called back and she said, "Okay, we will put the bishop on, who will be the translator." So I told him, still in that heavy accent, "Dees is Mr. Kissinger." And he said, "Listen, I just spoke to Mr. Kissinger an hour ago." You see, they had checked out my story and had called the real Kissinger in Moscow.

Ha! But I didn't hang up. I said, "You can verify my number. You can call me back." And I gave him a U.S. number that would call a loop-back number so they wouldn't find out my number. But they never called back, which was too bad.

Years later, though, I couldn't stop laughing when I saw an article about me where they were interviewing Captain Crunch. He said I was calling the pope to make a confession!

● ○ ●

For ages and ages, I always told people how I was the ethical phone phreak who always paid for my own calls and was just exploring the system. And that was true. I used to get huge phone bills, even though I had my Blue Box that would've let me make any call for free.

But one day Steve Jobs came alone and said, "Hey, let's sell these." So by selling them to others we really were getting the technology out to people who were using it to call their girl-friends and the like and save money on phone calls. So looking back, I guess that, yes, I aided and abetted that crime.

We had a pretty interesting way of selling them. What we would do is Steve and I would find groups of people in vari-ous dorms at Berkeley to sell them to. I was always the ring-leader, which was really unusual for me. I was the one who did all the talking. You know, I thought I'd be so famous doing this, but it's funny, I didn't know you had to talk to a reporter to get your phone phreak handle (mine was Berkeley Blue) in articles.

Anyway, the way we did it was just by knocking on doors. How do you know you're not walking up to somebody who's going to turn you in? Someone who might see it as a crime? Well, we'd knock on a door (usually a door in a male dorm) and ask for someone nonexistent like, "Is Charlie Johnson there?" And they'd say, "Who's Charlie Johnson?"

And I'd say, "You know, the guy that makes all the free phone calls." If they sort of seemed cool—and you could tell by their face if they wanted to talk about such a thing as illegal free phone calls—I'd add, "You know, he has the Blue Boxes?"

Sometimes they might say, "Oh my god, I've heard about those things." And if they sounded really cool enough, and every once in a while they did, then one of us pulled a Blue Box out of our pockets. They'd say something like, "Wow! Is that what they look like? Is that real?"

And that's how we knew we had the right guy and he wouldn't turn us in. Then one of us would say, "Tell you what, we'll come back at 7 p.m. tonight; have everyone you know who knows someone in a foreign country here and we'll give you a demo."

And we'd come back at 7 p.m. We'd run a wire across their dorm room and we'd hook it up to the tape recorder. That way, everything was tape-recorded—every single sale we ever did was tape-recorded. Just to play it safe.

We made a little money selling Blue Boxes. It was enough at the time. Originally I would buy the parts to hand-build one for $80. The distributor in Mountain View where I got the chips (no electronics stores sold chips) charged a ton for small quantities. We eventually made a printed circuit board and, making ten or twenty at a time, got the cost down to maybe $40. We sold them for $150 and split the revenue.

So it was a pretty good business proposition except for one thing. Blue Boxes were illegal, and we were always worried about getting caught.

● ○ ●

One time Steve and I had a Blue Box ready for sale. Steve needed some extra money, and he really wanted us to sell the box that day. It was a Sunday. Before driving up to Berkeley to sell the Blue Box, we stopped to eat at a Sunnyvale pizza parlor. While eating our pizza, we noticed a few guys at the next table. They looked cool, and we started talking to them. It turned out they were interested in seeing one and buying it.

We then went to a rear hallway of the pizza parlor, where there was a pay phone. Steve pulled out the Blue Box. They gave us a number in Chicago, in the 312 area code, to test it. The call went through to a ringing phone, which no one answered.

The three guys were really excited and told us they wanted the Blue Box but couldn't afford it. Steve and I headed out to the parking lot to get into Steve's car. And just very quickly, before Steve started the engine, one of the guys popped up next to the driver's-side window with a big long black gun barrel pointed right at us.

He demanded the Blue Box.

Steve nervously handed it to him. And the thieves went to their own car. As we sat there, stunned, an amazing thing happened. One of the guys came back to the car and explained he didn't have the money yet, but he did want the Blue Box. And that they would pay us eventually. And he wrote down a phone number and a name for us to call him at. His name was Charles.

After a few days, Steve called the number. Someone answered, and when we asked for Charles, he gave us the number of a pay phone. We knew it was a pay phone because back then, if the last four digits of any number started with a 9 or a 99, it was certainly a pay phone.

Steve called that number, and Charles answered. He said he would pay us eventually for the Blue Box, but he needed to know how to use it.

Steve tried to talk him into returning it to us. Charles said he wanted to meet us somewhere. We were too scared to meet him, even in a public place. I came up with the idea of telling him a method to use that would get him billed for every call—like, to start your call by dialing an 808 number, which is an area code for Hawaii. I also thought of telling him a way to use it that would get him caught. Like dialing 555 information calls, which look suspicious when they last for hours.

If only I'd been more of a joker, I would've thought to tell him to start by dialing the number of a police station.

But I didn't recommend any of those things, and in the end, Steve hung up. We were too scared to do anything, and for sure Charles and those guys never learned how to use it.

Chapter 8

HP and Moonlighting as a Crazy Polack

This much I know for sure: I was meant to be an engineer who designs computers, an engineer who writes software, an engineer who tells jokes, and an engineer who teaches other people things.

Now, finally, there was a time in my life—a time right after that third year at Berkeley—that I finally got my dream job. But it wasn't a job building computers. It was a job designing calculators at Hewlett-Packard. And I really thought I would spend the rest of my life there. That place was just the most perfect company.

This was January of 1973, and for an engineer like me, there was no better place to work in the world. Unlike a lot of technology companies, Hewlett-Packard wasn't totally run by marketing people. It really respected its engineers. And that made sense, because this was a company that had made engineering tools for years—meters, oscilloscopes, power supplies, testers of all types, even medical equipment. It made all the things engineers actually used, and it was a company driven by engineers on the inside so far as what engineers on the outside needed. Man, I loved that.

For just a few months before that, right after I finished Berkeley in June, I worked at a much, much smaller company, called Electroglas. That was a blast, too. Getting that job was almost too easy. I'd looked in the newspaper ads, and the first ad I saw was for an electronics technician for $600 a month, or close to that. I called them up and they said, "Come on down for an interview." Well, I went down and they gave me this incredibly easy written test—you know, with electronic formulas and all. Of course, I knew that stuff. I'd known it forever. They interviewed me and instantly hired me, so I had a job. And they paid me enough that I was actually able to get my first apartment. It was in Cupertino, just a mile from my parents' house. And it was just the greatest, greatest thing.

But six months later I heard from my old friend Allen Baum, who by then was working as an intern at Hewlett-Packard. He was excited, telling me he was actually hanging around the guys who'd designed the HP 35 calculator. This, to me, was the most incredible invention of all time.

I'd been a slide rule whiz in high school, so when I saw the calculator, it was just amazing. A slide rule was kind of like a ruler— you had to look at it precisely to read the values. The most accurate number you could get was only three digits long, however, and even that result was always questionable. With a calculator, you could punch in precisely the digits you wanted. You didn't have to line up a slider. You could type in your numbers exactly, hit a button, and get an answer immediately. You could get that number all the way out to ten digits. For example, the real answer might be 3.158723623. An answer like that was much more precise than anything engineers had ever gotten before.

Well, the HP 35 was the first scientific calculator, and it was the first in history that you could actually hold in your hand. It could calculate sines and cosines and tangents, all the trigonometric and exponential/logarithmic functions engineers use to calculate and to do their jobs. This was 1973, and back then calculators—especially handheld calculators—were a very, very big deal.

So Allen's internship was working in the calculator group. He told me he'd told his managers all about me, that I was a great designer and had designed all these computers and things, and all of a sudden I found myself interviewing with a vice president of engineering, and the people under him, and the people under them. I guess they were impressed, because they made me an offer right away to come work there. They told me I could help design scientific calculators at HP. I thought, Oh my God.

I did love my job at Electroglas. I got to stand up all day, which I like, and help test and repair circuits. (A lot of their chips went bad because, instead of sockets, they used the soldered resistor-transistor logic [RTL] method of attaching chips.) I liked everyone I worked with and I'd made a lot of good friends. So when I told them about the job offer at HP, man, they did everything to keep me. They told me they'd make me a full engineer, they would up my salary over what HP had offered, and I felt bad because I really did love that company.

But even though Electroglas was what I considered to be a great job, it was nothing compared to what I considered to be the ideal job in the whole world: working on handheld scientific calculators at the only company in the world that could build a product like that. How could you beat that?

I was already a big fan of Hewlett-Packard. When I was at Berkeley, I'd even saved up to spend $400 (that's about $2,000 in today's money) on the HP 35.

There was no doubt in my mind that calculators were going to put slide rules out of business. (In fact, two years later you couldn't even buy a slide rule. It was extinct.) And now all of a sudden I'd gotten a job helping to design the next generation of these scientific calculators. It was like getting to be a part of history.

This was the company for me because, like I said, I'd already decided that I wanted to be an engineer for life. It was especially neat because I got to work on a product that at the time was the highlight product of the world—the scientific calculator. To me, it was the luckiest job I could have.

As an example of how great a company HP was, consider this. During this time—the early 1970s—the recession was going on and everyone was losing their jobs. Even HP had to cut back 10 percent on its expenses. But instead of laying people off, HP wound up cutting everyone's salary by 10 percent. That way, no one would be left without a job.

You know, my dad had always told me that your job is the most important thing you'll ever have and the worst thing to lose.

I still think that way. My thinking is that a company is like a family, a community, where we all take care of each other. I never agreed with the normal thinking, where a company is more competition driven, and the poorest, youngest or most recently hired workers are always the first to go.

By the way, I was twenty-two when I got that job at Hewlett-Packard.

• ○ •

Once I got into HP, I met a lot of people there and became good friends with the engineers, the technicians, even some of the marketing people. I loved the environment. It was just very free. I still had long hair and a beard, and no one seemed to mind. At HP, you were respected for your abilities. It didn't matter how you looked.

We had cubicles, I remember. For the first time, I sat in a cubicle and was free to walk around and talk to other people. During the day, you could throw out ideas about products and debate them. And HP made it easy to do that. Every day, at 10 a.m. and 2 p.m., they wheeled in donuts and coffee. That was so nice. And smart, because the reason they did it was so everyone would

More on HP

Stanford 1934 graduates Bill Hewlett and Dave Packard founded Hewlett-Packard in their garage in 1939. Now, a lot of people confuse that story with Apple's, saying that we started Apple in a garage. Not true. HP started in a garage, true. But in the case of Apple, I worked in my room at my apartment and Steve worked in his bedroom in his parents' house. We only did the very last part of assembly in his garage.

But that's how it goes with stories.

HP's first product was a precision audio oscillator, called the Model 200A. It measured sound waves and cost under $50, which was a quarter of the price of other companies' less reliable oscillators. And here's a cool fact. One of HP's earliest clients was Walt Disney Productions, which used eight Model 200B audio oscillators for testing the sound system for the movie *Fantasia*.

gather in a common place and be able to talk, socialize, and exchange ideas.

A few years before, during those long walks I took during high school, I'd decided that I was into truth and facts and solid calculations. I knew I never wanted to play social games. The Vietnam War only solidified that attitude. That's why I was sure, even at twenty-two, that I didn't want to switch from engineering to management, ever. I didn't want to go into management and have to fight political battles and take sides and step on people's toes and all that stuff.

I knew I could do that at HP—that is, have a long career without ever having to get into management. I knew this because I'd met a couple of engineers who were a lot older than me, and they had no desire to be in management either. So after I met them, I knew that was possible.

I worked at HP for quite a while—about four years. I didn't have a college degree yet, but I promised my managers I would work toward one by taking night classes at San Jose State nearby.

I couldn't imagine quitting my job and going back to school full-time, because what I was doing was too important.

• ○ •

At HP, I got into calculator circuits and how they were designed. I looked at the schematics of the engineers who had invented this calculator processor, and I was able to make modifications to those chips.

But the longer I worked there, the more I found myself drifting away from the computers of my past: computers and processors, registers, chips, gates, building all these things I used to be fascinated by. Everything was so good in my life; I just set my computer ambitions aside.

I'd even missed the fact that microprocessors—the brain of any modern computer today—were getting more and more powerful and more and more compact. I lost track of the chips that were coming up. I lost track of the fact that we were almost at the point where you could get all of a computer's main brainpower—its central processing unit (or CPU)—onto just one small chip.

I stopped following computer developments so closely. And I didn't really think of our calculators as computers, though of course they were. They did have a couple of chips inside that added up to a little microprocessor—a very strange one, I admit, but in those days you had to design things strangely and come up with weird techniques. Your chips could really do only one thing at a time. Back then, chips were simpler, you couldn't fit more than a hundred or so transistors on a chip, compared to more than a billion today.

So everything was weirder then. And because I was so happy in my job, I didn't know what I was missing.

• ○ •

What's a CPU?

You hear the letters "CPU" thrown around a lot, but what does it actually mean? And what did its invention change in terms of today's computer revolution?

CPU, short for central processing unit, is a term that's usually used interchangeably with "microprocessor." That is, provided the CPU is on one chip. When I first started building computers, like the Cream Soda Computer, there was no such thing as a CPU on a chip—that is, a microprocessor.

As it turned out, Intel came out with the first true micro-processor in the mid-1970s. It was called the 4004.

The whole purpose of the CPU, which really is the brains of a computer, is to seek and execute all the instructions someone stored in the computer as a program. Say you write a program that spell-checks a document. Well, the CPU is capable of find-ing that program (which is represented in the machine as the binary numbers 1 and 0) and communicating with the other components of the computer to make it run.

Sometimes a bunch of us engineers would take small planes and fly to lunch somewhere. A lot of us had our pilot's licenses. For my first flight ever in a plane, I ended up in Myron Tuttle's plane. Myron was a design engineer, like me, a guy who worked with me in my cubicle. That day he let me sit in the copilot's seat, which I thought was so cool.

I remember there were two people in the back, other people in our group. So here we are, flying for lunch to Rio Vista, near Sacramento.

When Myron landed, we just bounced and bounced and bounced. I had never been in such a small plane before, so I just thought, Oh, this is interesting. So this is how a small plane is. Really bumpy when you land.

At lunch, the other pilots had this private conversation. (I found out later they were trying to decide whether they would let Myron fly us back!) Well, it turned out they decided, okay, it was just one flight, and the runway in San Jose was 10,000 to 12,000 feet long. They thought maybe Myron would be able to do a better job on the return flight.

So we flew back after lunch—and there it was again, another one of those really, really bouncy landings. Again I just thought that's how you land in small planes. There was a first bounce, then a second bounce that was pretty hard, then a scraping sound, and then it bounced, bounced, bounced, and bounced again for what seemed like the millionth time down the runway.

I must've been white as a sheet, I think everyone was. And not one of us could say a word. We taxied around the runway for a few minutes, and still the three of us didn't say a word to Myron. Not one word.

That silence was uncomfortable. Finally I felt like I had to say something, just anything technical, because he's an engineer and all. So after we got out of the plane, I said to Myron, "Hey, that's interesting that they bend the propeller like that—is that for aerodynamic reasons?"

And Myron said, "They don't." That's all he said.

I realized I had just said the worst possible thing.

Myron had bent his propeller on that landing.

To be fair to Myron, it's not impossible that I did something in my copilot seat that made the bounce worse. It's possible that in my own fright I touched something I shouldn't have.

At any rate, I heard Myron never flew again after that. As for the propeller he bent, he had to buy it. We mounted it on the lab wall, something for us to always look at and remember. Like it was a joke.

●   ○   ●

I think most people with day jobs like to do something totally different when they get home. Some people like to come home and watch TV. But my thing was electronics projects. It was my passion and it was my pastime.

Working on projects was something I did on my own time to reward myself, even though I wasn't getting rewarded on the outside, with money or other visible signs of success.

One such project I called Dial-a-Joke. I started it about two weeks before I went to work at HP, and it went on for a couple of years after that.

Now, a lot of people start companies, and I know a lot of people will probably be reading this book only because I started Apple. But what I wish more people knew about me is what I think I should really be famous for: creating the very first Dial-a-Joke in the Bay Area, which was one of the first in the world.

A dial-a-joke service was something I had wanted to do for a while, mostly because I'd been calling dial-a-joke numbers (remember Happy Ben?) all around the world with my Blue Box. So I knew there were dial-a-joke lines in places like Sydney, Australia, and Los Angeles, but there were none in the San Francisco Bay Area. How could that be? I couldn't believe it. And you know me; I always like to be in the forefront of things. So I decided I was going to be the first one to do it.

Before long I really did have the first dial-a-joke in the Bay Area, and it was unbelievably popular. In fact, it had so many calls that I could only keep doing it for a couple of years. I was fielding thousands of calls a day by the end of it. Eventually I couldn't afford it anymore.

• ○ •

To do a dial-a-joke system, the first thing was to get an answering machine. You couldn't just buy them. It was illegal to connect one to your phone line without actually renting it from a phone company. Keep in mind that there were no phone jacks in the walls back then. Just wires connected to screws.

I knew movie theaters had answering machines, though. That was for prerecording movie titles and showtimes. Somehow I managed to rent one of those machines for about $50 a month. That was pretty expensive for a young guy like me. But I wanted to do it for fun, and money wasn't going to stop me. Well, at least not at first.

Next, I needed jokes. I got them from *The Official Polish-Italian Joke Book*, by Larry Wilde. That book was the best-selling joke book of all time.

So I hooked up the machine and recorded a joke. Using my best Slavic accent, I'd say: "Allo. Tenk you fur dialing Dial-a-Joke." Then: "Today's joke ees: Ven did a Polack die drinking milk? Ven de cow sat down! Ah, ah. Tenk you fer dialin' Dial-a-Joke."

The first day, I just gave the number to a few people at work and told them to let their kids try it.

The next day, I read another joke into the machine. And every day I'd do that, reading a new Polish joke into the machine.

You wouldn't believe how fast Dial-a-Joke ramped up. The first day, there were just a couple of calls. Then there were ten. The next day, there were maybe fifteen. And then suddenly it spiked up to a hundred calls, then two hundred calls a day. Within two weeks, the line was busy all day. I would call it from work and I couldn't even get through. After school let out that year, there were like two thousand calls a day on a single line phone number. I made a point of keeping my jokes as short as I could—under fifteen seconds—just so I could handle more calls a day. I couldn't believe how popular it got!

I started to really have a blast with it. Every now and then, just for fun, I'd take live calls when I got home from work. I'd say, "Allo. Tenk you fur dialing Dial-a-Joke." I got to talk to lots of people and hear weird things about their schools and teachers and other students. I took notes. That way, if I asked someone (in my Polish accent, of course) what high school do you go to, and they answered "Oak Grove," I could say, "Hey, does Mr. Wilson still wear those weird red pants?"

So they were amazed by me. They heard the recordings and they knew I actually picked up the phone sometimes—they thought this old Polish guy knew everything about them! I told them my name was Stanley Zebrazutsknitski.

At one point I bought two books of insults—*2,001 Insults*, volumes 1 and 2. A lot of these insults were really funny. Sometimes I would say something a little critical to a caller—like, "You not so bright, are you?"—just to get them going. Usually they would retort by calling me something nasty, like an old fart. That's when I could start reading the insults out of the book, ones that were so clever no one could come back with anything good. As hard as anyone tried, I would always win the insult battle.

Somewhere around that time, I got complaints from the Polish American Congress that the jokes defamed people of Polish descent. Being a Polish Wozniak who tells and laughs at Polish jokes, I asked them if they would mind if I switched to Italian jokes. They said that would be fine.

See, the notion of political correctness didn't exist back then. The Polish-Americans didn't care if I told ethnic jokes as long as they weren't about Polish people!

Want to Hear a Dial-a-Joke?

The first dial-a-joke service is rumored to have been created by New York Bell in the early 1970s. Want to hear some examples? You can hear archived recordings at http://www.dialajoke.com.

And you know what? Twelve years later the same Polish American Congress gave me its Heritage Award, its highest award for achievements by a Polish-American.

● ○ ●

As it happened, most of my callers were young teenagers. Adults don't have the time or the patience to keep dialing a busy number over and over to get through.

But the kids, because they were dialing it over and over, frequently misdialed the number. One time, on a weekend, I took a live call from this woman who said, "Please, you've got to stop that machine. My husband works nights and he's got to sleep days, and we're getting a hundred calls a day that are meant for you." So the next day I called the phone company and had them change the number. I did that just for her.

I didn't hear any more complaints for the next month, so I assumed the phone number switch worked. But a manager at the phone company called me to tell me that a lot of other people were complaining.

And that was frustrating to me because I didn't want to make trouble for anyone. So I started thinking about getting an easy-to-dial number. I was in Cupertino where one of the prefixes was 255, so I thought, How about 255-5555? That would be easy to dial—you could keep dialing the same touch-tone, and your finger wouldn't have to leave the space. I tried calling this number, and I found out that no one had it. I also found out that nobody had 255-6666.

I called a manager at the phone company—Dial-a-Joke was such a big deal by now that even shy Steve Wozniak could talk to phone company managers. I suggested that the remedy for all the misdialing should be an easy-to-dial phone number. I asked first for the 255-5555 number, but they weren't allocating numbers in the 5000 range. So I said, "How about 255-6666?" He checked and said, "Fine." And he gave it to me.

I ended up getting some cards printed up that said: "The Crazy Polack. Heard a good one lately? Call 255-6666."

I figured that would be the end of the misdialing problems, but it wasn't. I remember coming home from Hewlett-Packard to the apartments in Cupertino, where I lived, and there were three people waiting. They said they worked at Any Mountain, which was and still is a major ski supply shop in California. And their number was 255-6667, one digit different. They said they were getting so many crank calls and weird people and kids calling they were afraid to answer their own phone! I was kind of proud of the fact that my little operation was able to affect that big a business, but I really did want to change my number again to protect them. So I did that. I changed it to a 575 prefix—575-1625—but that 575 prefix was actually set up for high-volume calls like radio station contests and that kind of thing. And I had that number until the end of Dial-a-Joke a couple of years later.

But Dial-a-Joke was hurting for money. The cost of the answering machine alone was breaking me.

At one point I thought maybe I could get money from the callers to help pay for Dial-a-Joke. I added the message, "Please send money to P.O. Box 67 in Cupertino, California." In three months I received only $11. Only once did I get a whole dollar. Usually I'd get a nickel, dime, or quarter taped to a piece of paper.

• ○ •

The biggest problem with Dial-a-Joke, like I said, was the expense. Not only did renting the machine cost a lot of money, but I was constantly having to rent new machines from the phone company.

To give you an idea, in theaters, these machines lasted years. But with me, they were lasting, like, a month. So every month I'd have to call up the phone company and say, "You've got to come over here to fix your answering machine, it's no good."

And really I loved doing that because they were charging me so much to rent it, it seemed only right that I wouldn't have to be stuck with it once it broke down. I liked to see them lose money, too. So this guy would show up at 5 p.m., when I got home from work, with a whole new machine. I'd meet the guy, let him into the apartment, he'd install the machine, and that was that.

One month, when I got home that day after five when the repairman was supposed to be there, there was instead a note from him saying he'd been there at 2 p.m.

Two p.m.? I called up the phone company. "He's always supposed to come after five. You better have him come after five tomorrow." Well, the next day I got a note saying he'd been there at 3 p.m. So now I called the phone company almost livid—and that is really unusual for me—and I said something like: "You'd better tell him to be there at 5 p.m. this time." But then the next day, again, there was a note saying he'd been there at 2 p.m. What was going on? I had no idea.

But I had gone three days with a nonworking machine that I was paying for, and that was no joke to me.

Now, I decided to play the game a different way. I called them and this time just very politely asked them to get the guy there at five. I hooked up an illegal but working answering machine to my Dial-a-Joke phone and left a message in my Slavic voice that told all the kids the machine was broken because of the phone company, and if they liked Dial-a-Joke they better call 611 (the number for telephone repair) to complain. And I told them to have all their friends call, too.

The next day I was pretty much in meetings all day at Hewlett-Packard, but I got home at 4:45 p.m., just in time to disconnect the illegal answering machine before the telephone guy got there. Then I called 611 and said, "I have a complaint."

She said, "I know. Dial-a-Joke."

"How did you know?" I asked.

A Good Number Is Hard to Find

I told you about 255-6666. That was the first good phone number of my life. Many years later, I got the home number 996-9999, which had six digits the same. That was a milestone for me. When I lived in Los Gatos, I got numbers like 353-3333 and 354-4444 and 356-6666 and 358-8888.

My main goal with phone numbers was to someday get a number with all seven digits the same. The way they divided phone numbers between San Jose and San Francisco, all of those numbers went to San Francisco. For example, 777-7777 was the *San Francisco Examiner*. But as the area codes started running out of phone numbers, they started duplicating the prefixes, allowing San Jose's area code to someday have numbers that started with 222, 333, 444, or whatever.

In the early days of cell phones, I had a scanner that would let you listen to people's cell phone calls. It would show me the phone numbers of callers. One day my friend Dan spotted a number in our 408 area code starting with 999. I immediately called the phone company to get 999-9999 for myself. Unfortunately, they couldn't pull that number out of a larger group of numbers someone else had reserved.

A few weeks later, Dan spotted a number starting with 888. This time I lucked out.

I got the numbers 888-8800, 888-8801, up to 888-8899. So by about 1992, I had achieved my lifetime goal of having the ultimate phone number.

I put the number 888-8888 on my own cell phone, but something went wrong. I would get a hundred calls a day with no one on the line, not once. Sometimes I would hear shuffling sounds in the background. I would yell, whistle, but I could never get anyone to speak to me.

Very often I would hear a tone being repeated over and over, and then it hit me. It was a baby, pressing the 8 button over and over. I did a calculation that concluded that perhaps one-third of the babies born in the San Jose 408 area code would eventually call my number. And basically this made my phone unusable.

I'll tell you about one last number. It was 221-1111. This number has a mathematical purity like no other. It's all binary numbers—magic computer numbers. Powers of two. But the real purity was how small the digits were, 1s and 2s. By the rules of allocating phone numbers in the United States, no other phone number could have only two 2s and the rest 1s. In that sense, it was the lowest number you could get.

It was also the shortest dialing distance for your finger to move on a rotary phone,

As with 888-8888, I got so many wrong phone numbers every day. One day I was booking a flight and noticed that Pan American Airlines had the number, 800-221-1111.

The next phone call I got, I heard someone start to hang up after I said hello. I shouted, "Are you calling Pan Am?" And a woman came on the line and said, "Yes." I asked her what she wanted and booked my first flight for a Pan Am passenger that day.

Over the next two weeks, I booked dozens of flights. I made up a game to see how crazy I could make prices and flight times and still have people book it. After a couple of weeks, I started feeling guilty. And vulnerable. I didn't want to get arrested. So for the next two years, I answered every phone call with, "Pan Am, International Desk. Greg speaking." My friends would have to yell, "Hey, Steve, it's me," when they called. I would trick people into booking the craziest things, but I would always tell them it was a prank and that I was not really Pan Am.

For example, I might tell them that their flight would leave San Jose at 3 a.m., so a lot of times they would be really relieved. I started booking callers on what I called the "Grasshopper Special." If they flew through our lesser-used airports, it would reduce their fare. I almost always told them to fly to Billings, Montana, down to Amarillo, Texas, then up to

Moscow, Idaho, then to Lexington, Kentucky, and *then* to their destination. Boston.

Hundreds of people took me up on this. Hundreds, maybe thousands, over the course of two years. Anyone who knows me saw me taking reservations constantly. I also booked Grasshopper flights to other countries, telling people they had to stop in Hong Kong, Bangkok, Tokyo, and Singapore to get to Sydney.

I told some callers they could fly "freight." But they had to wear warm clothing.

I kept a straight face because everyone always went for the lower fare. At some point I started telling them it was cheaper to fly on propeller planes than jets. The first time I did this, I tried to book a guy on a thirty-hour flight to London. But he would have nothing to do with it. I did get a number of people to buy into a cheap twenty-hour flight from San Jose to New York City.

The craziest one—and I still smile when I think about it—was the one I called the "Gambler's Special." I would tell them that the first leg of their flight had to go to Las Vegas. From there, they had to go to our counter at the airport. And if they rolled a "7," the next leg would be free.

"Every other call today has been for Dial-a-Joke," she said, sounding really frustrated. So I just got this big grin on my face. I felt like I had made the big time.

And yes, the guy did show up that day at 5 p.m.—with his supervisor. I let the guy in to replace it, but left the supervisor out in the rain with a book to read called *I'm Sorry, the Monopoly You Have Reached Is Not in Service*, by K. Aubrey Stone. It's a really lousy book, actually, but I thought he deserved it.

Eventually I had to give up Dial-a-Joke because I couldn't keep it up on my tiny HP engineer's salary. Even though I loved it so, so much.

• ○ •

There is one major thing I haven't yet told you about Dial-a-Joke. It is how I met my first wife, Alice. She was a caller one day when I happened to be taking live calls. I heard a girl's voice, and I don't know why but I said: "I bet I can hang up faster than you!" And then I hung up. She called back, I started talking to her in a normal voice, and before long we were dating. She was really young, just nineteen at the time.

We met, and the more I talked to her, the more I liked her. And she was a girl. I had only kissed two girls up to that point, so even being able to talk to a girl was really rare.

Alice and I were married two years later. And our marriage lasted just a little longer than my career at Hewlett-Packard, which is funny in a sad way.

Because I thought both of those arrangements were going to last forever.

Chapter 9

Wild Projects

During those four years at HP, from the time I was twenty-two to twenty-six, I constantly built my own electronics projects on the side. And that's not even including Dial-a-Joke. Some of these were really amazing.

When I look back, I see that all these projects, plus the science projects I did as a kid and all the stuff my dad taught me, were actually threads of knowledge that converged in my design of the first and second Apple computers.

After Dial-a-Joke, I was still dating Alice, still living in my first apartment in Cupertino, still coming home every night to watch *Star Trek* on TV and work on my projects. And there was almost always some kind of a project to work on, because after a while, people at HP started talking about my design skills to their friends, and I started to get calls from them. Like, could I go down to some guy's house and design something electronic for him? Gadgets, stuff like that. I would always do it for no money—I'd say, Just fly me down to Los Angeles and I'll bring the design down and I'll get it working. I never charged any money for it because this was my thing in life—designing stuff—this is what I loved to do. As I said before, it was my passion.

My boss, Stan Mintz, once came to me with a project to do a

home pinball game. These friends of his wanted to build a little pinball game with rockers and buttons and flippers, just like the ones you use in arcades. So I basically designed something digital that could watch the system, track signals, display the score, sound buzzers and all that. But there was one very tricky circuit that confused Stan, and I remember him telling me, "No, that's wrong. It won't work." But I showed him why it would work. And it did.

I just loved it whenever other engineers, especially my boss, would be surprised by my designs. That always made me happy.

● ○ ●

And soon I was getting involved in one of the most amazing projects. Someone asked me to help design the digital part of the first hotel movie system, which was based on the very earliest VCRs. No one had VCRs then, of course. I was thinking, Oh my god! This is going to be incredible—designing movies for hotels! I couldn't get over it.

Their formula was this. They'd line up about six VCRs. Then they had a method of sending special TV channels to everybody's room. They could play the movies on those channels. There was a filter in each room to block those channels. But the hotel clerk in the lobby could send a signal to unlock the filter in a particular room. Then the guest could watch the movie they ordered on their TV. Someone in the VCR room had to literally start the movie, but this was still a really cool system.

Another project I did was for a company that came out with the first consumer VCRs, and yes, it was before the Betamax. It was called Cartrivision, and the VCR had this amazing motor in it with its own circuit board that spun as it ran the motor. In other words, the spinning circuit board was actually the electronics that ran the motor! It was very strange.

Well, at HP I heard a rumor that this little company had gone bankrupt and they had about eight thousand color VCRs for sale, cheap. I mean, at the time a black-and-white VCR for a school cost almost $1,000. But Cartrivision was selling them at this super-low surplus price. So my friends and I would drive down to their San Jose tape duplication facility. And we'd walk through the building, just amazed at these hundreds of color VCRs in boxes. They weren't really cabinet VCRs like you've seen, but kind of open, where you could see all the circuitry. Anyway, we'd take a bunch of engineers down there and buy them for, like, $60.

This became a huge part of my life almost right away. I studied the kinds of circuits the VCR used, how it worked, went through all the manuals. I tried to figure out how they processed color, how color got recorded onto tape, how the power supply worked. This was all information that came in really handy when we did the color Apple computers. And then I would buy wooden boxes to put these naked color VCRs into. Listen, I had a working color VCR in my apartment in Cupertino when nobody, but nobody, in the world had a VCR at home.

There were only a few movies available at the time. The first one I watched at home was *The Producers*. I saw it right there on my Cartrivision. I opened up my TV, looked at the schematic to figure out where the video signal was, and figured out how to match it to the Cartrivision. That way, I could record shows, too. One of the things I actually recorded was Nixon's resignation on TV. So I must be one of the only people in the world to have a consumer tape of that, because if you go back to that date in time, 1974, you'll see that there were absolutely no VCRs on the market available to consumers.

● ○ ●

Now let me tell you about Pong. Remember Pong? It was the first successful video game (first in the arcade, later at home), and it came from a company called Atari. I remember I was at the Homestead Lanes bowling alley in Sunnyvale with Alice, who was by now my fiancée. And there it was, Pong. I was just mesmerized.

Pong really stood out for me because it was a full-size arcade game right there in a bowling alley. Back then, bowling alleys had a bunch of pinball machines everywhere, but never, ever anything electronic. And Pong was so different from those. It had this little black-and-white TV screen with digital sounds coming out of it—pong, pong, pong. You used the dials to move a paddle up and down to hit a little white ball and bat it to the other player's paddle. It was so simple, but so fun.

All I could do was stare at it in amazement. And I noticed that while pinball games cost a dime to play and required only one person to play, this game cost a quarter and needed two people.

The thing I thought was so incredible wasn't so much the game concept—I mean, it was very much like Ping-Pong or tennis or something like that—as the fact that somebody had come up with the idea that by controlling the white and black dots (pixels) on a TV screen, you could actually build a game. Wow!

And it was a game so different from pinball, but still very attractive. In fact, I found it even more attractive, because of its newness, than all those flashy pinball machines. I got some quarters and played a few games with Alice, and then I sort of stood there awhile and stared at it. Alice said, "What? What are you thinking?"

"What? Here's what," I said. "I could design one of these."

I knew the minute I started thinking about it that I could design it because I knew how digital logic could create signals at the right times. And I knew how television worked on this principle. I knew all this from high school working at Sylvania, from the hotel movie system, from Cartrivision, from all kinds of experience I'd already had.

So right there in that bowling alley I suddenly had this cool new goal. I was going to go back and start thinking about my first design that was actually going to put characters on a TV set. I remember how, way back in high school, I wondered how, if I ever did a computer, I would ever be able to afford one that could display characters on a screen. That was unfathomable back then. But now, I knew, something was different.

Everything had changed.

● ○ ●

I right away decided I was going to build my own Pong game, for my own use at home, and that meant I had to design it from scratch.

To understand how I did this, you have to know a little bit about how a TV set works. It draws a regular pattern, in little dots, in lines across the screen. Left to right for the top line, left to right for the next one, left to right for the next one down, and so on. When it gets done with all 575 lines, it starts again. There's a precise interval, too, between the drawing of each line. All of this is part of what's known as the National Television Systems Committee (NTSC) standard, which is the standard all TVs in the United States follow.

So I understood exactly what the right timings were. I figured out exactly how I could use chips to delay the amount of time the lines scanned on the TV and generated a dot on the screen at the right moment. I also kept track of where it was drawing dots at any point in time.

So if you look at an NTSC television set, there might be 300,000 total possible dot positions, each corresponding to where the line is at any point in time. And remember, each one of these dot positions is getting hit as the TV draws the picture line by line, left to right, from top to bottom, really fast. It happens about 60 times a second. I figured out that I should be able to design a circuit that could keep up with the timing and generate TV signals to draw dots in other places on the screen.

One of my skills was that I was really good at designing things with the absolute minimum amount of chips. That goes back to the Cream Soda Computer. So I figured out how to put just a few chips together and use a crystal clock chip (like the one in my Blue Box or the one that keeps time in your watch) to control the timing and keep count of what is happening.

TVs at that time didn't have any video input connections. There was no video-in like there is now. And I needed a video-in connection if I was going to design a game that would let you display the game on-screen. But how could I figure out where on the TV the video came in from the antennas?

Well, all TVs came with schematics back then. And if you read the schematics and you knew electronics, you could study the transistors and the filters and the coils and the voltages. You could trace your way through the circuit and find out where the video signal really exists in the TV.

So that's where the signal goes into the display circuits of the television set, the signal that carries the television picture according to NTSC standards. I tapped around with an oscilloscope, and with a few resistors and test points I was able to find the exact point of the video signal inside the TV. So I just applied my own video signal to that point, and from then on I could generate everything on the screen.

I also could've put my own TV signal on a TV channel through what is called a modulator. It's the same way a VCR, for instance, puts a TV picture on Channel 3. But my other method was more efficient—better and easier—for me at the time.

So this Pong game I did, it wasn't commercial, of course. I did it all on my own, at home. It had nothing to do with Atari, but I did do it at least a year before Atari came up with a home Pong game that worked with your TV.

All in all, I ended up with twenty-eight chips for the Pong design. This was amazing, back in the days before microprocessors. Every bit of the game had to be implemented in wires and small gates—in hardware, in other words. There was no game program—that is, a game in software form that someone could load. It was all hardwired.

Well, I wanted to make mine even more special, so in addition to showing the score on-screen, I programmed these little chips (called PROMs, for programmable read-only memory) to spell out four-letter words every time you missed the ball. You know. Like HECK or DARN. Not exactly those words, but this is a family book. Anyway, I could easily turn the four-letter-word feature on or off with a switch.

Once, while visiting Steve Jobs, who was working at Atari, I showed it to a bunch of engineers there and they loved it. Soon after, I showed it to Al Alcorn, who was one of the top guys (next to founder Nolan Bushnell) at Atari, and he was really impressed! They thought it was funny, with the dirty words and all.

They offered me a job right then and there, but I said, No way. I explained to them that I could never leave Hewlett-Packard. It wasn't possible. My plan, I told them, was to work at HP for life. It was the best company for an engineer like me.

• ○ •

A few months later—and of course I was still at Hewlett-Packard—I got a call from my friend Steve Jobs. He was getting excited about some interesting work he was doing at Atari. Atari was getting all kinds of attention by then for having started the video game revolution with games like Pong. Its chief at the time, Bushnell, well, he was just larger than life. Steve said it was a blast to work for him.

So anyway, Steve had this job at Atari. After the people designed the games at Atari's Grass Valley design facility, they'd send them down to Steve in Los Gatos. And he would look at those games and try to give them, you know, some final tweaks. Whatever could make them just a little bit better, he would do. Or he might find bugs.

Steve called me at work one day saying that Nolan wanted to do another Pong-like game. Nolan wanted me to do it because he knew how good I was at doing designs with the fewest possible chips. Nolan had been complaining that the Atari games were going higher and higher in chip count, approaching two hundred chips for a single game. He wanted them to be simpler. And he'd seen how good I was at that.

Steve said Nolan wanted a one-player version of Pong, but with bricks that would bounce the ball back to the paddle.

"You gotta get in here," he said. "They're right. You'd be perfect for it."

I was immediately excited because I could see that if one player could play it, instead of it needing two players, it could be a much more fun game. Because when the ball breaks enough bricks—do you remember this game?—it can then get behind the bricks and start bouncing them from behind, which bounces even more bricks out. So it's a little more complicated, and you don't need someone else to play.

So, not even thinking about it, I said, "Sure."

And then Steve says, "Well, there's a caveat. It has to be done in four days." Wow! Back then there wasn't a game you could do in four days. Plus, a game was all hardware. It was hardware where every single wire mattered and every single connection had to determine when signals would be on the screen. And then, I mean, there were the thousands of little connections between chips, and they all mattered, and I realized that this timetable was ridiculous. A game like that should take engineers working on a normal schedule a few months to complete.

I realized I could probably do this in a shorter time than anyone else, but I still thought it was an insane goal to do a hardware game in four days.

But I was up for the challenge.

•   ○   •

So I designed this game Breakout.

I began by actually drawing the schematics so a TV would display light on the screen—line by line. I didn't sleep for four days and nights during this project. During the day, I drew the design on paper, drawing it out clearly enough so that a technician could take the design and wire chips together. At night Steve would wire the chips together, using a technique called wire-wrapping. Wire-wrapping is a way of connecting chips with wires that does not require soldering. I prefer soldering, myself, because it's always cleaner, smaller, and tighter. But wire-wrapping is how most technicians do it. Don't ask me why.

With wire-wrapping, you hear a zipping sound of a little electronic motor, the sound of it wrapping a wire around a small metal pole. In about a second the wire-wrap gun wraps the wire about ten times around the metal pole. Then zip onto another one. Zip onto another one. Over and over. It actually gets kind of messy, with wires dangling everywhere between the metal poles. But like I said, that's how things are done—a lot of engineers still do it that way. I can't understand why, but they do.

Well, then Steve would breadboard it—that means putting all the components, wires, chips, and everything, onto a prototype board—and do the wire-wrapping.

It's funny how when you're up so late at night for so long your mind can get into these creative places, the kind of creative places that come to you when you're halfway between asleep and awake.

For instance, I remember Steve one night saying something about how Atari was planning on using a microprocessor in a game someday soon.

Whoa. I didn't know exactly what a microprocessor was, but I knew enough to know that what we were talking about is a whole little computer inside. And I thought, Wow, a little computer could be inside a game, which either meant that the computer would actually make all the decisions in the game or the game could be a program that used the microprocessor to make it powerful.

I imagined what it might look like someday when microprocessors could control games. My brain just took a leap there. There were so many ways it could go.

Then there was another night when some guys were overlaying colored cellophane over the TV screen to make our game look like it had colors in it. As things went from left to right, the colors would sort of shift. And I thought, Oh my gosh, color in computer games would be so neat, that would be just unbelievable!

I used to sit on a bench with Steve on the left-hand side of me breadboarding. And I'd be thinking about how I sort of knew what the waves for color would look like in an oscilloscope. I could imagine it. For instance, one nice pure wave is called a "phase shift." So the way color TV is designed is it has this one particular wave of a certain frequency, a certain number of times per second, which is roughly 3.7593-something cycles per second. Perfect.

According to the theory of phase delay, on an American TV set that particular signal will show up as a color. And there are complicated mathematics and circuits that can introduce the right phase delay to get the color you want. (Also, the signal itself that comes to a TV set can be higher or lower voltage. Higher voltage means lighter—more toward white—while lower voltage is darker—more toward black.)

So somehow this idea popped into my head that if you took a normal digital chip—a chip that works with 1s and 0s, not waves—and you spun this chip around with four little bits—call it 1, 0, 1, 0 (alternating high and low voltages)—what you would get out of the end is four 0s. And four 0s would look just like black on a TV. And what if you put four 1s in. Then you'd get white. Now, say, you put 1, 0, 1, 0, it's going to average out as gray. So if you could keep spinning this register at the exact right rate, it would come out as the United States color TV frequency, showing up as color on most TV sets. You could even put it through a small filter and round it off the way real color TV set waves work. The concept I came up with is that if I kept shifting this register around, it just might come out in purple, or red if it was shifted slightly the other way.

How amazing that one little digital chip doing nothing but 1s and 0s could do what color TVs could with waves! It would be so much simpler and more precise.

That was amazing because back then, color TVs operated with circuits a lot more complicated than any computer was back then. And the funny thing is, that very idea came to me in the middle of the night at that lab at Atari. I did no testing on it, but I filed it away in my memory, and eventually that was exactly how things like color monitors ended up on personal computers everywhere. Because of my wild idea that night.

● ○ ●

In addition to thinking, while I was waiting for Steve to finish breadboarding I also spent a lot of time playing what I thought was the best game ever: Gran Trak 10. In just those couple of nights, I got so good at it that many years later, when I found one in a pizza parlor, I was able to get the score you needed for a free pizza every time. After I did that twice, the pizza parlor got rid of the machine.

Maybe you're wondering why I didn't use the extra two hours to sleep instead of playing Gran Trak 10, a racing game I loved. It was because at any moment Steve might call me in and say, "Okay, I've got breadboard. Let's test it." And I had to be there for the testing because I was the one who'd understand the circuit I'd designed.

The bottom line of this story is that I actually did finish this project in four days and nights somehow, and it worked.

Steve and I both ended up with mononucleosis. The whole thing used forty-five chips, and Steve paid me half the seven hundred bucks he said they paid him for it. (They were paying us based on how few chips I could do it in.) Later I found out he got paid a bit more for it—like a few thousand dollars—than he said at the time, but we were kids, you know. He got paid one amount, and told me he got paid another. He wasn't honest with me, and I was hurt. But I didn't make a big deal about it or anything.

Ethics always mattered to me, and I still don't really understand why he would've gotten paid one thing and told me he'd gotten paid another. But, you know, people are different. And in no way do I regret the experience at Atari with Steve Jobs. He was my best friend and I still feel extremely linked with him. I wish him well. And it was a great project that was so fun. Anyway, in the long run of money—Steve and I ended up getting very comfortable money-wise from our work founding Apple just a few years later—it certainly didn't add up to much.

Steve and I were the best of friends for a very, very long time. We had the same goals for a while. They jelled perfectly at forming Apple. But we were always different people, different people right from the start.

You know, it's strange, but right around the time I started working on what later became the Apple I board, this idea popped into my mind about two guys who die on the same day. One guy is really successful, and he's spending all his time running companies, managing them, making sure they are profitable, and making sales goals all the time. And the other guy, all he does is lounge around, doesn't have much money, really likes to tell jokes and follow gadgets and technology and other things he finds interesting in the world, and he just spends his life laughing.

In my head, the guy who'd rather laugh than control things is going to be the one who has the happier life. That's just my opinion. I figure happiness is the most important thing in life, just how much you laugh. The guy whose head kind of floats, he's so happy. That's who I am, who I want to be and have always wanted to be.

And that's why I never let stuff like what happened with Breakout bother me. Though you can disagree—you can even split from a relationship—you don't have to hold it against the other. You're just different. That's the best way to live life and be happy.

And I figured this all out even before Steve and I started Apple.

Chapter 10

My Big Idea

I can tell you almost to the day when the computer revolution as I see it started, the revolution that today has changed the lives of everyone.

It happened at the very first meeting of a strange, geeky group of people called the Homebrew Computer Club in March 1975. This was a group of people fascinated with technology and the things it could do. Most of these people were young, a few were old, we all looked like engineers; no one was really good-looking. Ha. Well, we're talking about engineers, remember. We were meeting in the garage of an out-of-work engineer named Gordon French.

After my first meeting, I started designing the computer that would later be known as the Apple I. It was that inspiring.

Almost from the beginning, Homebrew had a goal: to bring computer technology within the range of the average person, to make it so people could afford to have a computer and do things with it. That had been my goal, too, for years and years before that. So I felt right at home there.

And eventually Homebrew's goal just expanded and expanded. It wasn't long before we were talking about a world—a possible world—where computers could be owned by anybody, used by anybody, no matter who you were or how much money you made. We wanted them to be affordable—and we wanted them to change people's lives.

Everyone in the Homebrew Computer Club envisioned computers as a benefit to humanity—a tool that would lead to social justice. We thought low-cost computers would empower people to do things they never could before. Only big companies could afford computers at the time. That meant they could afford to do things smaller companies and regular people couldn't do. And we were out to change all that.

In this, we were revolutionaries. Big companies like IBM and Digital Equipment didn't hear our social message. And they didn't have a clue how powerful a force this small computer vision could be. They looked at what we were doing—small computers, hobby computers—and said they would just remain toys. And a relatively minor business. They didn't imagine how they could evolve.

There was a lot of talk about our being part of a revolution. How people lived and communicated was going to be changed by us, changed forever, changed more than anyone could predict exactly.

Of course there was also a lot of talk about specific components that would make faster computers, and about technical solutions for computers and accessories themselves. People would talk about the humanistic future uses of computers. We thought computers were going to be used for all these weird things—strange geeky things like controlling the lights in your house—and that turned out not to be the case. But everyone felt this thing was coming. A total change. We couldn't always define it, but we believed it.

As I said, almost all of the large computer companies were on record saying that what we were doing was insignificant. It turned out they were wrong and we were right—right all the way.

But back then, even we had no idea how right we were and how huge it would become.

● ○ ●

It's funny and maybe a little bit ironic how my involvement in the whole Homebrew thing got started. Remember Allen Baum? He shows up again and again at a lot of important times in my life. He was my friend who sometimes worked at Sylvania with me in high school, whose dad designed the TV Jammer, who did the Homestead High prank with Steve Jobs and me, and also the one who helped get me that dream job at Hewlett-Packard.

I still had that HP job at the time. One day at work I got a call from Allen. It was a call that would change my life yet again, the call that introduced me to Homebrew.

Allen called and said something like, "Listen. There's this flyer I found at HP, it's for a meeting of people who are building TV and video terminals and things."

Now, TV terminals I already knew a little about. By this point, in 1975, I'd done all kinds of side projects, and had already learned a lot about putting data from computers onto TVs. Not

More About Homebrew

This Homebrew Club I belonged to since its first meeting in March 1975 led to other computer companies than Apple. It was incredibly revolutionary. Other members who started computer companies included Bob Marsh and Lee Felsenstein (Processor Technology), Adam Osborne (Osborne Computers), and, of course, me and Steve Jobs, who I later talked into going with me. I once wrote an article on the importance of Homebrew, and you can find it at: http://www.atariarchives.org/deli/home brew_and_how_the_apple.php.

only had I done my version of Pong plus that project at Atari, Breakout, but I'd already built a terminal that could access the ARPANET, the government-owned network of computers that was the predecessor to the Internet. My terminal even let you display a few letters, up to sixty characters a second. I know that sounds slow now, but this was about six times faster than most teletype systems at the time and a whole lot cheaper. Teletype systems cost thousands of dollars, way more than someone on an engineer's salary could afford, but I built a system using a Sears TV and a cheap $60 typewriter keyboard.

Just like my Pong design and the Cartrivision VCR, I connected my video signal into the test pin of my home TV, the one I found in the schematics.

Now, if Allen had told me that Homebrew was going to be about microprocessors, I probably wouldn't have gone. I know I wouldn't have gone. I was shy and felt that I knew little about the newest developments in computers. By this time, I was so totally out of computers. I was just immersed in my wonderful calculator job at HP. I wasn't even following computers at all. I mean, I hardly even knew what the heck a microprocessor was.

But, like I said, I thought it was going to be a TV terminal meeting. I thought, Yeah, I could go to this thing and have something to say.

I was scared, but I showed up. And you know what? That decision changed everything. That night turned out to be one of the most important nights of my life.

● ○ ●

About thirty people showed up for this first meeting there in that garage in Menlo Park. It was cold and kind of sprinkling outside, but they left the garage door open and set up chairs inside. So I'm just sitting there, listening to the big discussion going on.

They were talking about some microprocessor computer kit being up for sale. And they seemed all excited about it. Someone there was holding up the magazine *Popular Electronics*, which had a picture of a computer on the front of it. It was called the Altair, from a New Mexico company named MITS. You bought the pieces and put them together and then you could have your own computer.

So it turned out all these people were really Altair enthusiasts, not TV terminal people like I thought. And they were throwing around words and terms I'd never heard—talking about microprocessor chips like the Intel 8080, the Intel 8008, the 4004, I didn't even know what these things were. Like I said, I'd been designing calculators for the last three years, so I didn't have a clue.

I felt so out of it—like, No, no, I am not of this world. Under my breath, I am cussing Allen Baum. I don't belong here. And when they went around and everyone introduced themselves, I said, "I'm Steve Wozniak, I work at Hewlett-Packard on calculators and I designed a video terminal." I might have said some other things, but I was so nervous at public speaking that I couldn't even remember what I said afterward. After that, we all signed a sheet of paper where we were supposed to put down our name and what interests and talents we were bringing to the group. (This piece of paper is public now; you might be able to find it online.) The thing I wrote on that paper was, "I have very little free time."

Isn't that funny? These days I'm so busy and people are constantly asking for my autograph and stuff, but back then I was also just as busy: always working on projects, engineering for work and then engineering at home. I don't feel like I've changed much since then, and I guess this proves it, sort of.

Well, anyway, I was scared and not feeling like I belonged, but one very lucky thing happened. A guy started passing out these data sheets—technical specifications—for a microprocessor called the 8008 from a company in Canada. (It was a close copy, or clone, of Intel's 8008 microprocessor at the time.) I took it home, figuring, Well, at least I'll learn something.

• ○ •

That night, I checked out the microprocessor data sheet and I saw it had an instruction for adding a location in memory to the A register. I thought, Wait a minute. Then it had another instruction you could use for subtracting memory from the A register. Whoa. Well, maybe this doesn't mean anything to you, but I knew exactly what these instructions meant, and it was the most exciting thing to discover ever. Because I could see right away that these were exactly like the instructions I used to design and redesign on paper for all of those minicomputers back in high school and college. I realized that all those minicomputers I'd designed on paper were pretty much just like this one.

Only now all the CPU parts were on one chip, instead of a bunch of chips, and it was a microprocessor. And it had pins that came out, and all you had to do was use those pins to connect things to it, like memory chips.

Then I realized what the Altair was—that computer everyone was so excited about at the meeting. It was exactly like the Cream Soda Computer I'd designed five years before! Almost exactly. The difference was that the Altair had a microprocessor—a CPU on one chip—and mine had a CPU that was on several chips. The other difference was that someone was selling this one—for $379, as I recall. Other than that, there was pretty much no difference. And I designed the Cream Soda five years before I ever laid eyes on an Altair.

It was as if my whole life had been leading up to this point. I'd done my minicomputer redesigns, I'd done data on-screen with Pong and Breakout, and I'd already done a TV terminal. From the Cream Soda Computer and others, I knew how to connect memory and make a working system. I realized that all I needed was this Canadian processor or another processor like it and some memory chips. Then I'd have the computer I'd always wanted!

Oh my god. I could build my own computer, a computer I could own and design to do any neat things I wanted to do with it for the rest of my life.

I didn't need to spend $400 to get an Altair—which really was just a glorified bunch of chips with a metal frame around it and some lights. That was the same as my take-home salary, I mean, come on. And to make the Altair do anything interesting, I'd have to spend way, way more than that. Probably hundreds, even thousands of dollars. And besides, I'd already been there with the Cream Soda Computer. I was bored with it then. You never go back. You go forward. And now, the Cream Soda Computer could be my jumping-off point.

No way was I going to do that. I decided then and there I had the opportunity to build the complete computer I'd always wanted. I just needed any microprocessor, and I could build an extremely small computer I could write programs on. Programs like games, and the simulation programs I wrote at work. The possibilities went on and on. And I wouldn't have to buy an Altair to do it. I would design it all by myself.

That night, the night of that first meeting, this whole vision of a kind of personal computer just popped into my head. All at once. Just like that.

●　○　●

And it was that very night that I started to sketch out on paper what would later come to be known as the Apple I. It was a quick project, in retrospect. Designing it on paper took a few hours, though it took a few months longer to get the parts and study their data sheets.

I did this project for a lot of reasons. For one thing, it was a project to show the people at Homebrew that it was possible to build a very affordable computer—a real computer you could program for the price of the Altair—with just a few chips. In that sense, it was a great way to show off my real talent, my talent of coming up with clever designs, designs that were efficient and affordable. By that I mean designs that would use the fewest components possible.

I also designed the Apple I because I wanted to give it away for free to other people. I gave out schematics for building my computer at the next meeting I attended.

This was my way of socializing and getting recognized. I had to build something to show other people. And I wanted the engineers at Homebrew to build computers for themselves, not just assemble glorified processors like the Altair. I wanted them to know they didn't have to depend on an Altair, which had these hard-to-understand lights and switches. Every computer up to this time looked like an airplane cockpit, like the Cream Soda Computer, with switches and lights you had to manipulate and read.

Instead they could do something that worked with a TV and a real keyboard, sort of like a typewriter. A computer like I could imagine.

As I told you before, I had already built a terminal that let you type regular words and sentences to a computer far away, and that computer could send words back to the TV. I just decided to add the computer—my microprocessor with memory—into the same case as that terminal I'd already built.

Why not make the faraway computer this little microprocessor that's right there in the box?

I realized that since you already had a keyboard, you didn't need a front panel. You could type things in and see things on-screen. Because you have the computer, the screen, and the keyboard, too.

So people now say this was a far-out idea—to combine my terminal with a microprocessor—and I guess it would be for other people. But for me, it was the next logical step.

That first Apple computer I designed—even though I hadn't named it an Apple or anything else yet—well, that was just when everything fell into place. And I will tell you one thing. Before the Apple I, all computers had hard-to-read front panels and no screens and keyboards. After Apple I, they all did.

• ○ •

Let me tell you a little about that first computer—what is now called the Apple I—and how I designed it.

First, I started sketching out how I thought it would work on paper. This is the same way I used to design minicomputers on paper in high school and college, though of course they never got built. And the first thing was I had to decide what CPU I would use. I found out that the CPU of the Altair—the Intel 8080—cost almost more than my monthly rent. And a regular person couldn't purchase it in small or single-unit quantities anyway. You had to be a real company and probably fill out all kinds of credit forms for that.

Luckily, though, I'd been talking to my cubicle mates at HP about the Homebrew Club and what I was planning, and Myron Tuttle had an idea. (You remember him: the guy whose plane almost crashed when I was in it.) He told me there was a deal you could get from Motorola if you were an HP employee. He told me that for about $40, I could buy a Motorola 6800 microprocessor and a couple of other chips. I thought, Oh man, that's cheap. So very quickly I knew exactly what processor I would have.

Another thing that happened really early on was I realized—and it was an important realization—that our HP calculators were computers in a real sense. They were as real as the Altair or the Cream Soda Computer or anything else. I mean, a calculator had a processor and memory. But it had something else, too, a feature computers didn't have at the time. When you turned a calculator on, it was ready to go: it had a program in it that started up and then it was ready for you to hit a number. So it booted up automatically and just sat there, waiting for you to tell it to do something. Say you hit a "5." The processor in the calculator can see that a button is pushed, and it says, Is that a 1? No. A 2? No. A 3, 4 . . . it's a 5. And it displays a 5. The program in a calculator that did that was on three little ROM (read-only memory) chips— chips that hold their information even if you turn the power off.

So I knew I would have to get a ROM chip and build the same kind of program, a program that would let the computer turn on automatically. (An Altair or even my Cream Soda Computer didn't do anything for about half an hour after you set switches so you could put a program in.) With the Apple I, I wanted to make the job of having a program go into memory easier. This meant I needed to write one small program which would run as soon as you turned your computer on. The program would tell the computer how to read the keyboard. It would let you enter data into memory, see what data was in memory, and make the processor run a program at a specific point in memory.

What took about half an hour to load up a program on the Altair, took less than a minute using a keyboard on the Apple I.

What Is ROM?

Read-only memory (ROM) is a term you'll hear a lot in this book. A ROM chip can only be programmed once and keeps its information even if the power is turned off. A ROM chip typically holds programs that are important for a computer to remember. Like what to do when you turn it on, what to display, how to recognize connected devices like keyboards, printers, or monitors. In my Apple I design, I got the idea from the HP calculators (which used two ROM chips) to include ROMs. Then I could write a "monitor" program so the computer could keep track of what keys were being pressed, and so on.

If you wanted to see what was in memory on an Altair, it might take you half an hour of looking at little lights. But on the Apple I, it took all of a second to look at it on your TV screen.

I ended up calling my little program a "monitor" program since that program's main job was going to be to monitor, or watch, what you typed on the keyboard. This was a stepping point—the whole purpose of my computer, after all, was to be able to write programs. Specifically, I wanted it to run FORTRAN, a popular language at the time.

So the idea in my head involved a small program in read-only memory (ROM) instead of a computer front panel of lights and switches. You can input data with a real keyboard and look at your results on a real screen. I could get rid of that front panel entirely, the one that made a computer look like what you'd see in an airplane cockpit.

Every computer before the Apple I had that front panel of switches and lights. Every computer since has had a keyboard and a screen. That's how huge my idea turned out.

• ○ •

My style with projects has always been to spend a lot of time getting ready to build it. Now that I saw my own computer could be a reality, I started collecting information on all the components and chips that might apply to a computer design.

I would drive to work in the morning—sometimes as early as 6:30 a.m.—and there, alone in the early morning, I would quickly read over engineering magazines and chip manuals. I'd study the specifications and timing diagrams of the chips I was interested in, like the $40 Motorola 6800 Myron had told me about. All the while, I'd be preparing the design in my head.

The Motorola 6800 had forty pins—connectors—and I had to know precisely how each one of those forty pins worked. Because I was only doing this part-time, this was a long, slow process. And several weeks passed without any actual construction happening. Finally I came in one night to draw the design on paper. I had sketched it crudely before. But that night I came in and drew it carefully on my drafting board at Hewlett-Packard.

It was a small step from there to a completely built computer. I just needed the parts.

● ○ ●

I started noticing articles saying that a new, superior-sounding microprocessor was going to be introduced soon at a show, WESCON, in San Francisco. It especially caught my attention that this new microprocessor—the 6502 from MOS Technologies in Pennsylvania—would be pin-for-pin compatible with, electrically the same as, the Motorola 6800 I had drafted my design around. That meant I could just pop it in without any redesigning at all.

The next thing I heard was that it was going to be sold over the counter at MOS Technologies' booth at WESCON. The fact that this chip was so easy to get is how it ended up being the microprocessor for the Apple I.

And the best part is they cost half ($20) of what the Motorola chip would have cost me through the HP deal.

WESCON, on June 16–18, 1975, was being held in San Francisco's famous Cow Palace. A bunch of us drove up there and I waited in line in front of MOS Technologies' table, where a guy named Chuck Peddle was peddling the chips.

Right on the spot I bought a few for $20 each, plus a $5 manual.

Now I had all the parts I needed to start constructing the computer.

● ○ ●

A couple of days later, at a regular meeting of the Homebrew Computer Club, a number of us excitedly showed the 6502 microprocessors we'd bought. More people in our club now had microprocessors than ever before.

I had no idea what the others were going to do with their 6502s, but I knew what I was going to do with mine.

To actually construct the computer, I gathered my parts together. I did this construction work in my cubicle at HP. On a typical day, I'd go home after work and eat a TV dinner or make spaghetti and then drive the five minutes back to work where I would sign in again and work late into the night. I liked to work on this project at HP, I guess because it was an engineering kind of environment. And when it came time to test or solder, all the equipment was there.

First I looked at my design on draft paper and decided exactly where I would put which chips on a flat board so that wire between chips would be short and neat-looking. In other words, I organized and grouped the parts as they would sit on the board.

The majority of my chips were from my video terminal—the terminal I'd already built to access the ARPANET. In addition, I had the microprocessor, a socket to put another board with random-access memory (RAM) chips on it, and two peripheral interface adapter chips for connecting the 6502 to my terminal.

I used sockets for all my chips because I was nuts about sockets. This traced back to my job at Electroglas, where the soldered chips that went bad weren't easily replaced. I wanted to be able to easily remove bad chips and replace them.

I also had two more sockets that could hold a couple of PROM chips. These programmable read-only memory chips could hold data like a small program and not lose the data when the power was off.

Two of these PROM chips that were available to me in the lab could hold 256 bytes of data—enough for a very tiny program. (Today, many programs are a million times larger than that.) To give you an idea of what a small amount of memory that is, a word processor needs that much for a single sentence today.

I decided that these chips would hold my monitor program, the little program I came up with so that my computer could use a keyboard instead of a front panel.

What Was the ARPANET?

Short for the Advanced Research Projects Agency Network, and developed by the U.S. Department of Defense, the ARPANET was the first operational packet-switching network that could link computers all over the world. It later evolved into what everyone now knows as the global Internet.

The ARPANET and the Internet are based on a type of data communication called "packet switching." A computer can break a piece of information down into packets, which can be sent over different wires independently and then reassembled at the other end. Previously, circuit switching was the dominant method—think of the old telephone systems of the early twentieth century. Every call was assigned a real circuit, and that same circuit was tied up during the length of the call.

The fact that the ARPANET used packet switching instead of circuit switching was a phenomenal advance that made the Internet possible.

• ○ •

Wiring this computer—actually soldering everything together— took one night. The next few nights after that, I had to write the 256-byte little monitor program with pen and paper. I was good at making programs small, but this was a challenge even for me.

This was the first program I ever wrote for the 6502 microprocessor. I wrote it out on paper, which wasn't the normal way even then. The normal way to write a program at the time was to pay for computer usage. You would type into a computer terminal you were paying to use, renting time on a time-share terminal, and that terminal was connected to this big expensive computer somewhere else. That computer would print out a version of your program in 1s and 0s that your microprocessor could understand.

This 1 and 0 program could be entered into RAM or a PROM and run as a program. The hitch was that I couldn't afford to pay for computer time. Luckily, the 6502 manual I had described what 1s and 0s were generated for each instruction, each step of a program. MOS Technologies even provided a pocket-size card you could carry that included all the 1s and 0s for each of the many instructions you needed.

So I wrote my program on the left side of the page in machine language. As an example, I might write down "LDA #44," which means to load data corresponding to 44 (in hexadecimal) into the microprocessor's A register.

On the right side of the page, I would write that instruction in hexadecimal using my card. For example, that instruction would translate into A9 44. The instruction A9 44 stood for 2 bytes of data, which equated to 1s and 0s the computer could understand: 10101001 01000100.

Writing the program this way took about two or three pieces of paper, using every single line.

I was barely able to squeeze what I needed into that tiny 256-byte space, but I did it. I wrote two versions of it: one that let the press of a key interrupt whatever program was running, and the other that only let a program check whether the key was being struck. The second method is called "polling."

During the day, I took my two monitor programs and some PROM chips over to another HP building where they had the equipment to permanently burn the 1s and 0s of both programs into the chips.

But I still couldn't complete—or even test—these chips without memory. I mean computer memory, of course. Computers can't run without memory, the place where they do all their calculations and record-keeping.

The most common type of computer memory at the time was called "static RAM" (SRAM). My Cream Soda Computer, the

Altair, and every other computer at the time used that kind of memory. I borrowed thirty-two SRAM chips—each one could hold 1,024 bits—from Myron Tuttle. Altogether that was 4K bytes, which was 16 times more than the 256 bytes the Altair came with.

I wired up a separate SRAM board with these chips inside their sockets and plugged it into the connector in my board.

With all the chips in place, I was ready to see if my computer worked.

● ○ ●

The first step was to apply power. Using the power supplies near my cubicle, I hooked up the power and analyzed signals with an oscilloscope. For about an hour I identified problems that were obviously keeping the microprocessor from working. At one point I had two pins of the microprocessor accidentally shorting each other, rendering both signals useless. At another point one pin bent while I was placing it in its socket.

But I kept going. You see, whenever I solve a problem on an electronic device I'm building, it's like the biggest high ever. And that's what drives me to keep doing it, even though you get frustrated, angry, depressed, and tired doing the same things over and over. Because at some point comes the Eureka moment. You solve it.

And finally I got it, that Eureka moment. My microprocessor was running, and I was well on my way.

But there were still other things to fix. I was able to debug— that is, find errors and correct them—the terminal portion of the computer quickly because I'd already had a lot of experience with my terminal design. I could tell the terminal was working when it put a single cursor on the little 9-inch black-and-white TV I had at HP.

The next step was to debug the 256-byte monitor program on the PROMs. I spent a couple of hours trying to get the interrupt version of it working, but I kept failing. I couldn't write a new program into the PROMs. To do that, I'd have to go to that other building again, just to burn the program into the chip. I studied the chip's data sheets to see what I did wrong, but to this day I never found it. As any engineer out there reading this knows, interrupts are like that. They're great when they work, but hard to get to work.

Finally I gave up and just popped in the other two PROMs, the ones with the "polling" version of the monitor program. I typed a few keys on the keyboard and I was shocked! The letters were displayed on the screen!

It is so hard to describe this feeling—when you get something working on the first try. It's like getting a hole-in-one from forty feet away.

It was still only around 10 p.m.—I checked my watch. For the next couple of hours I practiced typing data into memory, displaying data on-screen to make sure it was really there, even typing in some very short programs in hexadecimal and running them, things like printing random characters on the screen. Simple programs.

I didn't realize it at the time, but that day, Sunday, June 29, 1975, was pivotal. It was the first time in history anyone had typed a character on a keyboard and seen it show up on the screen right in front of them.

Chapter 11

The Apple I

I **was never** the kind of person who had the courage to raise his hand during the Homebrew main meeting and say, "Hey, look at this great computer advance I've made." No, I could never have said that in front of a whole garageful of people.

But after the main meeting every other Wednesday, I would set up my stuff on a table and answer questions people asked. Anyone who wanted to was welcome to do this.

I showed the computer that later became known as the Apple I at every meeting after I got it working. I never planned out what I would say beforehand. I just started the demo and let people ask the questions I knew they would, the questions I wanted to answer.

I was so proud of my design—and I so believed in the club's mission to further computing—that I Xeroxed maybe a hundred copies of my complete design (including the monitor program) and gave it to anyone who wanted it. I hoped they'd be able to build their own computers from my design.

I wanted people to see this great design of mine in person. Here was a computer with thirty chips on it. That was shocking to people, having so few chips. It was like the same amount of chips on an Altair, except the Altair couldn't do anything unless you bought a lot of other expensive equipment for it. My computer was inexpensive from the get-go. And the fact that you could use your home TV with it, instead of paying thousands for an expensive teletype, put it in a world of its own.

And I wasn't going to be satisfied just typing 1s and 0s into it. My goal since high school was to have my own computer that I could program on, although I always assumed the language on the computer would be FORTRAN.

The computer I built didn't have a language yet. Back then, in 1975, a young guy named Bill Gates was starting to get a little bit of fame in our circles for writing a BASIC interpreter for the Altair. Our club had a copy of it on paper tape which could be read in with a teletype, taking about thirty minutes to complete. Also, at around the same time a book called *101 Basic Computer Games* came out. I could sniff the air.

That's why I decided BASIC would be the right language to write for the Apple I and its 6502 microprocessor. And I found out none existed for the 6502. That meant that if I wrote a BASIC program for it, mine could be the first. And I might even get famous for it. People would say, Oh, Steve Wozniak, he did the BASIC for the 6502.

Anyway, people who saw my computer could take one look at it and see the future. And it was a one-way door. Once you went through it, you could never go back.

● ○ ●

The first time I showed my design, it was with static RAM (SRAM)—the kind of memory that was in my Cream Soda Computer. But the electronics magazines I was reading were talking about a new memory chip, called "dynamic RAM" (DRAM), which would have 4K bits per chip.

The magazines were heralding this as the first time silicon chip memory would be less expensive than magnetic core memory. Up to this point, all the major computers, like the systems from IBM and Data General, still used core memory.

I realized that 4K bytes of DRAM—what I needed as a minimum—would only take eight chips, instead of the thirty-two SRAM chips I had to borrow from Myron. My goal since high school had always been to use as few chips as possible, so this was the way to go.

The biggest difference between SRAM and DRAM is that DRAM has to be refreshed continually or it loses its contents. That means the microprocessor has to electrically refresh roughly 128 different addresses of the DRAM every one two-thousandth of a second to keep it from forgetting its data.

I added DRAM by writing data to the screen—I held the microprocessor clock signal steady, holding transitions off, during a period called the "horizontal refresh."

You know how a TV scans one line at a time on your TV, from top to bottom? It takes about 65 microseconds (millionths of a second) to scan each line on a U.S. TV. Well, it turns out that about 40 of these microseconds are visible and the other 25 microseconds are not. During this 25-microsecond time, the so-called refresh period, I inserted 16 unique addresses to the DRAM. (I got these addresses for free, using the counters of the terminal, which were generating video signals.)

I had selection chips that selected the address to come from the horizontal and vertical counter chips of the terminal during this period. Amazingly, it only took two of these selection chips and maybe another chip or two worth of logic to do the whole thing. So I actually stole some cycles away from the microprocessor to refresh the DRAM.

I would've had no idea how to get a DRAM chip, but luckily, right around this time someone at the club who worked at AMI offered some 4K-bit DRAM chips for sale at a reasonable price. This was before they were even on the market. I see now that someone must've ripped them off from AMI, but I didn't ask any questions.

I bought eight of them from the AMI guy for about $5 each and modified my design. I added some wires to the memory connector on the Apple I board so it could accommodate either an SRAM or DRAM board. I plugged the new DRAM board in, and it worked the very first time.

• ○ •

I had been showing off this exciting design of mine to Steve Jobs. He'd gone with me to Homebrew a few times, helping me carry in my TV. He kept asking me if I could build a computer that could be used for time-sharing—like the minicomputer a local company called Call Computer used.

The year before, Steve and I had sold my ARPANET terminal to Call Computer in Mountain View, giving them the rights to build and sell it.

"Sure," I said. "Someday." It could be done, I thought, but it was ages off.

Then he asked if I could add a disk for storage someday. I said, again, "Sure. Someday." This all seemed a long way off.

Then, a few days after I got the AMI DRAMs working, Steve called me at work. He asked me if I'd considered using the Intel DRAMs instead of AMI's.

"Oh, Intel's are the best, but I could never afford them," I told him.

Steve said to give him a minute.

He made some calls and by some marketing miracle he was able to score some free DRAMs from Intel—unbelievable considering their price and rarity at the time. Steve is just that sort of person. I mean, he knew how to talk to a sales representative. I could never have done that; I was way too shy.

But he got me Intel DRAM chips. Once I had them, I redesigned around them. And I was so proud because my computer looked smaller yet. I had to add a couple more chips to my computer to make it work with the Intel DRAMs. But the Intel chips were physically so much smaller than the AMI chips.

I have to stop here and explain what the big deal about having a smaller-sized chip is. Remember when I said my goal since high school had always been to have the fewest chips? Well, that isn't the whole story. One time in high school, I was trying to get chips for a computer I'd designed. My dad drove me down to meet an engineer he knew at Fairchild Semiconductor, the company that invented the semiconductor. I told him I'd designed an existing minicomputer two ways. I found out that if I used chips by Sygnetics (a Fairchild competitor), the computer had fewer chips than if I used Fairchild chips.

The engineer asked me which Sygnetics chips I'd used.

I told him the make and model number.

He pointed out that the Sygnetics chips I'd used in the design were much larger in physical size, with many more pins and many more wires to connect, than the equivalent Fairchild chips. That added complexity.

I was stunned. Because he made me realize in an instant that the simpler computer design would really have fewer connections, not simply fewer chips. So my goal changed, from designing for fewer chips to trying to have the smallest board, in square inches, possible.

Usually fewer chips means fewer connections, but not always.

Back to the Intel DRAM design of the Apple I, switching from AMI to Intel DRAM memories meant I could reduce the total size of the board, even though I had to add a couple extra chips to do it.

And looking back, what a great, lucky decision it was to go with Intel's chips. Because that chip design eventually became the standard for all memory chips, even to this day.

• ○ •

By Thanksgiving of 1975, Steve had been to a few of the Homebrew meetings with me. And then he told me he'd noticed something: the people at Homebrew, he said, are taking the schematics, but they don't have the time or ability to build the computer that's spelled out in the schematics.

He said, "Why don't we build and then sell the printed circuit boards to them?" That way, he said, people could solder all their chips to a printed circuit (PC) board and have a computer in days instead of weeks. Most of the hard work would already be done. His idea was for us to make these preprinted circuit boards for $20 and sell them for $40. People would think it was a great deal because they were getting chips almost free from their companies anyway.

Frankly, I couldn't see how we would earn our money back. I figured we'd have to invest about $1,000 to get a computer company to print the boards. To get that money back, we'd have to sell the board for $40 to fifty people. And I didn't think there were fifty people at Homebrew who'd buy the board. After all, there were only about five hundred members at this point, and most of them were Altair enthusiasts.

But Steve had a good argument. We were in his car and he said—and I can remember him saying this like it was yesterday: "Well, even if we lose our money, we'll have a company. For once in our lives, we'll have a company."

For once in our lives, we'd have a company. That convinced me. And I was excited to think about us like that. To be two best friends starting a company. Wow. I knew right then that I'd do it. How could I not?

Chapter 12

Our Very Own Company

To come up with the $1,000 we thought we'd need to build ready-made printed circuit boards, I sold my HP 65 calculator for $500. The guy who bought it only paid me half, though, and never paid me the rest. I didn't feel too bad because I knew HP's next-generation calculator, the HP 67, was coming out in a month and would cost me only $370 with the employee discount.

And Steve sold his VW van for another few hundred dollars. He figured he could ride around on his bicycle if he had to. That was it. We were in business.

Believe it or not, it was only a couple of weeks later when we came up with a name for the partnership. I remember I was driving Steve back from the airport along Highway 85. Steve was coming back from a visit to Oregon to a place he called an "apple orchard." It was actually some kind of commune.

Steve suggested a name—Apple Computer.

The first comment out of my mouth was, "What about Apple Records?" This was (and still is) the Beatles-owned record label.

We both tried to come up with technical-sounding names that were better, but we couldn't think of any good ones. Apple was so much better, better than any other name we could think of.

Steve didn't think Apple Records would have a problem since it probably was a totally different business. I had no idea.

So Apple it was. Apple it had to be.

• ○ •

Really soon after that, we met with a friend of Steve's who worked at Atari. This guy said he'd be able to design the basic layout of my printed circuit board, based on my original design, for about $600. That was what we needed so we could take it into a manufacturing company that could mass-produce boards.

We also met with another guy from Atari, Ron Wayne, who Steve thought could be a partner. I remember meeting him for the first time and thinking, Wow, this guy is amazing. He could just sit at a typewriter and type out our whole legal partnership agreement like he's a lawyer. He wasn't a lawyer, but he knew all the legal words. He was a fast talker and he seemed so smart. He was one of those people who seemed to have a quick answer for everything. He seemed to know how to do all the things we didn't.

Ron ended up playing a huge role in those very early days at Apple—this was before we had funding, before we'd done much of anything. He was really the third partner, when I think of it. And he did a lot. He wrote and laid out the early operation manual. After all, he could type stuff. And he could draw. He was the one who did the etching of Newton under the Apple tree that was on the computer manual.

Underneath it was a line from a William Wordsworth poem describing Newton. It said: "A mind forever voyaging through strange seas of thought . . . alone."

Eventually Steve, Ron, and I figured out a partnership agreement that started Apple and included all three of us. Steve had 45 percent, I had 45 percent, and Ron got 10 percent. We both trusted him as someone who'd be able to resolve arguments. Ron started working on the paperwork.

• ○ •

Where Did That Weird Quote Come From?

I had to look this one up. It turns out it is from book 3 of *The Prelude* by William Wordsworth. (A Mind Forever Voyaging is also the name of a video game from 1985. Who knew?)

The lines in full read like this:

The antechapel where the statue stood
Of Newton with his prism and silent face,
The marble index of a mind for ever
Voyaging through strange seas of Thought, alone.

Before the partnership agreement was even inked, I realized something and told Steve. Because I worked at HP, I told him, everything I'd designed during the term of my employment contract belonged to HP.

Whether that upset Steve or not, I couldn't tell. But it didn't matter to me if he was upset about it. I believed it was my duty to tell HP about what I had designed while working for them. That was the right thing and the ethical thing. Plus, I really loved that company and I really did believe this was a product they should do. I knew that a guy named Miles Judd, three levels above me in the company structure, had managed an engineering group at an HP division in Colorado Springs that had developed a desktop computer.

It wasn't like ours at all—it was aimed at scientists and engineers and it was really expensive—but it was programmable in BASIC.

I told my boss, Pete Dickinson, that I had designed an inexpensive desktop computer that could sell for under $800 and would run BASIC. He agreed to set up a meeting so I could talk to Miles.

I remember going into the big conference room to meet Pete, his boss, Ed Heinsen, and Ed's boss, Miles. I made my presentation and showed them my design.

"Okay," Miles said after thinking about it for a couple of minutes. "There's a problem you'll have when you say you have output to a TV. What happens if it doesn't look right on every TV? I mean, is it an RCA TV, a Sears TV, or an HP product that's at fault?"

HP keeps a close eye on quality control, he told me. If HP couldn't control what TV the customer was using, how could it make sure the customer had a good experience? More to the point, the division didn't have the people or money to do a project like mine. So he turned it down.

I was disappointed, but I left it at that. Now I was free to enter into the Apple partnership with Steve and Ron. I kept my job, but after that I was officially moonlighting. Everybody I worked with knew about the computer board we were going to sell.

Over the next few months, Miles would keep coming up to me. He knew about BASIC-programmable computers because of his division out in Colorado, and even though they didn't want my design, he said he was intrigued by the idea of having a machine so cheap that anyone could own one and program it. He kept telling me he'd been losing sleep ever since he heard the idea.

But looking back, I see he was right. How could HP do it? It couldn't. This was nowhere near a complete and finished scientific engineer's product. Everybody saw that smaller, cheaper computers were going to be a coming thing, but HP couldn't justify it as a product. Not yet. Even if they had agreed, I see now that HP would've done it wrong anyway. I mean, when they finally did it in 1979, they did it wrong. That machine went nowhere.

A few weeks after the meeting, the PC board was finished and working. I was so proud of it. I was at HP showing it off to some engineers when the phone rang at the lab bench.

It was Steve.

"Are you sitting down?"

"No," I told him.

"Well, guess what? I've got a $50,000 order."

"What?"

Steve explained that a local computer store owner had seen me at Homebrew and wanted to buy one hundred computers from us. Fully built, for $500 each.

I was shocked, just completely shocked. Fifty thousand dollars was more than twice my annual salary. I never expected this.

It was the first and most astounding success for Apple the company. I will never forget that moment.

• ○ •

Well, I decided I should run the whole thing by HP one more time. I spoke to Pete again. He told me to run it by legal.

The legal department ran it by every single division of HP. That process took about two weeks.

But HP still wasn't interested, and I received a note from HP's legal department saying they claimed no right to my design.

• ○ •

It turned out that a guy named Paul Terrell was starting a new computer store, called the Byte Shop in Mountain View.

As I said, Terrell had seen me demonstrating my computer at Homebrew, and he'd told Steve to "keep in touch," and Steve followed up with him the next day. Steve showed up barefoot at his office the next day, saying, "Hi. I'm keeping in touch."

What Steve didn't know was that Paul was looking for a product just like ours. Terrell wanted to sell a complete computer to his customers, fully assembled. And that had never been done before. Before us, Paul had been buying Altairs or kits like that, and had technicians soldering them together in the back. Every time he got one built, he could sell it. But he thought he had a lot of interest, a lot more potential customers. Steve told him about the Apple I I'd designed and Paul realized it was a completely built board, so it was a great product for him.

So suddenly, with Terrell's order, I could see that someone else was interested in the Apple I. That was so unexpected and exciting—and so easy. I mean, we already had a little company that was set up to mass-produce our boards down in Santa Clara. Now, all we needed to do was supply the additional parts and they would solder them on.

But how would we get the parts? That would cost money we didn't have. Allen Baum and his dad, Elmer, loaned us $1,200 to buy some of the parts. But we did end up finding a chip distributor (Cramer Electronics) and got the parts on a thirty-day credit. The chip distributor had to call Paul Terrell to see if he was really going to pay us.

The deal Steve worked out with Paul Terrell was he would pay us cash on delivery for the computers. So Paul Terrell was really financing this whole project, it turned out. When he paid us, we were able to pay for the chips.

The distributor gave us the parts, and then they went into a sealed closet at the Santa Clara company that was manufacturing the boards. On the day they were ready for them, the parts came out of the closet, were accounted for and soldered on, and then we had thirty days to pay for them.

Our first batch of boards was finished in January 1976. There were kits like the Altair out there, but nothing like what we were doing. I remember how, waiting for them, I was just the happiest person in the world. I was so happy around this time. I never truly thought we were going to make money with Apple. That was never in my mind. The only thing on my mind was, Wow, now that I've discovered what a microprocessor can do, there are so many places I can take it. I knew that for the rest of my life, I would have a computing tool for myself.

The potential with the Apple I was blowing my mind. I mean,

I'm around video games, and suddenly I realize that my little computer is going to be able to play games. I imagined word-processing software replacing typewriters someday. I was a fast typist, and I could see we were nowhere near where we needed to be for a computer to replace a typewriter yet, though I could imagine it. I imagined how a computer could help me with all my design work at HP. It just blew me away. Every single thing I thought about on the computer was going to be valuable. I could see it so clearly. And that was all I could think about.

After the boards were finished, we rounded up Steve's friend Dan Kottke and Steve's sister, Patty, to plug chips into sockets for $1 a board. Steve would bring us maybe ten or twenty assembled boards at a time from the manufacturer. And there we would sit on a lab bench in the garage of Steve's parents' house at 11161 Crist Avenue. Then I would plug each assembled board into the TV and keyboard we had there and test it to see if it worked.

If it did, I put it in a box. If it didn't, I'd figure what pin hadn't gotten into the socket right or what circuit was shorted. I'd fix the bad ones and put them in the box. After a dozen or two were in the box, Steve would drive them down to Paul Terrell's store and get paid in cash.

These weren't finished computers as you would think of them today. Paul Terrell ended up having to supply monitors, transformers, keyboards, and even the cases to put the computers in. I'm not sure that's what he expected. I think he thought, based on what Steve Jobs told him, that he was getting a fully built computer.

Back then, we didn't have the volume to do plastic. So Paul would put them into wooden cases—often a Polynesian wood called koa—which was a style thing for us.

We had to come up with a retail price for our literature. After all, we weren't going to sell them just to Paul.

We decided to price them at $666.66 each—a price I came up with because I liked repeating digits. (That was $500, plus a 30 percent markup.)

And you know what? Neither of us even knew the number's satanic connections until Steve started getting letters about it. I mean, what? The number of the Beast. Truly, I had no idea. I hadn't seen the movie *The Exorcist*. And the Apple I was no beast to me.

• ○ •

By now, writing the BASIC interpreter was turning out to be the longest, most complicated single project I'd ever do for Apple.

Man, I sniveled at BASIC back then. Compared to FORTRAN, it was a weak, lightweight language. I thought no one would ever use it, for example, to create the kind of sophisticated programs engineers and scientists use. I could just see where things were going. That book I told you about, *101 Basic Computer Games*, meant you could just type in the programs and have these games.

I'd been writing a BASIC interpreter to run on the Apple I, which was based around the MOS 6502 processor. I figured if I wrote this language really fast—if I worked on it day and night and turned my ideas into something that worked within a couple of months—well, then I would get almost famous. People would say that Steve Wozniak wrote the first BASIC for the 6502, just like they knew Bill Gates for writing the BASIC for Altair. I would be the source, and that was kind of exciting.

I had never taken a class on writing a computer language. In my early college years, Allen Baum would Xerox textbooks at MIT, where he went to school, and send those pages to me. I learned a little that way.

So I understood that computer languages had a grammatical syntax, just like any language, and I knew how they were organized.

I didn't know that the BASIC interpreters that existed for different computers, like DEC's and HP's, were different in any way.

I assumed they were all the same, and I assumed Bill Gates's was the same as those.

So, back at work, I grabbed some HP BASIC manuals and studied them. I started writing on paper a syntax table. This is what describes the grammar of the computer language. It defines what commands a programmer can enter.

For instance, if English had a syntax table, it would explain that personal pronouns like "he" and "she" are nouns and usually subjects in a sentence such as, "He threw the ball." It would list all the possible verbs, of which "threw" would be one. And it would tell you what all possible "objects" would be, such as "ball." In English, there are millions of possibilities for subjects, verbs, and objects, but in a language like BASIC you can limit them to a certain number of items.

Then there are the rules you need. Say you wrote out the equation $5 + 3 \times 7$. When you write that out with no parentheses, a mathematician would know that you execute multiplication and division first, addition and subtraction second. So really that equation would be $5 + 21$. So that rule, about what terms to execute first, is an example of something that has to be defined in the syntax table.

I had no idea what other people did in their computer languages, but I felt it was obvious that you needed a noun stack to hold things like numbers, a verb stack (which would include actions like multiplication or addition), and a set of priorities for every single verb that was typed in.

It took me about four months to come up with the core of my BASIC interpreter. I ended up leaving out the ability to type in decimal numbers (called "floating point arithmetic"), and instead handled everything with integers—that is, whole numbers. That saved me about a month of work, I figured. I decided that for games and computer simulations—the two main things I was writing the BASIC for—I would just get by with integers.

Many of the key programs in my life, including those back in Colorado, used only integers. So I designed my BASIC to only work with numbers from −32,768 to +32,787.

I wrote the whole program on paper—with machine instructions on the left and the equivalent in hexadecimal (equivalent to 1s and 0s) on the right. I had to do this by hand because I couldn't afford to use an assembler program, which is the typical way you'd do this. This is the same way I had to write the little monitor program.

So I figured, Hey, I'm able to write the program with the code by myself, by hand. Who needs a computer to do this for you?

By the way, I still have the notebook I wrote my BASIC interpreter in. I'm not sure, but I bet it could be worth a lot to a museum now!

Anyway, the end result of all this was, when my 6502 BASIC was in the computer, I could type in little programs with the keyboard. Like I could have the computer ask you, "What's your name?" And if you typed it in, it would fly your name all around the screen. This sounds so simple now, but back then, nobody had ever seen a small computer where you could actually type in programs with a regular keyboard and have it execute.

Even with machines like the Altair, it was very expensive to add a plug-in card and a big cable that would connect to an enormous ugly teletype that had the keyboard to type on.

I showed my computer running BASIC at Homebrew after the main meetings a few times, and people were just blown away by it.

But there was one problem. The Apple I had no permanent storage—no hard disk drive or floppy or CD drive like you see today. This was way, way before that. So every time I wanted the BASIC to run, I had to turn on the computer and literally type my whole program in from my notebook. This was a 4,000-byte program—it took almost forty minutes for me to type it all in every time. And when I turned off the computer, because there was no

The Basics on BASIC

The BASIC computer language, the one I told you I sniveled at, was designed from the start to be an easy-to-program language for writing computer programs. Created in 1963 by Dartmouth College professors John Kemeny and Thomas Kurtz, the BASIC acronym stands for Beginner's All-purpose Symbolic Instruction Code. There's no question that BASIC is an easier-to-learn language than languages such as Pascal or C. It's also smaller and slower. But it worked just perfectly with my first Apple computers.

permanent storage and only RAM, the whole program would be gone. I ended up having to either leave my computer on all the time—which meant I couldn't transport it very well—or come up with a solution.

That's how I developed the cassette tape interface for the Apple I. Aside from changing the type of RAM from static to dynamic, this was the only change to my original design from the very first days of Homebrew in the spring of 1975. I designed a circuit so that a regular cassette tape could hold the BASIC, and when I turned the computer on, it would automatically load my BASIC into memory so the computer was usable.

Once the BASIC was done and easily loadable from a cassette tape, I discovered something terrible. I had miscalculated. I had thought that all versions of BASIC were more or less the same, and that all the 101 games in BASIC that I had in that book would automatically run if you typed them in. That turned out not to be the case. It turned out that the type of BASIC I'd written—as well as the HP BASIC I'd originally studied—was totally different from Bill Gates's Microsoft BASIC, which was based on the DEC BASIC at the time. Bummer!

So anyone who wanted to put those games on the Apple I was going to have to make changes to the games to do it.

I did manage to get some games working on the Apple I, though. There was a popular game, in BASIC, called Star Trek. Like the show. I adapted it to my BASIC and it ran just fine.

● ○ ●

After we started selling the boards to Paul Terrell—working day and night to get them to him on time—we had profits like I never imagined. Suddenly our little business was making more than I was making at HP. That wasn't very much, admittedly. But still, it was a lot. We were building the boxes for $220 and selling them wholesale to Paul Terrell for $500.

And, of course, we didn't need a ton of money to operate. I had a day job, so I looked at it as, Hey, cool. Extra money for pizza! As for Steve, he was living at home. I was twenty-five and he was only twenty-one at the time, so what expenses could we have, really? Apple didn't have to make that much to sustain itself and be ongoing. We weren't paying ourselves salaries or paying rent, after all. We didn't have any patents to pay for. Or lawyers. It was a small-time business, and we weren't worried that much about anything.

My dad, watching this, pointed out that we weren't actually making money because we weren't paying ourselves anything. But we didn't care, we were having too much fun.

● ○ ●

Right after we delivered to Paul Terrell, Steve arranged for me to show the Apple I PC board during the main meeting of Homebrew in about March 1976. I had shown off my computer after the meeting for months by then, but I'd never talked about it formally to the whole group.

Of course, I'd never spoken in front of a group of people this large. This was the largest spotlight I had ever been in. I mean, by now Homebrew had grown to about five hundred or more people. The meeting was being held at the auditorium at the Stanford Linear Accelerator Center (SLAC). So I just stuck to the facts after I walked down the aisle with my printed circuit board in my hands. This was the first of only two times I ever spoke in front of the Homebrew meeting. (The other was when I introduced the Apple II.)

I knew that many people in the club had seen me running my prototype. So I just stood there in front of everybody and described the chips on the board—what they were and all—and talked about the specifications and the architecture. I talked about how I built it. And I talked about the main thing, as far as I was concerned: having a human-typable keyboard instead of a stupid, cryptic front panel with a bunch of lights and switches.

I explained that I'd used dynamic RAM instead of static RAM and why. I pointed out that my board had 8K bytes RAM and compared that to the Altair motherboard, which had only 256 bytes. I talked about a little BASIC program—the one that moved your name around on-screen when you typed it in. I described the video circuitry, the connectors, the voltages needed, everything. And finally I got to tell everyone the price—$666.66.

I'm not sure if we were a big hit or not. You'll have to ask someone there who saw me giving the talk. After all, by that time a lot of Homebrew members were either starting or working for little computer companies. So maybe they couldn't see that the Apple I was that special.

But I could. And Steve could. We were so proud.

We were participating in the biggest revolution that had ever happened, I thought. I was so happy to be a part of it. It didn't have to be a big business. I was just having fun.

Ron Wayne, the third partner, wasn't having as much fun, I guess. He was used to big companies and big salaries. We bought him out for $800 after we delivered some of the first boards to Paul Terrell and well before we got our first outside investment.

Chapter 13

The Apple II

By early 1976 we had sold maybe 150 computers. Not just through the Byte Shop but through other little stores that were popping up all around the country. We would drive around California, just walk into a store, and ask if they wanted to carry the Apple I. We did sell a few that way.

But this was nothing. Because we were watching other companies that sprang up around Silicon Valley at this time. And one of them, Processor Technology it was called, was supposedly selling more than a thousand units a month of their SOL-20 computer. It was the hit of the hobby computer world. It was also the hobby computer that supported a keyboard, which is how they designed it after I showed the Apple I at a main meeting at Homebrew. The Apple I started that trend.

Lee Felsenstein, the guy who emceed the Homebrew meetings, had actually designed the SOL. And Gordon French worked there. So we heard things.

I thought the Processor Technology SOL computer wasn't that impressive. Steve and I were sure we could sell more than what they were selling. But by then we had a prototype of the next Apple, the Apple II, and it was ten times better than the Apple I.

With that computer, we knew we could easily sell as many

computers as Processor Technology if we just had the money to build them.

The Apple II, which I started working on almost as soon as the Apple I was complete, was a phenomenal improvement over what I'd done before. I knew I wanted to have a computer that did color, for instance. I had built the Apple I from the beginning with chips working at the frequencies you would need to generate color on an American television, and I had planned to add color. But though I'd designed the Apple I so I could add a color to it, I decided it would be better to design a fresh computer instead.

You see, the add-on to color wasn't just a matter of buying more chips. It was a matter of efficiency and elegance of design. I wanted to design color from the ground up, not just as an add-on to an existing computer. That way, the Apple II would be designed with color ability on those chips from the start.

Another Apple II improvement I thought of was to design the whole new computer around text and graphics, with all of it coming out of the system's own memory.

So rather than having a whole separate terminal to do the on-screen stuff and other memory to do the other computations, I decided to combine all the memory into one bank—one section of DRAM. A portion of the DRAM the microprocessor used could also be continually tapped for whatever needed to be displayed on the screen.

In doing this, I knew I would save some chips. In fact, the Apple II ended up with half as many chips as the Apple I in the end.

It was also quite a bit faster. Remember how I told you how the Apple I had to constantly keep the contents of its DRAM memory alive by refreshing them? Well, by now I had faster DRAM chips. And instead of the microprocessor being able to access (write from or read to) the RAM once every millionth of a second, these new chips could do it twice every microsecond.

In fact, it even worked out that the microprocessor could access the RAM in one-half of a microsecond (millionth of a second) while the circuitry that refreshed the RAM could access during the other half. That's why the new computer I designed, this Apple II, actually ran faster. It was also smaller and cheaper. And that is always the goal with me.

The Apple II had countless improvements over the Apple I. Some people consider the Apple II to be a second design built from the Apple I, but I want you to know that that is not so. Not so at all.

The Apple I was not a computer designed from the ground up. It was a quick extension of my ARPANET terminal to a microprocessor, with virtually no electronic innovations except for the DRAM.

The Apple II, on the other hand, was designed and engineered from the ground up. Also solely by me.

Looking back now, I could've done the Apple II first—color and all—but I chose to go with the design I could come up with most quickly.

It's true that both machines brought striking advances to the computer world. The Apple I made history by being the first personal computer that could work with a keyboard and a display. But the Apple II brought color, high-resolution graphics, sound, and the ability to attach game paddles. It was the first to boot up ready to use, with BASIC already built into the ROM.

Other computers eventually caught up, but it took years for them to match what I'd done. Eventually every one of them would have to offer that same list of features.

The Apple II was the first low-cost computer which, out of the box, you didn't have to be a geek to use.

• ○ •

But no one had seen the Apple II yet. I was still finalizing it, and we were still working in our houses at this point. I was working out of my apartment and Steve was working the phones in his bedroom. We were still testing computers in his garage. I was still building calculators at HP, and I still thought this was just a hobby. I was still planning on working at HP forever.

But it was very soon after delivering the Apple I boards to Terrell that I had a working Apple II. And like I said, it wasn't just twice as good. It was like ten times better.

By August 1976, I had completed it—the board, I mean, which was the center of the Apple II. I remember that so well because that was the month Steve and I flew out to the PC '76 show in Atlantic City.

● ○ ●

We got on the plane in San Jose, and Steve and I sat together with the Apple I and II with us on board. And the funny thing was, a bunch of the people we knew from Homebrew, who now worked at all these little competing computer companies, were seated around us on the same plane. We could hear them talking in advanced business talk—you know, talking about proposals and using businesslike acronyms we'd never heard before. We felt so left out of these discussions.

But inside, we knew we had a secret. A big secret. Maybe we weren't part of the business-type groups, but we knew had a better computer. Actually, we had two better computers. The Apple I and the Apple II. And no one in the world knew about the Apple II yet.

When the show started in Atlantic City, I was lucky because I didn't have to hustle the Apple I at the booth. I'm not a sales type. Steve Jobs and Dan Kottke did that. I was upstairs getting the very last BASIC sequences finished up.

The show was full of young, barely financed companies like Apple. The proprietors looked like us. I mean, there weren't any nicely dressed company executives, company owners, or company managers really attending the show. It was a pretty sloppy group of people, come to think of it.

They were in our business and most of them were competitors. We were all friends, but we were still competitors.

Even though we didn't let the Apple II out of the bag at that show, there was one guy not associated with any of these companies or businesses who saw it. He was a convention guy setting up a projection TV for the convention goers. Steve and I went down the first night, after everyone else had left, and met with this projector technician. I think we had told him to stay. It was probably about 9 p.m. You see, I had this different method of generating color and I was still amazed at how many TVs it worked with. In fact, I never found a TV that it didn't work with. But I figured that a projector might have different color circuitry that would choke on my color method. I wanted to see if the Apple II would work with it.

So I hooked the Apple II prototype up to this projector and it worked perfectly. That technician, who was seeing every low-cost computer in the world as he was setting up the show, told me that of all of them, this was the only computer he would buy.

I only smiled. The Apple II wasn't even announced yet.

● ○ ●

After the show, the biggest, earthshaking Eureka moment ever was the day I got Breakout, the Atari game, working on the Apple II.

I had put enough capability in BASIC that you could read where the game paddles were. It could sound the speaker as needed, and it could plot colors on the screen. So I was ready.

I sat down one day with this little blank board with chips on the top side of it and little red and blue wire-wrapped wires all soldered underneath and connected it with some wires to transformers and then connected it all to my color TV.

I sat down and started typing in BASIC the commands I needed to make one row of bricks—just like the ones in Atari's arcade game—and it worked! I had a row of bricks. I played around with different color combinations until I had the brick color that worked.

I made eight rows of bricks lying side by side. I figured out the right colors, I figured how the bricks should be offset to look more realistic. Even and odd rows. And then I started programming the paddle. I made the on-screen paddle go up and down with the game control knob. And then I put in a ball. I started giving the ball motion. Then I started telling the ball when it hits bricks, here's how it gets rid of the bricks and here's how it bounces. And when it hits the paddle, here's how it bounces and here's how it changes direction vertically and horizontally.

And then I played with all these parameters and it only took a half hour total. I tried dozens and dozens of different variations of things until, finally, I had the game of Breakout completely working on the Apple II, showing the score and everything.

I called Steve Jobs over. I couldn't believe I'd been able to do it, it was amazing. I sat him down and showed him how the game came up with the paddle and the bricks. And then I said, "Watch this." And I typed a couple of BASIC statements, changed the color of the paddle, and the color of the bricks, and where the score was.

I said, "If I had done all these varieties of options in hardware the way it was always done, it would've taken me ten years to do. Now that games are in software, the whole world is going to change."

That was the exact moment it sank in. Software games were going to be incredibly advanced compared to hardware games— games that were hardwired into arcades and systems like that.

These days, the graphics are so great in games. They have gotten incredibly complicated and huge in size. If they had to be in hardware, there wouldn't be enough time in the universe to design them.

I thought, Wow. Nobody in the club is ever going to believe

that an arcade game could be written in BASIC. It was a first in
the world. I put a secret into my Breakout game for the Apple II,
too. If you hit CTRL and Z on the keyboard, the game went into
a mode where the paddle would always jiggle but could never
miss the ball.

What a great feature. It tricked people into thinking they were
just really lucky in hitting it. The paddle was so shaky and jiggly
that a person could never tell it wasn't really because of their
own skill and their own movements that they were hitting it.

One day I sat down with John Draper (Captain Crunch,
remember?). We were at Homebrew right after the main meeting, the time people could demo stuff.

John had never played an arcade game before.

I said, "Here. Play this game." I showed him how you turned
the dial so the paddle went up and down. And he sat there and
played it. Everyone in the room watched him for about fifteen
minutes. The ball was going so fast, and he, even though he
didn't really know what he was doing with the control, kept hitting it. People just thought he was a superior game player.

After about fifteen minutes, he finally won the game. And all
of us were congratulating him like he was the best game player
in the world. I don't think he ever knew it was a setup.

• ○ •

In the spring of 1976, as I was working on the Apple II, Steve
and I got into our first argument. He didn't think the Apple II
should have eight slots. Slots are connectors you can plug extra
circuit boards into in case you want to expand the functionality
of the computer. Steve wanted only two slots—one for a printer
and one for a modem. He thought that way you could build a
cheaper, smaller machine that was good enough for today's tasks.

But I wanted more slots, eight of them.

I had the idea that there would be a lot of things people would
want in the future, and no way did we want to limit people.

Usually I'm really easy to get along with, but this time I told him, "If that's what you want, go get yourself another computer." There wasn't a single chip I could save by reducing the number of slots from eight to two, and I knew people like me would eventually come up with things to add to any computer.

I was in a position to do that then. I wouldn't always be. A couple of years later, Apple went on to design the Apple III, which was just a disaster, and it had fewer slots.

But in 1976 I won that argument, and the Apple II was designed and eventually came out the way I wanted it to.

•   ○   •

I remember coming in one day to HP—where I was still working—and showing the other engineers the Apple II. I demoed it doing color swirls. The other engineers would come up to me and say this was the best product they'd ever seen. And yet HP still couldn't find a way to do it right, a way to do this kind of project.

One day my boss, Pete Dickinson, told me that some people in my calculator division had created a new project that had gotten through levels of corporate approval to build a small desktop machine with a microprocessor, DRAM, a small video screen, and a keyboard. They even had five people assigned to write BASIC for it.

The awful thing about this was they all knew what I had done with the Apple I and even the Apple II. Yet they had started up this project without me! Why would they do that? I don't know. I think they just saw what they wanted to do as a project was what I'd done.

But I went to talk to the project manager, Kent Stockwell. Although I had done all these computer things with the Apple I and Apple II, I wanted to work on a computer at HP so bad I would have done anything. I would even be a measely printer interface engineer. Something tiny.

I told him, "My whole interest in life has been computers. Not calculators."

After a few days, I was turned down again.

I still believe HP made a huge mistake by not letting me go to its computer project. I was so loyal to HP. I wanted to work there for life. When you have an employee who says he's tired of calculators and is really productive in computers, you should put him where he's productive. Where he's happy. The only thing I can figure is there were managers and submanagers on this computer project who felt threatened. I had already done a whole computer. Maybe they bypassed me because I had done this single-handedly. I don't know what they were thinking.

But they should've said to themselves, "How do we get Steve Wozniak on board? Just make him a little printer interface engineer." I would've been so happy, but they didn't bother to put me where I would've been happiest.

•   o   •

Like I said before, we needed money. Steve knew it and I knew it.

So by that summer of 1976, we started talking to potential money people about Apple, showing them the Apple II working in color in Steve's garage.

One of the first people we showed it to was Chuck Peddle. Remember him? He was the guy from MOS Technologies who'd sold me the 6502 processor I designed the Apple I around the year before at the WESCON show.

By this time Chuck was working at Commodore, a consumer electronics company rumored to be shopping around for a personal computer to sell. I remember I was so impressed to meet him after the role his chip, the MOS 6502, had played in the Apple I. We'd opened Steve's garage to the sunlight that day, and he came walking in wearing a suit and a cowboy hat. Wow, I was excited to see him and couldn't wait to show him the Apple II. This was a very important person in my mind.

I typed in a few BASIC programs, showed some color spirals

on-screen, showed him how many chips and how it worked and everything. Just to show him what we were doing. Chuck was in good spirits throughout the meeting, laughing and smiling. He told us we should make a presentation to the company bigwigs, which we did a few weeks later.

I'll never forget how, in that conference room, Steve Jobs made what I thought was the most ridiculous statement. He said, "You might just want to buy this product for a few hundred thousand dollars."

I was almost embarrassed. I mean, there we were, we had no money, we had yet to prove to anybody there was going to be any money in this thing. Steve added, "A few hundred thousand dollars, plus you have to give us jobs working on this project."

Well, we left and heard back a few days later that, no, they'd decided they would build their own machine, it was cheaper. They didn't need to support fancy things like color, sound, and graphics, all the cool things we had. Chuck Peddle, in the garage, had told us he thought it was possible for them to do their own computer in four months. I didn't see how anyone could, but I guess after he saw the Apple II, it would be a lot easier to design something like what he wanted.

I saw the Commodore PET, the computer they came up with so quickly, a few months later at the West Coast Computer Faire, by the way. It kind of sickened me. They were trying to do something like what we'd shown Chuck in the garage that day, with a monitor and programming and a keyboard, but they made a real crappy product by doing it so quick. They could've had Apple, you know? They could have had it all if they'd had the right vision. Bad decision.

It's funny. I think back on it now—the Apple II would turn out to be one of the most successful products of all time. But we had no copyrights or patents at all back then. No secrets. We were just showing it to everybody.

• ○ •

After Commodore turned us down, we went over to Al Alcorn's house. He was one of the founders of Atari with Nolan Bushnell, and he was the one who'd hired Steve to do video games there two years before.

Now, I knew Al knew me. He knew I had designed Breakout, the one-player version of Pong. I remember that when we went to his house I was so impressed because he had one of the earliest color projection TVs. Man, in 1976, he would have been among the first people to have one. That was cool.

But he told us later that Atari was too busy with the video game market to do a computer project.

A few days after that, venture capitalists Steve had contacted started to come by. One of them was Don Valentine at Sequoia. He kind of pooh-poohed the way we talked about it.

He said, "What's the market?"

"About a million," I told him.

"How do you know?"

I told him the ham radio market had one million users, and this could be at least that big.

Well, he turned us down, but he did get us in touch with a guy named Mike Markkula. He was only thirty, he told us, but already retired from Intel. He was into gadgets, he told us. Maybe Mike would know what to do with us.

• ○ •

The very first time I met Mike, I thought he was the nicest person ever. I really did. He was this young guy. He had a beautiful house in the hills overlooking the lights of Cupertino, this gorgeous view, amazing wife, the whole package.

Better still, he actually liked what we had! He didn't talk like a guy who was hiding things and thinking about ripping you off. He was for real. That much was obvious right away.

What a major thing this was.

He was truly interested. He asked us who we were, what our backgrounds were, what our goals were with Apple, where we thought it might go. And he indicated some interest in financing us. He was talking about $250,000 or thereabouts to build 1,000 machines.

Mike was just talking in normal commonsense terms about what the future of a new home computer industry might be like. Now, I had always thought of the Apple computer as being something for a hobbyist who wanted to solve a work simulation or play a game.

But Mike was talking about something different. He talked about introducing the computer to regular people in regular homes, doing at home things like keeping track of your favorite recipes or balancing your checkbook. This was what was coming, he said. He had a vision of the Apple II as a real home computer.

Now, we'd already been kicking around this idea a little, of course. I mean, out-of-the-box and ready-to-use was something Paul Terrell at the Byte Shop had asked for. And we were planning on doing that, as well as a plastic case. We had even planned to hire a friend of Steve's, Rod Holt, to build a switching power supply. That kind of power supply was so much more efficient than what was previously available—we knew it would generate less heat. That was necessary if you were going to fit a board and our power supply into a plastic case.

But when Mike agreed to sign up, he told us, "We're going to be a Fortune 500 company in two years. This is the start of an industry. It happens once a decade."

I believed him only because of his reputation and position in life, you know? He was the sort of person who if he said it—and you can tell sincerity in a person—he really believed it. I thought Fortune 500 might be out of the range, though. I mean, a $5 million company would be immense and unbelievable.

But if somebody knows how to make certain judgments better

than I do, I don't try to use my own logic and reasoning to challenge them. I can be skeptical, but if someone really knows what they're talking about, they should be trusted.

It turned out that even Mike was underestimating our success. But look, I'm getting ahead of myself.

• ○ •

Well, after Mike agreed to do our business plan—after he started working on it—he asked to talk to me. He said, "Okay, Steve. You know you have to leave Hewlett-Packard."

I said, "Why?" I mean, I'd been at HP the whole time I'd designed the Apple I and Apple II. And all the time I was moonlighting, I set up interfaces, did the color, the graphics, wrote the BASIC, just did the whole thing. I said, "Why can't I keep doing this on the side and just have HP as my secure job for life."

But he said, "No, you have to leave HP." He didn't give me any reasons. He told me I had to decide by Tuesday.

And I went and thought and thought and thought. I realized I had a lot of fun designing computers and showing them off at Homebrew. I had fun writing software and I had fun playing with the computer. I realized I could do all those things for the rest of my life. I didn't need my own company.

Plus, I felt very insecure in starting a company where I would be expected to push people around and run their affairs and control what they did. I'm not a management kind of person. I told you before: I'd decided long ago that I would never become someone authoritative.

So I decided I wouldn't do Apple after all. I would stay at HP for my full-time job and design computers for fun.

I went to the cabana—Mike had a cabana on his property—on ultimatum day and told Mike and Steve what I'd decided. I told them no. I'd thought about it, and I'd come to the conclusion that I wasn't going to leave HP.

I remember Mike was very cool about it. He just shrugged and said, "Okay. Fine." He was really terse about it. It was like he thought, okay, fine, he would just get what Apple needed somewhere else.

But Steve was upset. He felt strongly that the Apple II was the computer they should go with.

• ○ •

Within a couple of days my phone started ringing. I started getting phone calls at work and home from my dad, my mom, my brother, and various friends. Just phone call after phone call. Every one of them told me I'd made the wrong decision. That I should go with Apple because, after all, $250,000 is a lot of money.

It turned out that Steve had talked them all into calling me. Apparently he thought I needed an intervention.

But it didn't do any good; I still was going to stay at HP.

Then Allen Baum called.

Allen said, "Steve, you know, you really ought to go ahead and do it. Think about it. You can be an engineer and become a manager and get rich, or you can be an engineer and stay an engineer and get rich." He told me he thought it was absolutely possible for me to start a company and stay an engineer. He told me I could do it and never get into management.

That was exactly what I needed to hear. I needed to hear one person saying that I could stay at the bottom of the organization chart, as an engineer, and not have to be a manager. I called Steve Jobs right away with the news. He was thrilled.

And the next day I came in early, walked over to a couple of friends at HP, and told them, "That's it, I am going to leave HP and start Apple."

Then I realized, Oh, you should always tell your boss first. So I went over to tell him quickly, but he didn't show up at his table. I waited and waited, and finally it was like four in the afternoon, and he still wasn't at his table. Everybody kept coming up to me as I waited there, saying, "Hey, I hear you're leaving," and I didn't want my boss to hear it from someone else.

Finally my boss showed up near the end of the day. I told him I was leaving to start my own company. He asked me when I wanted to go. I told him, "Right away." So he took me over to human resources and they interviewed me and all of a sudden I was gone. It was that quick.

But I never doubted my decision. I mean, I'd made my decision. Apple was the main thing for me from that point on.

• ○ •

Just before we met Mike, Steve and I made plans to move Apple from his house and my apartment to a real office. We had something like $10,000 in the bank from the Apple I sales, so we were able to do this. The office was on Stevens Creek Boulevard in Cupertino, just a few blocks away from where the huge Apple campus would eventually be on Bandley Drive.

Then, when Mike joined us, we had even more money in our account. We moved into our little office. There were about five or six desks around. There was a little room to set up a lab bench to do some testing and debug work. It was a real long lab bench. And we had our key staff in place. Steve, me, Mike Markkula, Rod Holt, and, now, a guy named Mike Scott.

We'd hired Mike Scott to be the president just before Mike Markkula got there. (So now we had two Steves and two Mikes.) Mike, or "Scotty," as we called him, was a guy with experience running things. He came from National Semiconductor, where he'd been a director.

I think a lot of people have forgotten him today, but Mike was Apple's president and leader for four years—he took us public four years later.

We had this idea that we would announce and show the Apple II at the West Coast Computer Faire, which was about four months away. The Faire, started by Jim Warren, another

Homebrew member, would be in San Francisco in January of 1977.

So I had four months to finish things up. I was completing the 8K bytes of code we had to release to Synertek, the company that was going to make the ROMs for the Apple II. Those were the ROMs that would make it an Apple II running BASIC.

Then there was the project surrounding the plastic case. We were going to be the first computer ever in a plastic case. I did not have to deal with this at all, thank god. It was a rough project. Steve Jobs, Rod Holt, and Mike Scott dealt with that. They had a guy in Palo Alto who was signed up to make plastic cases for us. The process was time-consuming and laborious, and it turned out there was a limit to what this guy could do. He was using a process to build the cases, but it turned out he could only do a really small number per day.

It was only about three days before the West Coast Computer Faire that we got our first three plastic cases as samples. They came in, and we actually assembled the whole complete computer with the board inside. It sort of looked like what the Apple II would look like, and now we could show it off at the Faire.

Finally, in the days before the West Coast Computer Faire, Mike Markkula explained how we would all have to dress up nicely, how we should appear and look, how we should act. He coordinated how we would talk to people and show them things.

Of course, on the side, I started thinking of how I could do a prank at the show. First, I wrote a little joke program that would tell jokes about people's ethnicity. Then I set up a huge prank that would take a lot more effort than just a regular joke. And I thought I would play this joke on the big company that started it all for me. I'm talking about the company that made the Altair: the MITS Corporation.

●　○　●

Well, we had a list of everyone who was going to show computers and equipment at the West Coast Computer Faire, and I thought it was so strange that MITS wasn't going to be there.

I thought, What a great opportunity to pull a prank on them!

I got an idea from something I'd read in the Pentagon Papers. There was a part in there all about political trickery and a guy named Dick Tuck who played dirty tricks, clever little psychological tricks like putting out fake memoranda, fake notices to alarm people that were written in such a way that they couldn't really be denied as being lies. So I decided I'd put out a fake memo of my own—a fake ad, like a leaflet, for a fake product from MITS. After I heard from Mike Markkula that we were going to hand out twenty thousand brochures for the Apple II, I realized it would be possible to get thousands and thousands of fake ads out.

The first thing I did was call Adam Schoolski, who was a thirteen-year-old phone phreak when I'd first met him a few years earlier. He'd gone by the handle Johnny Bagel. Anyway, I told him that I wanted to do this prank but didn't want to do it near the San Francisco Bay Area. I had a lot of good experience with pranks by then, and I knew that you don't get caught if you keep people out of the loop, you don't do things nearby, and you keep a level of secrecy. And this was going to be a major prank, I told Adam, because I wanted to print up eight thousand leaflets to distribute. I was able to come up with the $400 I needed to print eight thousand copies on different colors of paper.

Adam and I made it together. The product we made up was called the Zaltair. You see, there was a new company at the time, called Zilog, that was making a chip that was compatible with the Intel 8080. It was called the Z-80, and at the time there were lots of hobby computers coming out that were built around it. They were called the Z-this and the Z-that. All these companies were always using Z words. So I came up with the Zaltair, a made-up computer that was also built around the Z-80.

I came up with all kinds of dumb computer-y Z words, too. Like Bazic. And Perzonality. Then I needed copy for the leaflet. I looked in a computer magazine, *Byte*, for an ad that was the worst ever. And I found it. It was from a company called Sphere. And it said dumb stuff like, "Imagine this. Imagine that. Imagine some other thing." So I wrote copy that said, "Imagine a race car with five wheels." I made up the stupidest things any idiot dork would laugh at, but if they saw it in a nicely done leaflet with good fonts, they would think it's all real and legitimate. Imagine something going faster than the speed of light. Imagine a banjo with six strings. I came up with the dumbest things.

Also, I made a play on what was called the S-100 bus, the connection the Altair used to plug in expansion boards. I named the Zaltair's equivalent the Z-150 bus. I wrote, "We have 150 slots. We call it the Z-150 bus." I even said it was compatible with the S-100 bus, but with 50 extra pins. If you think about this, these are just the dumbest statements, but I knew people would read stuff into it as if these were fantastic advances, just because our leaflet was going to look so professionally created.

Then I decided to make this prank on the MITS Corporation look like Processor Technology had done it. After all, they did a competing computer, the SOL. I got this idea from my experience at the University of Colorado, when I was able to make it look like another guy had jammed the TVs in my class. Two pranks for the price of one! So the way I did this was I made up a totally phony quote that would raise anybody's eyebrows. They would think, Whoa. What the hell is he saying? I attributed it to the president of MITS, Ed Roberts, and put it at the top in italics.

The quotation was completely and utterly nonsensical: "Predictable refinement of computer equipment should suggest online reliability. The elite computer hobbyist needs one logical option-less guarantee, yet." You see? The first letter of each word in those two sentences spells out Processor Technology!

Then, on the reverse side of the paper, I put a comparison chart. That was the common way magazines like *Byte* would compare computers. How fast are they? How big are they? How much RAM do they have? What processor do they use? Well, in my chart I made up the dumbest categories. Like, I had a cate-gory just generally called "hardware." A computer would get from 1 to 10. Then, software. I rated these computers on unique-ness, on personality, on just the dumbest, most generic terms you would never see a computer rated on. I gave the Zaltair a 1 in every category, of course, and I always made the Altair come in second. Then all the computers that were actually better than the Altair would rate behind that. That way, it looked like they were worthless by comparison, even though anybody at that show probably knew that the competitors were so much better. Of course, I included the Apple II.

I hoped it would look like MITS was lying in their comparison chart anyway.

I realized that, man, this was so big, and there was no way I could get caught at this thing. I couldn't let it happen. I had two young friends, Chris Espinoza and Randy Wiggington, who knew about it—they were teenagers back then. And I told each of them that, no matter what, they could never tell anyone about it. Even if you get called by the police and they tell you that your partner told them everything, you should still deny everything. We are going to stonewall this, I told them, and never ever admit it to anyone.

Adam Schoolski lived in Los Angeles but he came up for the Faire. And when the four of us got there with the eight thousand handouts, we saw these huge tables where all the companies were putting out their brochures and flyers. We brought two thousand in at first and just set them on a table like what we were doing was normal. And then we went around the Faire, kind of chuckling a little.

But Adam came up to me an hour later and told me the whole box was gone. Carton and everything. Gone.

So we went to our hotel and got another box of two thousand and brought them in. We stood around and watched until eventually some guy walks up, looks at one of the handouts, then picks up the box and takes it away. So we realized that a representative was there from MITS after all, intercepting them!

Now, we went back to the hotel and got a bunch more handouts. This time we didn't just put the carton down. Instead we carried them in our hands, under our coats, in our backpacks, and we put them in pay phones, corners, tables and everywhere. All over the Faire. We would find stacks of handouts—other companies' real handouts—and slip a few of ours underneath. So if somebody ran over right away, they wouldn't think we had slipped in bad stuff. Onesy, twosy, and we didn't get caught.

Thank god Steve and Mike didn't find out I'd done this. Mike, at least, would've said, "No, don't do pranks. Don't do jokes. They give the wrong image to the company." That's what any professional type would've said. But hey, they were dealing with Steve Wozniak. I did take work seriously—I had engineered a fantastic product, and everyone knew it—and I was serious about starting a company and introducing a product. But to me, that goes along with having fun and playing jokes. I'd spent my whole life like that. If you think about it, even a lot of the personality of the Apple computer was about fun. And that really came about just because my style was to have fun. Jokes make things worth doing.

I couldn't stop laughing the next day at Apple when Steve saw the comparison chart and started talking all positively about how we actually didn't perform too badly in the comparison. We were pretty lousy, of course, like everyone else but my made-up Zaltair, but he said, "Hey, we didn't do too bad, because, after all, we rank better than some of the others." Oh my god. Randy Wiggington had to run out of there, we were in such tears of laughter!

And the next night, which was the regular Wednesday night Homebrew meeting, I couldn't wait to see if people had caught on. Sure enough, someone held my thing up in the air and started talking about the Zaltair, saying he'd called the company and this was a fake. A hoax.

It turned out about a third of the people in there, a couple hundred, had actually gotten the handout. So it did get around.

About a week later, Gordon French, who started Homebrew and by now had left his job at Processor Technology, was kicking around Apple to see if there was any consulting work he could do for us. I remember thinking he was just such a nice, pleasant, easygoing guy.

I took the opportunity and said to him, "Oh, did you ever hear about that Zaltair that got introduced?" I could barely hold my laughter when I asked him.

"Oh yeah," he said. "That hoax. And I know who did it."

Randy and I both perked up at this. I said, "Who? Who did it?"

He said, "It was Gary Ingram at Processor Technology. He has a strange sense of humor."

This was exactly what I'd hoped for! Someone else getting the blame—and that someone else happened to be at our rival, Processor Technology. So it was a success.

I said, "You know, I heard there was kind of a code in the handout." And I pulled the brochure out and looked at the letters like I was discovering this for the first time. "P . . . R . . . O . . . C . . ."

I'm sure that for years and years after this, everyone thought Processor Technology had done it. I never admitted it to anyone until many years later, when I was at a birthday party for Steve Jobs.

It was there that I presented him with a framed copy of it. As soon as he saw it, Steve broke up laughing. He'd never even suspected I'd done it!

Chapter 14

The Biggest IPO Since Ford

Right after we officially incorporated as Apple Computer Corporation in early 1977, Mike had us go down to Beverly Hills and talk to patent lawyers. They said that any ROM chips we had around that had any code in them—any PROMs, any EPROMs—every single one of them needed a copyright notice. I had to put "Copyright 1977" on them all.

I sat down with one of the patent lawyers, Ed Taylor, and went through all the clever things in my design that other people definitely wouldn't have done before. How I did the color, for instance, and how I did the timing for the DRAM.

We ended up with five separate parts of a patent. It was a good, secure patent that was going to wind up being one of those patents in history that become very, very valuable. It was going to be the heart of lawsuits to come. For instance, it would come in handy when people tried to copy, or clone, the Apple II and other products after that.

Back then, there were no ideas of how software could be patented. This was such new stuff. We found out that copyrights were a better way to deal with people copying our technology. Copyrights were an easier, quicker, and less costly way than patents to stop people who tried to copy our computer outright.

• ○ •

Soon after the West Coast Computer Faire, where we introduced the Apple II, a couple of other ready-to-use personal computers came out. One was the Radio Shack TRS-80, and the other was Commodore's PET. These would become our direct competitors.

But it was the Apple II that ended up kicking off the whole personal computer revolution. It had lots of firsts. Color was the big one.

I designed the Apple II so it would work with the color TV you already owned. And it had game control paddles you could attach to it, and sound built in. That made it the first computer people wanted to design arcade-style games for, the first computer with sound and paddles ready to go. The Apple II even had a high-resolution mode where a game programmer could draw special little shapes really quickly. You could program every single pixel on the screen—whether it was on or off or what color it was—and that was something you could never do before with a low-cost computer.

At first that mode didn't mean a lot, but eventually it was a huge step toward the kinds of computer gaming you see today, where everything is high-res. Where the graphics can be truly realistic.

The fact that it worked with your home TV made the total cost a lot lower than any competitors could do. It came with a real keyboard to type on—a normal keyboard—and that was a big deal. And the instant you turned it on, it was running BASIC in ROM.

As I said, Commodore and Radio Shack within a few months came out with computers that also ran BASIC out of the box. But the Apple II was far superior to them. The Radio Shack TRS-80 and Commodore PET did have DRAM like the Apple II, but they were limited to only 4K bytes of it. The Apple II could expand up to 48K bytes on the motherboard, and even more in the slots.

The TRS-80 and PET only came in 4K or 8K models, and they weren't expandable. The Apple II had eight slots for expansion; the other two had none. Finally, the PET and TRS-80 screens were black-and-white. No color like ours. And they had rickety keyboards with small keys.

The Apple II could grow into the future and had so much versatility built in. That's why it became the leader.

•   ○   •

The Apple II was also an ideal computer for anybody who wanted to design a computer game.

We provided documentation and tools, making it really easy for programmers to create games in BASIC (at a hundred commands a second), or machine language (at a million commands a second), or both. The only way you could create a game for computers like the PET and TRS-80 was strictly in BASIC, and only with text characters on-screen. Unlike the Apple II, these machines didn't have graphics. It was inconceivable that anyone could've created a compelling arcade game on any of those computers.

Within months dozens of companies started up and they were putting games on cassette tape for the Apple II. These were all start-up companies, but thanks to our design and documentation, we made it easy to develop stuff that worked on our platform. Generally these little companies amounted to little more than a single guy in his house who figured out how to write a neat game, wrote it, and copied it onto a bunch of cassette tapes that he then sold through specialty computer stores.

And back then, there wasn't software rip-off happening like there is today. The stores weren't, for example, taking one cassette tape and making a bunch of copies and not paying the original guy. None of that was going on because there wasn't much money in the business yet. Ethics could still be high. It wasn't as if there was that much more money to be made by stealing.

So all the tapes the stores sold were legitimate, and the stores were taking a cut on the games they sold. Within a year a whole Apple II industry sprang up with dozens and dozens of companies of little guys—just onesy-twosy companies, really—at home writing software for the Apple II.

And then little companies started building circuit boards that fit into the Apple II slots. Boards were easy to design for the Apple II because we gave complete documentation on how our boards worked. Also, I had included some great tools: the Apple II had a little operating system developers could access, as well as a set of easy-to-use software debugging tools I had written myself.

So how do you design a printer board that will attach a printer to the Apple II? How do you design a scanner or a plotter board? It was all so well documented that within a year of the Apple II shipping that June, all of a sudden there were all these Apple II add-on products being sold by people.

People who wanted to do an add-on board not only had to design that board, but they had to write a little program—a device driver program that translates between computer programs and the actual hardware. The predecoded addresses I had for all eight slots would be connected to a ROM or PROM chip on the board containing this program. The program could be 256 bytes long with just a single PROM chip, but each slot had another 2K bytes of predecoded address space for a larger amount of code. You had to be aware that this second address space went to every board, so in order to use it, there had to be some other circuits that knew which board was in control.

Otherwise, when one of these 2K bytes of addresses came along, a bunch of boards would put data to the processor, and the boards would conflict. Each board also had 16 predecoded addresses intended to trigger hardware—to control and sense the hardware devices.

There were so many options available to a board designer that it led to a lot of very creative designs. The best designs made the most of the least, just as I like to do.

The computer magazines had tons of Apple II product ads for software and hardware. Suddenly the Apple II name was everywhere. We didn't have to buy an advertisement or do anything ourselves to get the name out. Our name was suddenly all over the place. We were just out there, thanks to this industry of software programs and hardware devices that sprang up around the Apple II.

We became the hot fad of the age, and all the magazines (even in the mainstream press) started writing great things about us. Everywhere you looked. I mean, we couldn't buy that kind of publicity. We didn't have to.

● ○ ●

Like I said, the Apple II used a cassette tape for data storage. I had never been around or even used a floppy disk in my life. They did exist, though. I'd heard of floppy disks you could buy for Altair-style kit computers, and, of course, the expensive minicomputers of the time used them. Now, all these were in the big, eight-inch floppy format. That means they were spinning magnetic disks that measured eight inches in diameter. And you could only hold about 100K bytes of data on each floppy disk. That's not very much by today's standards. Totally, it's only about 100,000 typed characters.

But Mike Markkula told me at a meeting that we really should have a floppy disk on the Apple II. He was annoyed at the way it took forever to get his little checkbook program to load from cassette. A floppy disk, because it spins so much faster and stores data more densely, would load the checkbook program much more quickly.

For instance, a computer could read 1,000 bits per second off a tape, but it would go 100,000 bits per second off a floppy.

I knew that the Consumer Electronics Show (CES) in Las

Vegas was coming up. It would be the first CES where companies could demonstrate computers, and only marketing people from Apple were going.

I asked Mike, if I finished the disk drive in time, could I go to Vegas for the show, too? He said yes.

That gave me only two weeks to build a floppy drive for the Apple II, a device I had never seen working before or ever used in any way, but I now had this artificial motivation (artificial, because of course I could've gone to the CES if I wanted to) to try to astound people at Apple again.

I worked all day, all night, through Christmas and New Year's trying to get it done. Randy Wiggington, who was actually attending Homestead High by now, the school Steve and I had graduated from, helped me a lot on that project.

• ○ •

To help me get started, Steve told me he'd heard that a company named Shugart, which was the main floppy drive manufacturer at the time, was coming up with a 5-inch format. (Alan Shugart had invented the floppy years before when he was at IBM.) Steve was always looking for new technologies that had an advantage and were likely to be the trend, and this was definitely a case like that.

He got one of the new Shugart 5-inch drives for me so I could see if I could make it work with the Apple II. What I had to do was design a controller board—a card that would plug into the Apple II—that would let you read and write data from the floppy. The first thing I did was examine the drive and its controller board and how they worked. I scanned the manual. Finally I studied the schematics of their circuitry, and I analyzed Shugart's floppy disk circuit too. It had a connector and a protocol for how signals would be applied to write data. In the end, I decided that of the twenty-two or so chips, about twenty of them weren't needed. To make the floppy disk work required a combination of a circuit I had to design and the existing circuit on the Shugart drive. I stripped out twenty of their chips, so that reduced twenty of my total end product. That's the way I always think about things. I could run data right from my own floppy controller to the read/write head and implement any start/stop protocols of my own in code on the computer. To tell you the truth, it was less work on the computer than generating the funny protocol Shugart wanted. Then I sat down and came up with a very simple circuit that would write data at floppy disk rates and read it. This turned out to be a real challenge.

● ○ ●

In the case of the cassette tape interface I'd designed, I had a signal that constantly varied from high to low and low to high and so on. The signal could never stop as long as the tape was running. The circuit handling signals to a cassette recorder weren't designed to let a signal stop changing.

And the tape wasn't able to store a signal that stayed the same for too long. So I had the microprocessor time the low-high-low transitions according to the 1s and 0s of the data being written. I chose the rates of this cassette data to be between 1,000 and 2,000 hertz. Those were typical voice frequencies that a cassette tape was designed to record and play. That's approximately one millisecond (a thousandth of a second) between transitions from high to low to high and so on signals.

But the signals to a floppy disk needed transition times that were much shorter—only four to eight microseconds (or millionths of a second). There was no way to get my microprocessor to generate these timings directly from the 1s and 0s. It was just too fast. After all, the 6502 microprocessor inside the Apple II ran at a clock speed of approximately 1 MHz. The fastest instruction took two microseconds and would take many instructions to generate the timing for 1s and 0s. This was a problem.

I came up with an answer, thankfully.

The Apple II was designed to read and write bytes of data to cards plugged into the eight free slots, and it could do that really efficiently. So I came up with a scheme to output 8 bits (that's one byte) of data to the floppy controller, which would output those bits every four microseconds on its own, one bit at a time.

The 8-bit data code came from 4 bits of real computer data. I used a lookup table to do this efficiently.

Even so, it was barely possible for a perfect program, a program I had to write to myself, to keep up with this rate. And I had to count the exact number of clock cycles, in microseconds, for every step. That way, when I output 8 bits of code data to the controller, exactly every thirty-two microseconds, it matched the rate it had to be written onto the transfer rate. No matter what paths my program took, how many instructions, how many branches, how many loops, it always happened exactly every thirty-two microseconds, when the next batch had to be written.

This sort of precision timing is a software job only a hardware person could deal with. Software programmers don't have to deal with precise timing ever.

• ○ •

This is as tricky as code gets. Even a minor change in the microprocessor could have killed it. For example, if they came out with a version of the 6502 that took three microseconds for a particular instruction instead of four, it would have screwed up all my calculated timing and the floppy controller for the drive would no longer work.

The floppy controller card had to accept 8 bits and merely shift it out to the floppy disk, through a magnetic write head, similar to writing to a cassette tape. That was how you saved data to the floppy, and that part was easy. An 8-bit shift register (registers hold data) could be loaded off the bus and do the four-microsecond shifting of the data.

Coming back from the other direction, reading data from the floppy was more of a challenge. I came up with the idea of creating a tiny processor—a tiny microprocessor, actually—I had to implement as what is called a state machine.

I did this using two chips, which was a remarkable achievement. One chip was a register and one was a PROM. I think I used a 6-bit register. Some of its bits were like maybe six of the 1s and 0s in this register, corresponding to a particular "state" the machine might be in. They functioned as address bits to a PROM.

The PROM would take as address inputs the bits indicating the current state—from the register—and also the bits of data from the floppy disk. Every microsecond, this PROM would output as data the next state number (which might be the same) and also a couple of bits that controlled the 8-bit shift register. That would shift the 0s and 1s to it in the appropriate time—when the time came to make decisions. That next state number would be reloaded into the register that held the state number.

Basically this little state machine was analyzing what was coming from the floppy disk every microsecond, and saving it in the master 8-bit chip register. Don't confuse this 8-bit shift register with the register that held the state number for the state machine.

I had to fill the state machine PROM with 1s and 0s that caused the right actions in my machine. This was much more difficult than writing a program on a microprocessor, because every 1 and 0 had a specific, important meaning on that PROM.

I completed the state machine and was sure it would work. It was elegant—in fact the whole design was elegant, and I was proud of it.

Now, all this data (1s and 0s) was coming from the floppy disk, but I had to be able to determine which 0 or 1 would be the start of a byte. (Remember, 8 bits together form a byte.) Also, when this four- and eight-microsecond timing between transitions came from the floppy disk to my controller, I didn't know which of the 0s and 1s was the start of a byte.

I was scared for a week or so as I built my controller that I wouldn't be able to solve this. But I did come up with some abnormal patterns that could be written onto the floppy disk but didn't translate back to data.

I would write about sixteen of these patterns in a row, and when they read back into my state machine, they automatically kept shifting it in time until it lined up with where the bytes would actually be. Then my read program, in the computer, continually looked for a couple of start bytes, called "mark bytes," which I'd write to indicate the start of a small section of data, called a "sector." Along with the data for each sector, I'd write the sector number of data on the floppy so that the reading program would be sure it was writing the correct sector. (If the reading sector ever determined the data was wrong, it would try again.)

● ○ ●

For the floppy, I did the hardware design and the state machine coding. I also wrote the very tightly timed code to read and write specially coded data to and from the floppy disk. This was my forte.

Randy Wiggington wrote a higher-level routine, more useful to application programmers and operating system programmers.

After I was able to read and write data, I wrote routines to step the head to any of the thirty-six tracks on the floppy disk. It would step for a long time to position itself on track 0, the innermost track. Then I'd give a sequence of pulses to a stepper-motor to step the head to track 1, then track 2, and so on, to get to the point where the data it needed was. I had to wait a certain time between this track-stepping, as specified by Shugart.

At one point it occurred to me that moving the magnetic read/write head was like moving a heavy car. It has inertia. It's slow to get started, but once you get it moving it rolls on its own inertia and you can push it to make it faster, and then faster yet. I decided I could probably safely accelerate the head as it crossed multiple tracks and then decelerate it to get it going slow enough not to overshoot the last track. Even if it overshot, it would read the track number it got to and then back up.

I experimented and came up with a table of acceleration/deceleration numbers for timing that worked fine. Now, instead of a click-click-click sound like the burst of a machine gun, as the head moved around it made a nice-sounding whoosh. We had the fastest floppy disk access times in the industry because of this.

This sounds very complicated, I know. But it had very few parts. Making it work was incredibly hairy. It was one of those things you don't even know is possible. You can get an idea of just how much I sweated in those two weeks.

I know all this got really technical, but I had to explain because to this day, engineers are always walking up to me and saying how great that floppy controller I did was. And in just two weeks. Now you know how I did it.

● ○ ●

The code was just about to the point where we could type "R Checkbook" to run the checkbook program or "R Color Math" to run the math program. I didn't actually have a floppy disk operating system in two weeks, but we had a table on the disk that tracked and sectored each program occupied. Normally an operating system would read an index to the whole disk and when you requested "Color Math" it would look up in the index the list of tracks and sectors it occupied. We didn't have this quite working the day we had to fly to Las Vegas, but Randy and I were sure we'd have it done in a few hours after we got there.

So we got on the plane in San Jose and flew to Las Vegas.

● ○ ●

That was a night Randy and I will never forget. It was our first time seeing the lights of Las Vegas. We were stunned by it. It was a much different and smaller strip than today, with much smaller hotels. There weren't even as many of them as there are now, and many were old and tiny. But it was impressive. We'd never seen anything so lit up, that is for sure!

Our motel was the cheapest place in town, the Villa Roma. It was near Circus Circus and we learned the route from there to the Las Vegas Convention Center. Randy and I did a lot of walking that night. I showed Randy, who was seventeen at the time, how to play craps and he won something like $35. At the convention center, we watched the late-night setup of all the booths. We set up in our booth and worked until about 6 a.m., finally getting everything working.

At that point I did one very smart thing. I was so tired and wanted some sleep but knew it was worth backing up our one good floppy disk, with all the right data.

I had some short programs that allowed me to read and write entire tracks. The floppy disk had thirty-six tracks. I decided to make a copy of this one floppy disk we had worked so long and hard to prepare. I only had two floppy disks with me so I decided to copy the good one to the blank. I inserted the good floppy and entered some data into memory to cause it to read track 0. Then I put in the blank floppy and used that data to write "track 0" on it. I did the same sequence for all thirty-six tracks. Backing up is smart, I always say.

But when I finished this backup, I looked at the two unlabeled floppy disks and got a sinking feeling that I'd followed a rote pattern but accidentally copied the bad floppy to the good one, erasing all the good data. A quick test determined that this is what happened. You do things like that when you are extremely tired. So my smart idea had led to a dumb and unfortunate result.

It meant that we would not, due to our tired state, have the floppy ready to show when the CES started in a few hours. What a bummer.

We went back to the Villa Roma motel and slept. At about 10 a.m. I woke up and got to work. I wanted to try to rebuild the whole thing. The code was all in my head, anyway. I managed to get the good program reestablished by noon and took it to our booth. There we attached the floppy and started showing it.

I can't tell you how successful and noted it was at this show, particularly in comparison to the Commodore PET and Radio Shack TRS-80, which were at the CES as well.

● ○ ●

The floppy disk made the computer fast, but it was a program named VisiCalc that made it powerful.

Two guys in Boston, Bob Frankston and Dan Bricklin, worked closely with Mike Markkula to design it. And boy, was this the right product at the right time! And it was definitely the right program for the right machine.

VisiCalc was a software product for business forecasting—it was designed to answer "what-if" scenarios. For instance, if we sell $100,000 worth of product X, how much revenue will we get? What if we sell half that? It was the earliest software program for doing spreadsheets on a personal computer, so that regular people working in business really had a high-tech tool.

And VisiCalc was so powerful it could only run on the Apple II. Only our computer had enough RAM to run it. The Radio Shack TRS-80 and the Commodore PET definitely weren't powerful enough. But we had the RAM, we had graphics on-screen and a two-dimensional display, and we were easy to use out of the box. And VisiCalc came out not on cassette, but on floppy disk. What a match.

Our business just exploded when VisiCalc came out. And the Apple II market suddenly moved from hobbyist people playing games who didn't mind waiting a few minutes for the program to load from tape, to business-type people who could load VisiCalc instantly.

After a couple of months, the businesspeople were something like 90 percent of the market. We had totally missed this audience, we never thought of it. But it took Apple in a whole new direction.

From 1,000 units a month, suddenly we went to 10,000 a month. Good god, it happened so fast. Through 1978 and 1979 we just got more and more successful.

By 1980 we were the first company to sell a million computers. We were the biggest initial public offering since Ford. And we made the most millionaires in a single day in history up to that point.

I believe the whole reason for this was the combination of the Apple II, VisiCalc, and the floppy disk.

● ○ ●

Remember when I told you Mike had us copyright the software? Well, what a good move.

After the CES, we found out about a new computer from a company called Franklin. It supposedly looked a lot like ours. It arrived at our building, and it looked so much like the Apple II I was very interested.

I thought, Hey, great. They copied my design. I wonder how much of it they copied. I didn't expect they would've copied much of it. I figured engineers are trained to invent and design their own things. An engineer would never look at another person's design and copy it, would they? No, that's what they go to school for. They go to learn how to design their own things.

I walked over to the main building to look at it. There it was, and I was shocked. The printed circuit board inside was exactly the same size as ours. And every single trace and wire was the same as ours. It was like they'd taken our Apple II board and Xeroxed it. It was like they'd just Xeroxed a blank Apple II board and put in the exact same chips. This company had done something no honorable engineer would've done in their effort to make their own computer.

I couldn't believe it.

Well, at the next computer show I attended, I immediately went up to their booth and told the president, who was in the booth, "Hey, this is just a copy of ours." I was all upset.

"This is ridiculous," I told him. "You copied our board. You just copied it. Which means I am your chief engineer, and you don't even give me credit for being your chief engineer."

The president looked at me and said, "Okay. You're our chief engineer."

And I was happy and walked away, but now that I think of it, I should've asked him for a salary!

We did sue them later, and I found out their argument for doing it. They claimed there were legal reasons that gave them the right to copy the Apple II. They were arguing that because there was such a huge software base of programs for the Apple II, it was unfair to exclude them. They claimed they had a right to build a computer that could run that software base, but that argument sure didn't make sense to me.

The case took a couple of years. They lost, and we did get money from them. Just a few hundred thousand dollars, not the millions I thought it was worth. But it was enough to stop them.

More About the Floppy Disk

The floppy disk was invented by Alan Shugart in 1967, when he was working at IBM. The first floppies were 8 inches across—and they were called floppies because they were on a thin, bendable piece of magnetic material. Later, floppies went to a smaller format, the 5.25-inch format.

Later on, when they were in an even smaller 3.5-inch format and in a nonbendable plastic cover, people started calling floppies "diskettes."

Chapter 15

The Woz Plan

Just before we went public in late 1980, a guy called me and asked whether he could buy some shares of my stock at $5 a share. He wanted to buy 10 percent of it.

I loved the idea, because it meant I could afford to buy Alice and myself a house. We were still living in the Park Holiday Apartments in San Jose, paying a rent of $150 a month.

But I like to do things different. I valued the employees at Apple—there were more than a hundred by then—as a community. I'd had that philosophy about a company being like a community since my first job, and maybe even earlier.

So I decided it would be better to sell some of my stock to employees and let them benefit, rather than some outside investor.

It was apparent to a lot of people at this point that Apple was going to have a very successful IPO—that, reasonably, the stock was going to be worth a whole lot more than $5, at any rate. And top executives and founders at Apple had a lot of stock. We were all likely to make millions. But a lot of other employees were left out, the majority of them.

I decided I was going to offer to sell some stock really cheap to people who deserved it. Regular employees didn't get all the stock options the executives got. Which wasn't fair. So I came up with something I called the Woz Plan. Any engineer or marketing person could buy 2,000 shares from me at a really low price of $5.

Almost everybody who participated in the Woz Plan ended up being able to buy a house and become relatively comfortable. I'm glad of that. But at first our lawyers told me I wasn't going to be allowed to sell stock to all these people. They told me they had to be sophisticated investors or something. But finally our attorney, Al Eisenstat, said, "Okay, Steve, you can do it."

Then there was the matter of some of our earliest employees who didn't get stock at all. Randy Wiggington, who'd helped me do the floppy disk, had been there before we started Apple even. Chris Espinoza, Dan Kottke, and my old neighbor Bill Fernandez were other examples. These employees weren't just around, they offered the inspiration that really allowed me to do the great stuff. I thought of them as part of the family, part of the family that had helped me design the Apple I and Apple II computers.

I gave each of them stock worth about a million dollars.

In those days, giving stock away to people you thought deserved it was just unheard of. Companies at the time just didn't give stock to all the workers. They were like, "Why should we give these people stock? They did what they did for what they got paid and they didn't have stock." Never would any company go back and say, "Okay, well, you were real nice. So now I'll give you some stock." So this was different because I was giving them my own stock—like a gift—it wasn't coming from the company.

• ○ •

I think behind the scenes Steve thought I was weak because of this—sort of ditching the company a little bit in kind of a sellout. But I sold that stock at about $5 a share to forty people in the Woz Plan—2,000 shares a pop—and then I was able to buy a really nice house for me and Alice. I bought it in cash. I figured, once you own a house, it's great. All you have to worry about is the maintenance of the house if you don't have a job or anything. So I bought it and owned it outright.

It wasn't a very big house, but it was a nice house. It was probably the very favorite house of my life. It was just beautiful—located in the middle of the Santa Cruz Mountains, in Scotts Valley. It was an all-wood house—knotty pine with the holes in the wood. There was a big master bedroom upstairs. And I remember I could walk upstairs through the bedroom and walk out onto a balcony and look down into the family room and a little aviary with a bunch of windows. I had a gate out front with a wooden mural I had done of dogs. I got my first huskies there. I loved everything about that house.

Alice and I didn't stay together in that house very long, though. Even though we now had money like we'd never dreamed of, it wasn't enough to make up for the fact that we had different interests. She wanted to go out every night with her friends. I wasn't into that. I wanted to stay home and work. I didn't want to get divorced—I never wanted to get a divorce, ever. I'm the kind of guy who always wanted to get married to someone forever, and I wanted that with Alice.

But what could I do? I mean, by then the Apple stock was worth so many hundreds of millions of dollars, and she just told the counselor we were seeing that she wanted to see who she was without me and be on her own in life. She never once said to the counselor that I worked too hard, which is kind of a myth about my divorce that got in the press later. No, that's not what she said. She said she wanted to be on her own.

Let me tell you that I opposed that divorce as strongly as I could. I never wanted to get divorced in my life. But finally I realized there was no way to stop it. So I just took Alice to a park in Cupertino and wished her well and said goodbye. I walked back to Apple feeling really different. Different like it was time to move on. Alice was gone.

My friend Dan Sokol gave me this framed Apple I circuit board as a thirtieth birthday gift. It was displayed in the Apple lobby for years. *(Photograph courtesy of Dan Sokol)*

Before we had the volume to pay for plastic cases, a lot of our customers would cover the Apple I board with a wooden case, often made of Koa wood. *(Photograph courtesy of Wikipedia)*

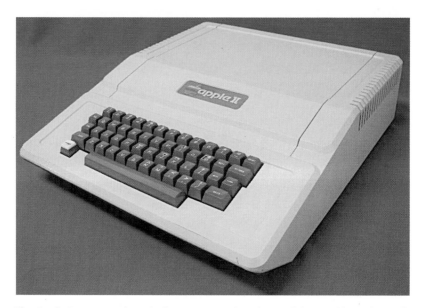

The Apple II—my creation—is the computer that changed the world. So they tell me. *(Photograph courtesy of Wikipedia)*

The Apple III was the computer that was designed by committee. Apple pushed it like crazy, but the majority of people still wanted the Apple II. *(Photograph courtesy of Wikipedia)*

U.S. President Ronald Reagan awarded Steve and me the U.S. Technology Medal in 1985. *(Photograph courtesy of The White House)*

Here I am the day we opened up the US Festival in 1983. It lost money, but I enjoyed every minute of it. *(Photograph courtesy of Dan Sokol)*

Here I am with my then wife, Candi, and then Van Halen front man David Lee Roth. We were at the party before one of Van Halen's US Festival appearances. *(Photograph courtesy of Dan Sokol)*

Singer Emmylou Harris is a longtime friend of mine. She sang at my wedding and played at my US Festival. *(Photograph courtesy of Dan Sokol)*

Here I am with my second wife, Candi. She is the mother of my three children. *(Photograph courtesy of Dan Sokol)*

Steve Jobs and me sharing a laugh at Macworld 2005.
(Photograph courtesy of Alan Luckow)

Here I am with one of my Segways. I ride one all the time. It's a great personal transportation device invented by Dean Kamen. *(Photograph courtesy of Dan Sokol)*

• ○ •

By this time Apple had its own building on Bandley Drive. By 1981 computers all of a sudden became the happening thing in life. There were articles in newspapers and magazines and TV shows talking about computers; it was just immense. Computers, personal computers, and home computers—suddenly everyone was wondering if they were going to make our lives better in the future, lead to better education systems, cause us to be more efficient and more productive. It looked like computers were going to enlighten us, improve our brains, let us think less and get correct answers sooner.

There was also a constant stream of articles in the trade press comparing our product with others on the market, and because we were the best technically, we were always rated as the best product. We were the one everyone wanted the most.

There were also stories about how we were just two people, Steve and I, and how we'd started with nothing and suddenly were so successful. We got all this publicity and all the benefits from it. Sales. Fame. We were just the hot, shining star.

In December of 1980, Apple's stock went public on the NAS-DAQ exchange.

• ○ •

It was the most successful IPO up to that time. It was on the front page of every major newspaper and magazine. Suddenly we were legendary. And rich. Really rich.

This was a pretty amazing accomplishment. After all, we had started from virtually nothing. It turned out Mike Markkula was right. We really were going to be a Fortune 500 company in five years.

Just a year later, we were going head to head with IBM's first personal computer, the IBM PC. Nonetheless, we had this major, major IPO. We also had the Apple III, a machine targeted to business, coming out—there were just rumors of it—and I think that was part of the reason the timing was right. (Another reason was that because so many people had received shares, the reporting hassle to the SEC was harder than going public!)

That computer, the Apple III, was a strong, strong statement to the business world. It was like, after this incredible Apple II phenomenon, we were suddenly going to be able to compete with the then-new IBM PC.

● ○ ●

The Apple III had some terrible problems, though. It was nothing like the Apple II, which was reliable all the time. I'm serious. You could buy an Apple II on eBay today, and it'll work. There is no modern product that is as reliable. In every speech I give, I talk to people who are still running Apple IIs, and they say those machines are still running after this many years.

No, the Apple III had hardware problems, serious ones. It would get to a store, for instance, boot up a couple of times, and then it would crash. Sometimes it wouldn't even boot up at all. My brother had a computer store by this time in Sunnyvale, and he told me Apple engineers would come down to fix it, but they could never get a machine that worked. Never. The first few months of the Apple III went by, and many of the stores had the same experience. Every Apple III came back not working. And what do you do when you're a computer dealer and this happens? Well, you stop selling it and you keep selling the original machine, the Apple II. That's why the Apple II was going to be the largest-selling computer in the world for at least three more years. In fact, by 1983 it would hit a huge milestone—it was the first computer to sell a million units!

So why did the Apple III have so many problems, despite the fact that all of our other products had worked so great? I can answer that. It's because the Apple III was not developed by a single engineer or a couple of engineers working together. It was developed by committee, by the marketing department. These were executives in the company who could take a lot of their power and decide to put all their money and resources in the direction of their own ideas. Their own ideas as to what a computer should be.

Marketing saw that the business community would be the bigger market. They saw that the typical small businessman went into a computer store, bought an Apple II, a printer, the VisiCalc spreadsheet program, and two plug-in cards. One was a memory card, which allowed them to run larger spreadsheets. And the other was an eighty-column card, which allowed them to present eighty columns of characters across the video display, instead of the normal forty. Forty columns was the limit of American TVs.

So they came up with the idea that this should all be built into a single machine: the Apple III. And it was built.

Initially there was virtually no software designed for the Apple III. Yet there were hundreds of software programs you could buy for the Apple II. So to have a lot of software right away, Apple built the Apple III as a dual computer—there was a switch that let you select whether the computer started up as an Apple II or as an Apple III. (The Apple III hardware was designed to be extremely compatible with the Apple II, which was hard to improve on.) It couldn't be both at once.

And it was here they did something very wrong. They wanted to set the public perception of the Apple III as a business computer and position the Apple II as the so-called home hobby machine. The little brother of the family. But get this. Marketing had us add chips—and therefore expense and complexity—to the Apple III in order to *disable* the extra memory and eighty-column modes if you booted it up as an Apple II.

This is what killed the Apple III's chances from the get-go. Here's why. A businessman buying an Apple II for his work could easily say, "I'll buy an Apple III, and use it in the Apple II mode since I'm used to it, but I'll still have the more modern machine."

But Apple killed the product that businessman would want by disabling the very Apple II features (extra memory and eighty-column mode) he was buying the computer for.

Out of the chute, the Apple III got a lot of publicity, but there was almost nothing you could run on it. As I said, it wasn't reliable. And in Apple II mode, it was crippled.

To this day, it boggles my mind. It's just not the way an engineer—or any rational person, for that matter—would think. It disillusioned me that big companies could work this way.

• ○ •

Finally, finally, about a year after Apple was able to make the Apple III reliable enough so it wouldn't break constantly, the computer still wouldn't sell. Because by then it had such a bad rep as a terrible, unreliable machine. You see, first impressions matter. When a computer passes by its period of acceptance, you just aren't going to get people jumping on the bandwagon by fixing the problem.

My feeling was, Hey, try to forget about it, and just change the name of the Apple III to the Apple IV and make it look different on the outside, and maybe then you could sell some.

• ○ •

From the years 1980 to 1983, Apple made the Apple III its highest priority. It's fair to say that Apple became the Apple III company. An Apple III company that just happens to sell Apple IIs.

By 1983 everybody at Apple was forced to have an Apple III on their desk. Suddenly, whenever I walked into the company, they'd be talking like, "Oh my god, did you see such and such new piece of software running on the Apple III?" And it was like, Who cares? I would go around the country in those days and give speeches to computer groups. I would talk to computer groups all over the place, and everywhere I went there would be ninety people with Apple IIs and three people with Apple IIIs.

Why would Apple pretend it was an Apple III company when it wasn't? That was my question.

After all, during these years the Apple II was the largest-selling computer in the world. The Apple II was carrying us. In those days, almost every ad Apple ran in major magazines like *Time* and *Newsweek* showed an Apple III. They never showed an Apple II. The executive staff cut plans for all Apple II products. Totally. There were only a couple of education-related products left.

Despite all this, the Apple II was still paying everyone's salaries and making a huge profit for the company. And it wasn't even being advertised. About the only salary Apple spent on the Apple II during that period—1980 to 1983—was on the guy who printed the price lists.

• ○ •

It was terrible. I mean, we had everybody at Apple—all the employees and all the money—going into the Apple III and nothing was coming out. And accounting didn't account for it that way. The company lost so much money on the Apple III in those days—in today's money, it would be at least a billion. I calculated at the time that we lost about $300 million. That's just my own estimate.

And not only was the Apple II carrying the whole company and carrying a debacle like the Apple III, it was hiding the Apple III's real deficiencies from the world. Nobody in the real world, but nobody, treated the Apple III as if it was significant.

All of our users had no idea, I'm telling you. Because if you opened up a computer magazine, all you saw were fifty ads for the Apple II—not by Apple, but by resellers and small mom-and-pop shops who were building all those games and add-ons for the Apple II.

As for the computer magazines, in their reviews of the Apple III, almost every one of them acknowledged it was a failure in the marketplace. Never did they acknowledge that it was a prominent part of Apple's business. They gave consumers the impression that we were largely an Apple II company—with this hugely successful product—and that there was this big group still working on the flawed Apple III for some reason.

● ○ ●

Now, I accept that Apple had to work the way a company has to. There are a lot of people who operate the company, and there are a lot of people on the board who run things. So the reasoning is very difficult to see. I mean, this was a time when the company had one reputation but it was totally different on the inside. It very much bothered me that you can get away with all kinds of things when you are successful. For example, a bad person can get away with a lot of things if they have a lot of money. And a bad person can hide it—hide behind the money—and keep on being a bad person.

In this case, we had a bad computer, the Apple III, even though the Apple II was selling like hotcakes. It had taken over the world. The IBM PC didn't overtake it until 1983. So it was a leader.

I still don't understand it.

● ○ ●

To be fair, the Apple III had some serious competition. In about 1981, IBM finally came out with its answer to the Apple II. It was selling great almost right away. It was truly becoming a huge success really rapidly. So we had some serious competition all of a sudden, and we'd never had that before.

All those big companies with big IBM mainframe and other large computers were already IBM customers, and it didn't take much for the IBM rep to sell them an IBM PC to go with it all. As a matter of fact, there used to be a saying that "you can't get fired for buying IBM."

When the IBM PC first came out, we were kind of cocky about it. We took out a full-page ad in the *Wall Street Journal* that said, "Welcome IBM. Seriously."

And like I said, the PC passed by the Apple II, the largest-selling computer in the world, in 1983.

● ○ ●

By this time, I should point out, Mike Scott—our president who took us public and the guy who took us through the phenomenally successful IPO—was gone. During the time the Apple III was being developed, he thought we'd grown a bit too large. There were good engineers, sure, but there were also a lot of lousy engineers floating around. That happens in any big company.

It's not necessarily the lousy engineer's fault, by the way. There's always going to be some mismatch between an engineer's interests and the job he's doing.

Anyway, Scotty had told Tom Whitney, our engineering manager, to take a vacation for a week. And meanwhile he did some research. He went around and talked to every engineer in the company and found out who was doing what and who was working and who wasn't doing much of anything.

Then he fired a whole bunch of people. That was called Bloody Monday. Or, at least, that's what it ended up being called in the Apple history books. I thought that, pretty much, he fired all the right ones. The laggards, I mean.

And then Mike Scott himself was fired. The board was just very pissed that he'd done this without a lot of backing and enough due process, the kind of procedure you're supposed to follow at a big company.

Also, Mike Markkula told me Mike Scott had been making a lot of rash decisions and decisions that just weren't right. Mike thought Scotty wasn't really capable of handling the company given the point and size it had gotten to.

I did not like this one bit. I liked Scotty very, very much as a person. I liked his way of thinking. I liked his way of being able to joke and be serious. With Scotty, I didn't see many things fall through the cracks. And I felt that he respected the good work that I did—the engineering work. He came from engineering.

And as I said, Scotty had been our president, our leader from day one of incorporation until we'd gone public in one of the biggest IPOs in U.S. history. And now, all of a sudden, he was just pushed aside and forgotten.

I think it's sad that none of the books today even seem to recall him. Nobody knows his name. Yet Mike Scott was the president that took us through the earliest days.

• ○ •

I learned a lot of things at Apple those first few years. I learned right away that in a company, you can have different ideas about what ads look like or what the logo looks like, even different ideas about the name of the company or a product it has. People have different and often conflicting ideas about all these things.

One thing I've learned directly from this new experience of creating and working at a company with so many different people is: Hey, never pretend you can do someone's job better than someone who's been doing it for years.

I was much better keeping quiet and just focusing on my particular talent of engineering. That guaranteed that I would be productive at what I do and could let other people be productive at what they did best.

So few companies were like this. But companies don't always evolve the way you want them to. After all, when we first started Apple, Steve and I really had this engineering-centric model in mind. We wanted Apple to have the amazing employee morale we think HP got as a result of treating its engineers like upper-class citizens, you know?

But we knew what were getting into because Mike Markkula told us. He said, "This is going to be a marketing company." The product is going to be driven, in other words, by demands that the marketing department finds in customers. This is just the opposite of a place where engineers just build whatever they love, and marketing comes up with ways to market them. I knew this was going to be a challenge for me.

● ○ ●

Back in high school, I read a book called *The Loneliness of the Long-Distance Runner* by Alan Sillitoe. It just grabbed me. It was about a criminal going through this big mental discussion. It really showed how he was thinking very independently—it showed the way people in general who are inwardly driven think—and he's trying to decide whether he should win this big footrace while he's in jail. The bad governor will become famous if the criminal wins.

And he's trying to decide, Should he win the race, or shouldn't he? Should he let the governor have all the fame? Or should he try to run away, and keep running, and just escape?

The whole thing had a huge impact on my own thinking. In life, there is an "us" and a "them." A "we" and a "they." And the "they" is the administration, the authorities. And sometimes they're on the wrong side and we're on the right side.

Chapter 16

Crash Landing

Before Alice and I were divorced, Alice told me about a friend of hers, Sherry, who was interested in buying a movie theater. A real running theater. It was the Mayfair Theater in San Jose. Alice thought I should buy it, and I could never turn Alice down when it came to anything she wanted to do.

So I bought it.

Sherry and Alice had gotten involved with a group called Eastern Star, a group of women who had relatives in the Freemasons. Because she was in Eastern Star, she was spending a lot of time there, a lot of nights away there. In order to have more time with her, I decided that I would become a Freemason. Freemasons, after all, regularly have joint events with Eastern Star. So I went down to the Masonic lodge and did a lot of training, and after some period of time and three big events, I became a third-degree Mason. Then I got more time with Alice. I eventually became an officer and everything.

I should tell you that although I am a lifetime Freemason, I'm not like the other people who are Freemasons. My personality is very, very unlike theirs. To get in, you have to say all this stuff about God, the Bible, words that sound a little bit like they come from the Constitution, and none of this ritual stuff is the way I think, you know? But I did it, and I did it well. If I'm going to do something, I always try to do it well. And I did this for one reason, as I said: to see Alice more. I wanted to save the marriage. I would go so far as to join the Freemasons if that's what it took. That's how I was.

So anyway, pretty much near the end of the marriage, I was a Freemason and I bought that theater. Alice's friend Sherry and Sherry's boyfriend, Howard, would run it. It had been their idea from the start, to run a theater. They'd gotten to Alice, as a friend, so she got to me. And now I owned it.

The Mayfair Theater was in kind of a low-income area of town. I remember we had to paint the bathroom black because of all the graffiti, and even afterward, people would still put graffiti in it, only in white paint. At least we could wash the walls.

I felt like making it into something special. I never had the idea that it was going to make a lot of money, but I wanted it to be kind of special and I put in nice seats and a good sound system. I had a couple of guys running it, and they scraped off a wall one day and found there was this beautiful natural wood artwork underneath this blah wall someone had tacked up on top of it. So we actually brought in some experts who sanded everything down, and they were able to recover the original artwork. I loved that theater.

But then Alice and I got divorced, and I was stuck with the theater. I went there every day after work at Apple. I drove down there, set up my computer so I could get some work done, saw what movies were playing, and said hi to everybody. The theater was this fun group of people, a really small operation. It was neat to see how it operated. I mean, it was a small, low-budget theater. We didn't get that many customers. And we only got pretty low-rate movies. For instance, we had *Friday the 13th*. That was probably the biggest movie we ever showed, and we only got it long after it opened.

Actually, the only movies we ever sold out on were gang movies, like *The Warriors*. That made sense, considering what part of town we were in!

I'd only been single a few weeks when I asked out the woman who would be my second wife, Candi Clark. I knew her because once, when I bought a bunch of advanced tickets to a *Star Trek* movie and offered them half price to Apple employees, she'd asked for a bunch because she had a lot of brothers. I thought she was pretty cute, so I asked her to come to one of those low-budget science fiction movies we were showing at my theater, and she did. The next day, we raced bumper cars at the Malibu Grand Prix track near the San Francisco airport and I beat her really well.

I thought she was just super pretty. She was blonde, medium build, and it turned out she had been an Olympic kayaker. (I found that out when I saw a picture of her and Ronald Reagan on the wall of her apartment after our second date.) She worked at Apple creating database reports for managers, that sort of stuff.

So now I had a girlfriend and that was it. It was all really quick.

• ○ •

It wasn't very long after I'd divorced Alice and met Candi that we decided to get married. She had an uncle down in San Diego who made jewelry, and I had this idea. Let's get a ring for me, I said, that has the diamond on the inside so nobody can see it. I thought that would be more special than a normal ring. We would know there was a diamond, but the world wouldn't.

So we decided to fly down on a plane, on my V-tail Beechcraft, which I'd bought right after getting my pilot's license six months before. I think today that it was the most beautiful and unorthodox single-engine plane there is. It was so distinctive, the shape of its tail was so unique, and I was so proud to fly it. I had it painted—by a painter named Bill Kelly, he'd done PR for Apple—in the nicest earth tones.

The first time in my life that I was able to take a passenger alone, it was with Candi. I took her down to San Jose one night and it was raining. Of course, I had never flown in the rain at night, but I did and we got back safely. I think that might have been my best landing ever.

But no, I wasn't at all cocky about my flying. I knew how to do a flight plan and how to do flights. I knew the rules to follow. But still, I was a beginner pilot. I was still a pretty rough new trainee. But anyway, Candi and I took a few trips in the new plane, and then one day we decided to fly down to San Diego where Candi's uncle could design that wedding ring with the diamond on the inside.

Candi and I flew from San Jose to a small airport in Scotts Valley to pick up Candi's brother Jack and Jack's girlfriend, Chris. Usually I would just taxi around and then take off, you know? So I'm going around, and suddenly I notice I'm blocked by another plane that's just sitting there, stalled on the taxiway. I'm thinking, Great. Great. I can't even get out of there.

So I looked around—I think we turned the airplane around—and I go off some other side way. By then the stalled airplane was gone and finally I got to the start of the runway. And I did all the little start-up procedures and reached for the throttle and you know what?

I remember reaching for the throttle at the start of the runway, and that's it. I can remember every other detail of the airport and everything that day up to that point. But I can remember absolutely nothing about what happened after that point. I have no memory of what happened next. (Later, I figured out that maybe Candi, who was sitting in the front, accidentally leaned on one of the controls, but we'll never know exactly what caused that accident.)

I woke up in the hospital, so they tell me, but it wasn't until five weeks later that I was able to remember that I was in a plane crash.

My friend Dan Sokol later told me that he saw news of the accident on TV. He said he turned on the TV and clicked onto the news channel when he heard something about an executive of a Silicon Valley computer company crashing his plane in Scotts Valley. And he immediately turned around just in time to see about two seconds of the Beechcraft upside down. I had crashed in the parking lot of a skating rink.

Of course, as I told you, I remember absolutely nothing about what happened, not even about being in the hospital or anything. It was some head injury! Dan told me my room was filled with gifts and toys and stuff from people at Apple. Handmade cards, off-the-shelf cards, and junk food. It was all there, Dan said, but I have no memory of it. Zero memory. Dan even told me that I asked him to smuggle in a milk shake and pizza for me, which sounds exactly like me, so at least I know that I was really in there. I mean, people took pictures of me in there playing computer games, which is what I would do, but I have no memory of that. No memory at all.

At some point, I guess a week or two later, I was finally released and allowed to go home. I didn't go to Apple to work, I presume because I thought every day was a weekend. That's the only explanation I can think of now as to why I didn't go to work, and also why I didn't notice my dog was missing. (He'd been checked into a kennel.)

For a few weeks after, I was living in my house in Scotts Valley in this weird, not-fully-functional state. I mean, people later told me I seemed hazy. They say I was driving around on my motorcycle, but people really had to direct me to do things. Like: "You go here. You have to do this now. Now you have to do this." I was apparently functioning, but I hardly have any memories of it. I was living this halfway weird life. I didn't realize that my dog had been boarded for five weeks away from me, for instance. It just seemed like every day was the same day. I didn't even realize I was missing a tooth for five weeks—one of my front teeth! How do you not spot something like that? I don't know, I can't explain it.

Now, Candi and her brother, I found out much later, were also injured in the crash. She even had to get some plastic surgery afterward. But I was the one who was the hardest hit. As I said, I ended up having what is known as anterograde amnesia, even though the doctors didn't know it at first. Anterograde amnesia means that you don't lose memories; you just lose the ability to form new ones.

But I guess, when I think about it now, it was actually a good thing because in my mind, I never had a plane crash to get over. It just isn't there. I underwent hypnosis to see if I could come up with any recollection of what happened to cause the crash. I really would've liked to know. But nothing came to me.

So in those five weeks—the weeks of my amnesia—I remembered everything from before that. I had all my old skills and memories, and those memories are still there up till that point. But during that five-week period, whatever I was doing, I wasn't remembering it.

And then suddenly I came out of it.

The first, the very first, memory I had was that I was somehow at the Macintosh building talking to associates I'd been working with on the Macintosh. And they were telling me something about how the project was going. And I don't remember exactly who, but I think it was Andy Hertzfeld (designer of the Macintosh graphical user interface) who mentioned something about a plane crash. A plane crash? And the instant he said the words "plane crash," I knew there was this thing about a plane crash in this dream I'd been having.

So I said to myself, Oh, this is a dream I'm having right now. And in a dream, I can always tell myself that I can just turn around and walk the other way. You can go any which way and a dream follows you. But this time I thought, No, I'll play by the rules of this dream and I'll keep talking to Andy. So I sat there talking to him, and that's my very first memory. But it was a very weak memory.

That night, I remember Candi and I went to see the movie *Ordinary People*. I don't remember a single detail of that movie, only that we saw it. Then we got home and we were in bed. I was lying on my back and thinking, Wait, did I have a plane crash that I heard about and kept dreaming about, or didn't I? I mean, I didn't have any memories of such a crash, and it seems like you would remember such a thing, wouldn't you?

Is it possible I had a plane crash and didn't remember it?

So I turned over and asked Candi, "Did I have a plane crash or was it a dream?"

I guess she thought I was joking, because she said, "It was a dream, Steve." That's what she said. That it was a dream. She wasn't playing with my head. She just had no idea that I had no idea I'd been in a plane crash.

This was a mental dilemma because I was struggling to prove in my head that it could be true.

So now I'm sitting there wondering if I'm ever going to get anybody to tell me if I had a plane crash or not. I suppose if I'd been smart, I would have looked in the newspaper or asked other people, but this was actually the first time I was starting to think that maybe I had in fact had a plane crash and it wasn't a dream.

So I sat there that night, feeling my body. And my body didn't have any broken bones or signs of a plane crash. Ha. I didn't think to look for a missing tooth!

So I kept thinking. I kept trying to pin it down. How do you figure out if something didn't happen? I could remember every single detail of that day up to the point of reaching for the throttle, but I couldn't remember pushing it. And then I thought of something logical. I thought, Wait a minute. I don't remember landing in Santa Catalina. If I had landed the plane, there's absolutely no way I would've forgotten that landing.

As soon as I thought that thought, I realized that my brain had been working very strangely. I realized that I'd been in a plane crash and it was real. And I just jerked my head up right away and realized that everything I was starting to suspect was real. My head started working immediately and retrieving and forming memories, I could feel it. And what was strange was, I could feel both states of mind. I had just come from a state where I wasn't forming memories, and now I was moving into this different state where I was forming memories. I could feel both states of mind at the same time, which was so strange.

Then I looked at the bed stand next to me, and there were something like a hundred cards from people I had received while I was in the hospital. They were sending me best wishes, saying get well and all that. And I read them. They were all from my very closest friends and associates.

And I said, Oh my god, I didn't even know they were there.

But I must have seen them every single night. Because they were there every single night. So it was like coming out of a very strange state and realizing that your head has not been forming any memories. That's what I deduced.

The very next day, my father called to remind me that I was supposed to show up for an appointment with the psychologist I'd been seeing. I had no memories of ever seeing a psychologist. But I went up to Stanford to see that psychologist and I kind of excitedly started explaining to him that I hadn't been forming memories or remembering the plane crash, and suddenly I'd come out of it. My head just switched over, I told him. It was amazing.

And would you believe it? He didn't believe me! I suppose I was so excited when I told him about this that he kept telling me I was a manic-depressive. I was stunned, and told him that I didn't have big highs or big lows like a manic-depressive would. I told him I was a very stable person. He said, "Well, manic depression usually starts when you're thirty." I was thirty. He had interpreted my excitement about my memory returning as being manic. What a quack.

Well, those five weeks after the plane crash, when I was finally and fully out of the amnesia, I decided this was a lucky opportunity. I should finish college, and not go back to Apple right away.

I realized it had been ten years since my third year of college, and if I didn't go back to finish up now, I probably never would. And it was that important to me. I wanted to finish. And I had already been out of Apple for a while anyway—five weeks without knowing it, actually—so that made it easier to just go back to school and not go back to Apple right away. I decided that life is short, right? So I decided.

I applied and got accepted and registered under the name Rocky Raccoon Clark. (Rocky Raccoon was the name of my dog, and Clark was my fiancée Candi's soon-to-be maiden name.)

And soon after I made that decision, Candi and I set the date to get married: June 13, 1981. It was an amazing party. We had the Apple hot-air balloon there in the front yard of Candi's parents' house. It was a spectacular party. Emmylou Harris, the famous folksinger, sang at the reception.

● ○ ●

The day after the wedding, I got an apartment in Berkeley to get ready to begin my fourth year of college. And on the weekend, the plan was that I would go back to this house we had bought on the summit of the Santa Cruz Mountains. It was amazing. Just a huge castle of a place.

It had a lot of flat land, which is unusual, so I had tennis courts built. And Candi turned a little pond into a nice little lake. I also bought an adjoining property, making twenty-six acres in all. It was a paradise. (Candi, now my ex-wife, still lives in that paradise.)

Candi stayed there working on the house while I spent the week in this college apartment a couple of hours north, in Berkeley. It was a great year, and a fun year. Because I was going under the name Rocky Raccoon Clark, no one knew who I was. I had fun posing as a nineteen-year-old college student, and the engineering classes were so easy for me. Every weekend, I went back home to the castle.

One of the first things I did at Berkeley, in addition to taking engineering courses for my degree, was to enroll in both psychology courses (for majors) and two courses specifically about human memory. After my accident and amnesia, I was intrigued by such strange aspects of memory, and I wanted to understand it more.

As far as my own condition went, it turned out to be relatively well known. It happens frequently to people after car and plane accidents, and it's associated with damage near the hippocampus section of the brain. It was a typical condition. There is no excuse for why my doctors—especially my psychologist—didn't figure this out.

Chapter 17

Have I Mentioned I Have the Voice of an Angel?

After the plane crash in 1981 and after I decided to go back and finish my degree at Berkeley, something else happened that I never would have expected.

It was during that first quarter at summer school when I was taking a class in statistics so I could enroll the following year. I was driving around in my car listening to a radio station—KFAT out of Gilroy, California—a station that had heavily influenced me during the Apple days. You see, I'd changed my music tastes from normal rock and roll to a type of really progressive country by then.

This was a new and strange type of music I'd never been exposed to before—a lot of folk, a lot of country, and a lot of comedy. It wasn't some dumb old countryish beat and song and themes; these songs were a lot about life. They very much reminded me of the sort of thinking Bob Dylan did, being as familiar with his lyrics as I was. And these songs went as deep— they pointed out what was right and wrong in life. The way they were written and the way I experienced them brought out a lot of emotion in me. I mean, there was a real meaning attached to these songs, and I was heavily influenced by this station.

At around this time, I recall seeing the movie *Woodstock*.

There was a meaning attached to that movie, too. A meaning that had to do with young people growing up and trying to find alternative ways of living. And so much of that was brought up in the words of these new progressive country songs I was listening to, like a music revolution was starting all over again.

And it hit me. I thought: Why not? Why not try to do a kind of Woodstock for my generation? I realized at this point that I had so much more money than I could ever dream of spending. I was thirty at the time and probably worth a hundred million dollars or more. I thought: My god, why not put on a big progressive country concert with these groups I loved? A lot of people might come.

At the time, I thought of it as kind of an unplanned event that would just happen.

Of course, I knew I didn't know enough to manage a concert or put one on. I didn't know the first thing about it. So I talked to a friend of mine, a friend who ran a nightclub in Santa Cruz. His name was Jim Valentine. I told him about my idea and convinced him that the kind of concert I had in mind would really draw a lot of people. Jim agreed, and man, it was nice to have one person agree with me. Most people didn't think progressive country could draw a crowd.

Now, Jim owned a nightclub in Santa Cruz called the Albatross, a strange name for a place like that. He ran it. He had comedians on his stage, he had singers and songwriters come in, he had musicians play. And he had some connections to the early big music concerts—things like Altamont in 1969 and the early San Francisco Bill Graham days. So even though I had these connections, I thought, Well, maybe in a few years. I'll finish at Berkeley and then do it.

But then Jim called me and said he had a guy who could put this thing on. He said he'd found the one guy he knew who could organize and manage a project this large. But it was going to run many millions of dollars to create. That guy's name was Pete Ellis.

After talking about this to Jim, I realized this concert was going to be huge. Huge. We were envisioning a huge outdoor space where people could just drive up and camp out for three days, like a Woodstock thing. But maybe better.

By the time we'd gotten to this point, I'd already started going back to school. (And at school, remember, I'd tricked everyone into thinking I was a student named Rocky Raccoon Clark.) I'd also just gotten married to Candi, and we'd just bought that castle of a house—with the house number of 21435. (I liked that number mathematically because it had all the first five digits appear exactly once.)

Candi was also supportive of the idea of a concert, probably because her background was kind of a hippieish Grateful Dead thing. I told her I thought if enough people came, it would make money. I wasn't sure enough people would come, but I didn't care. I knew I could afford it. I didn't know how much money would come back, exactly, but I was willing to take the risk. And after I was introduced to Peter Ellis, he put out that it would take a budget of $2 million to get started, and I was willing to pay that.

For that money, the starting amount needed, I could basically form a corporation (the UNUSON Corporation, short for UNite Us in SONg), hire people, do the planning, get the site, and put the whole thing together.

I remember when he came up to my apartment in Berkeley on Euclid Avenue one evening. I presented him with a check for $2 million. Then he knew it was for real.

Well, I should mention here that two weeks after I wrote that $2 million check, I read a book called *Barefoot in Babylon*, by Bob Spitz, which was about the entire progression of creating Woodstock from day one. It was about finding staff, getting permission for sites, publicity, getting groups signed up, overcoming political hurdles, changing sites at the last minute, inadequate preparations for the numbers of people who would show up, and more mishaps. Every chapter took my breath away and had me thinking, Oh my god, what a disaster. That book really chilled me. I thought, What have I gotten myself into?

Let me tell you, if I had read that book two weeks earlier, I never would have done it. Period. I absolutely wouldn't have done it.

I mean, according to that book, Woodstock broke even only because of the movie. Also, the expenses involved in putting on Woodstock were small enough because they didn't do an adequate job of setting up for and handling a large audience. Had they spent that money, they would've lost everything. And Woodstock was a rainy, swampy mess. It wasn't what we all imagined after seeing the movie. In fact, in putting together the US Festival, I later did talk to one of the two guys who'd created Woodstock, and he didn't want to work with us. He'd consult, that's it. He didn't want to do it again. He said he was just a music company executive and it was kind of like they got started on this thing and ended up captives to it.

In a way, that happened to me. The US Festival was exactly the opposite of the Apple experience for me. It didn't come easily. It involved having plans to get certain groups, and having those groups cancel. It involved having plans for sites, and having those sites cancel. It involved having plans for equipment, and having the equipment not come through. It was a costly battle to do all the right things, but we did them anyway.

I'd written a check. I had confidence in my people. I'd already taken a stand, and when you take a stand, you don't back away from it. Sometimes this has been a big problem in my life—especially marriage-wise—but if I'm in, I'm in. I don't back out. And by the time I could see this was a disaster, I had this guy, Pete Ellis, and all the people he'd hired, counting on me. I couldn't just all of a sudden pull the rug out. And we'd already planned the date: the first US Festival would be the Labor Day weekend of 1982, right after my first year back at school.

We finally secured a site, a county park near San Bernardino. It was in kind of a depressed area. The county park needed money, and they saw us as a way to get those funds.

There were some great things about this site. For one thing, it was an enormous area which would let us bring lots of trucks and stuff into the amphitheater. This place had the capacity to easily hold about 400,000 people, and hopefully as many as a million. That's twenty times what the Shoreline Amphitheater in Mountain View holds. (I built Shoreline years later with concert promoter Bill Graham and heiress Ann Getty. I put in $3 million of the $7 million total.)

We didn't want to use a preexisting arena or stadium, we wanted more of a campout-style setup. And they had a lake and a big area. We had to groom it with all these trucks going day after day after day digging up dirt and getting the right shape. And then we had to quickly plant some fast-growing grass sod to create sort of a grass liner that would span many, many acres.

We of course had to plan for the huge number of people we thought would come. We actually even got a temporary freeway exit, and we got some top highway patrol people who were on our side. They got things approved. The sheriffs of San Bernardino County were behind us, too. We were given this kind of support because we were sending out a good message of people working together, cooperating, getting things done, and putting education and technology shows in tent after tent we set up. So it was obvious to them that we weren't just rowdy concertgoers, but sort of good guys. In fact, the sheriffs were so behind us they even gave me an honorary sheriff's badge.

We started contracting with companies that put up sound systems and stages and artwork. We also had the most incredible sound system ever done. Not only did we have speakers at the main stage, but we also had extra speakers deep into the audience. This meant the sound in the back was delayed exactly to the point where it would match the front ones. So everyone could hear the music at the same time.

We also had groups to set up lots of concessions. We set up a technology fair with companies like Apple in air-conditioned tents, where they could show off computers and other products. We even had carnival rides planned. I ended up paying a total of about $10 million to complete that amphitheater. That was the biggest expense.

There were also very high payments to the artists to get exclusives for all of Southern California for that year—so bands we signed like Oingo Boingo and Fleetwood Mac, for instance, couldn't play anywhere else in Southern California that summer.

What I'm trying to get to is this: if I compare the US Festival to starting Apple, there's a huge difference. With Apple, I designed those computers alone. I could make every decision by myself and there were very few little changes and trade-offs. It was like I had total autonomy and total control, and that's how I was able to make everything work.

But with the US Festival, I had to deal with all kinds of people and lawyers. And let me tell you, in my experience, the music industry is the worst of all. And then I had to deal with all the construction and costs and funding everybody trying to get some bucks off the top. So the US Festivals were a much larger business to start than when I designed computers. In fact, it was the opposite. It was much better funded, it had many more people, and it was a trial, a real trial, from the start.

And I was the only one writing checks. This was my show, from that standpoint. But I felt that in booking groups, I just didn't have the experience. And none of my people did, either. They knew how to organize a company but not book groups. I talked to the concert promoter Bill Graham and signed him up. Now, if you've heard any of the legends surrounding Bill Graham, you know that he normally likes to run the whole show. But he'd been in Europe with the Rolling Stones, and we'd already been doing the engineering, coming up with what the stage would look like, the signs, the companies that would be hired, the sound system, the video. It was the first time ever that a big Diamond Vision display would be used at a concert in the United States.

But Bill had some definite ideas. For one thing, he totally nixed my progressive country idea, and he pretty much laid it out like this: You can't have that kind of music. He said, "If you want the kinds of numbers of people you're after, it's going to have to be a modern rock concert." If I really must, he said, I could add some country in.

He also said you have to have what kids in the high schools are listening to. So I actually went to some high schools and talked to kids. And when they threw out lists of the groups they wanted, all they were doing was relaying what the radio and MTV were playing. It was like all they wanted was two performers: Bruce Springsteen and Men at Work. It wasn't as if they had any special knowledge we didn't have. That was disappointing.

But we put the US Festival together anyway, and soon we were there. In 1982, over the Labor Day weekend. Candi was almost nine months pregnant, and we rented a house overlooking this huge venue. I mean, it was kind of scary to look down one day and see the hugest crowd down there. But we were going to pull it off, I knew it.

And we did, we really did. Though I lost money, that was not the biggest thing. The biggest thing was that people had a good time—and that facilities like the food stalls and bathrooms worked without a hitch. It was over 105 degrees that summer, and we set up a huge row of sprinklers people could run through all day to keep cool.

I still get emails and letters from people who say it was the greatest concert event of their lives. I just wanted everyone to smile, and I think everyone did. And we had a lot of firsts, that's for sure. We were the first non-charity concert ever of that size. We were the first to combine music and technology. We were the first to use that huge Diamond Vision video screen to bring the concert to people sitting way in the back, as well as to people at home watching on MTV, and we also had a satellite space bridge connecting our concert to some musicians in the then Soviet Union. We had Buzz Aldrin, the astronaut, involved in the space bridge, too, and we had him talking to a cosmonaut!

This was still during the Cold War. Back then, people in the Soviet Union, mainly Russians, were much more feared than Al Qaeda is today. The fear at the time was that the communist regime of the USSR would annihilate us with their weapons. Some of our UNUSON group had peace-oriented contacts with people in the USSR, though, including technicians who proposed the first-ever satellite linkup (space bridge) between the two countries.

I liked being the first at things—I always have—so I approved this instantly. Here's how we decided it would work: we would transmit live shows from our stage to a group in Russia. They would transmit a live show back to us on the Diamond Vision. The key to making it possible was that before the U.S. pulled out of the 1980 Olympics in Moscow, NBC had left a lot of satellite equipment behind. So all that equipment was still in a warehouse in Moscow.

Our technician friends in the USSR pulled this equipment out of its boxes and set up a satellite link on the specified date of the US Festival. There was no way we could know if it would even work. Back then, it took two weeks sometimes just to get a phone call into the USSR. We had to get the president of GTE to approve a constant phone call on the date of the transmission just so parties in both countries could talk to each other and make sure it was working.

On the date of the transmission, we weren't even sure it would work. Right up to the second their transmission appeared on our screen—the first day of the US Festival—we weren't sure. But then it came up.

Bill Graham was supposed to announce what was happening to the giant crowd. But he didn't. I ran across the stage to where Bill was viewing some TV monitors and told him to announce it.

Me and the USSR

Doing the satellite bridge to the Soviet Union at the US Festival led me to devote more than a million dollars over the next ten years to U.S./USSR peace efforts. The idea was personal diplomacy. I tried to get normal people, not officials, from each country to meet each other.

In 1988, on July 4, I sponsored the first big stadium concert in the USSR, just outside Moscow, with major Soviet and U.S. groups on the stage. The U.S. groups included the Doobie Brothers, James Taylor, Santana, and Bonnie Raitt. I found a cheap $25 guitar at a store in Russia, and got all the groups to sign it. I still have it. That concert was at the end of a great peace march there.

For doing things like the first space bridges between the US Festival and the USSR and this concert, I became pretty well known in the USSR. But you know what? The U.S. press didn't care one whit. There was almost no coverage.

In 1990 I sponsored two-week trips for 240 regular people—teachers, for instance—to tour the U.S. and stay in the homes of Rotary Club members here.

So I had done the first three space bridges in the Soviet Union. Somewhere around this time, maybe 1989, ABC put on a national TV show purporting to be the first space bridge ever. I actually paid for the connections of this hookup, but ABC never even mentioned my name and took credit for being first. Actually, they were fourth!

But he was certain that the Soviet signal was a hoax and coming from a studio in Southern California. He said, "No way would the Soviets permit a link like this."

But I knew the truth. So I went to the microphone and announced to the crowd that this was a historic transmission from Russia. There was some booing—remember, they were Cold War Enemy No. 1—but I knew we were making history.

To the USSR, we transmitted Eddie Money. They loved it.

• ○ •

The US Festival was also the first huge concert where anyone got to hear me sing! Have I mentioned I have the voice of an angel? I got up and sang with Jerry Jeff Walker, the singer known for the 1960s song "Mr. Bojangles." The song we sang was "Up Against the Wall Redneck Mother." Good thing they didn't give me a microphone! Walker was actually the only country guy we ended up getting that year. Remember, I originally wanted the whole concert to be country.

I also got to meet some of the other musicians! I was sticking around with my new baby, Jesse; I mostly avoided meeting the celebrities. I did meet Chrissie Hynde of the Pretenders—she had a baby, an infant, with her, too. And I remember how Jackson Browne came up and introduced himself to me. I was nearly tongue-tied—I was pretty intimidated talking to such a great performer.

The main thing for me was the audience.

I remember riding around with my friend Dan Sokol on little scooters and being just blown away by how much fun people were having.

• ○ •

And I was exhausted. I'd been up practically all of the last two nights, because Jesse was being born. He was two weeks early! It was September 1, two days before the concert began, we'd just finished the sound check, and at about 2 a.m. Candi woke up with labor pains. So, yikes, we hadn't made any plans for the delivery, none at all.

I mean, we'd been taking birthing lessons and all that up in Northern California. I called the midwife, and she recommended a natural birthing center over in Culver City, which was more than an hour and a half away. We borrowed one of the cars at the house we were renting and drove to the birthing center. But we didn't tell anyone.

I'm sure that the next morning, the morning before the day of the concert, everyone was wondering where the heck I was. But it wasn't until that afternoon that Jesse was born. He was a beautiful baby.

When Candi and I were discussing what to name the baby, I'd gotten the idea that we might have trouble agreeing on a name. I proposed a simple, conflict-free solution: if it was a boy, I'd name it; and if it was a girl, she'd name it. Candi thought this was fine. So when the baby was born, I named him Jesse, a name I'd already planned. First I'd thought Jesse James, but then I settled on Jesse John.

The name Jesse sounded funny with Wozniak, though. So I decided that if the baby was a boy, I would name him Jesse John Clark. So when the baby came out, I exclaimed loudly, "It's a boy!" But no, it was the umbilical cord I was seeing.

But then it turned out the baby really was a boy, and I simply announced, "Jesse John Clark."

● ○ ●

I was so tired, walking around the concert when it started, and there was a doctor who kept injecting me with something to keep me up—vitamins, he said. But I had to do all these interviews— one with Peter Jennings, for instance, and one with Sting beside me. And they were asking me questions about this enormous crowd, and I just did a horrible job because I was so tired.

But there is a wonderful picture—my favorite picture ever. It's a picture showing the moment when I got up on stage on the first day of the concert with one-day-old Jesse in my arms. I told everyone that this was the birth of something great. I meant Jesse, of course, but also the concert. People went wild, cheering and everything.

I will never forget that moment.

• ○ •

I loved that first US Festival concert, and I knew I'd made so many people happy doing it. We thought from press reports that enough people—nearly half a million—had shown up. So we thought that would make us money. But we lost money, nearly $12 million, because it turned out we didn't sell as many tickets as there were people.

A Big 8 accounting firm we hired explained to me that the reason was that people had been sneaking in. And I believed them.

So I decided to do it again. I said to everyone involved, "Let's do another show. We got such great publicity the first time around. We're hot, it's a sure go." And it was hot. So I thought, This time we'll just have to have supertight controls and make sure everybody has a ticket.

This time, in 1983, we did it over Memorial Day weekend. (We had a country music day the following Saturday.) This time we tried to stick with more of the new-wave music at the time—the alternative stuff. We had the Clash, Men at Work, Oingo Boingo, the Stray Cats, INXS, and a bunch of other bands. That was the first day. And on the second day, we did heavy-metal day.

We did the Soviet satellite link again. We had two more space bridges with the USSR. But we didn't transmit music shows this time. Instead we transmitted groups of us in tents speaking to groups of them, person to person. U.S. astronauts and Soviet cosmonauts were involved, too. It was a very big deal. What struck me emotionally was how similar our values were. Those exchanges dissolved forever in me the effects of a lifetime of propaganda about the Soviet people being our enemies.

• ○ •

But even though we were more careful in counting the tickets this time, we still lost money.

Another $12 million! You know, I was overpaying bands like crazy. I mean, with Van Halen, I paid a million and a half for its one appearance. I later heard that was the single highest amount paid for a band. And David Lee Roth, though he was nice and cordial when I met him, was practically falling down onstage. He was so drunk, slurring and forgetting lyrics and everything.

But this time we had installed very tight controls, collecting ticket stubs and keeping them. We had turnstiles to count everyone who came in. We also had aerial photographers to get an accurate head count. Plus we knew how many tickets we had sold, making sure people didn't slip in like the last time.

But it turned out that the Big 8 accounting firm was full of crock. The problem hadn't been that people were getting in for free. It was that press estimates of attendance were greatly exaggerated. Both times. So we lost the money because not as many people came as we thought. We didn't sell enough tickets to cover costs.

Still, I think of the US Festival as the biggest, hugest success. I'd do it again in a minute, I really would. It was a tremendous experience for me. Everyone had fun! Smiles everywhere. But on the economic side, well, not so hot. I lost a lot of money, and that was a big disappointment.

One of the most memorable moments for me was when concert promoter Bill Graham came up to me near the end of the concert the first year. There was a huge full moon, and Sting and the Police were onstage. And Bill put his arm around me and said, "Look at this, Steve, just look at it. You're not going to see this but once in a decade. This is so rare."

He told me that afterward, everybody was going to be doing these US Festivals because it was so popular, so fun, and so rare.

Later on, he was right in a way, there were all these huge con-

Paranoia?

On my first trip to the USSR, I decided to bring a number of friends with me.

One afternoon my friend Dan Sokol was trying to take a nap, but he was bothered by some Russian music in his room. I guess Dan was too tired to find the little music knob near the door. That's all you needed to turn the in-room music down.

Instead he propped open a ceiling tile near where the sound was coming from. He saw some wires and yanked them hard. They came loose but the music continued. So Dan got up on a chair and found another speaker in the ceiling. He yanked the wire off that one but the sound continued. He probed until he found another speaker, part of an intercom.

Hey, he thought, this is how they listen to you! When he ripped that one out, the sound stopped. Dan took credit for finding the USSR surveillance system. Like they were spying on him. Ha. I laughed because I thought, Well, that's Dan for you, paranoid and into conspiracy theories.

We told this story about the Russian surveillance device to some of our friends who went to the USSR later. The next year, a friend of Jim Valentine's went to St. Petersburg to install some sound equipment in a disco. Thinking of Dan's story, he scoured his room looking for the hidden surveillance device Dan had described. Under the rug he found some lumps. He lifted the rug and saw a brass plate secured by four large screws. He undid the four screws with a screwdriver.

When the last screw came out, a chandelier crashed on the floor below.

Also, around this time I met a girl (I was separated from Candi by this time), a Russian girl—Masha. She was to become a long-distance girlfriend for the next half year. She was an interpreter.

In Russia, my friends would point out several signs that I myself was being "watched." They thought certain Russian officials—car drivers and the like—were KGB agents staying extra close by me at all times.

One time, to get some time alone with Masha, I actually pulled a stunt to ditch the concert in a way that might lose the people who might be tailing me. So instead of leaving the concert in my own Soviet-provided car, I got someone else's driver to take Masha and me back to my hotel, where we had about twenty minutes alone to talk.

The next day, Masha and I toured an art museum at the Kremlin. Inside, she told me matter-of-factly, without even a raised eyebrow, that I was being followed by the KGB. I pooh-poohed this, but Masha pointed to a youngish man in a nice suit standing in the hall we were in. She said, "He's KGB."

She said she could always identify the KGB because she knew a bunch of guys in the KGB school, and she could always spot them by the way they stood and the way they looked. I decided to call Masha's bluff. I said, "You mean, if we backtrack through a couple of halls, he'll follow us?" She said, matter-of-factly and with total confidence, "Yes."

So we went back through a couple of rooms, and we were talking about things and admiring an icon on the wall when I glanced sideways. And there he was. The same guy, across the hall, looking into a glass enclosure.

I lost that bet.

certs: Live Aid, Farm Aid, all of those. They were concerts in stadiums, though, that were all in prebuilt places. Who else in history ever went out and actually built a facility like this, really a pretty good facility to support and maintain that many people?

For them and for me, it was the highlight of my life. Making money, losing money, that's important. But putting on a fine show is most important of all!

Chapter 18

Leaving Apple,
Moving to Cloud Nine

After the US Festivals and graduating from Berkeley, I went back to Apple to work as an engineer again. I didn't want to manage people or be an executive or anything like that. I wanted just to be there and design new circuits and come up with clever ideas and apply them.

But once I got there, it was weird, because I was already in the media mainstream and had so much other stuff to do. A ton of stuff. I was being called by a lot of people—the press, computer groups I had to speak to—and I was working on these philanthropic projects like the San Jose Ballet and a local computer museum. I was sort of splattered all over the world and in all these countries and in all these different areas—beyond just working on circuits.

So I could get the engineering sort of started and come up with an architecture idea. For instance, it could be something that might speed up the processor five times, but the other engineers had to do most of the actual designing of the chips and the connections and the laying out of the printed circuit boards. So truly I felt it wasn't critical for me to be there, even though I loved Apple still.

I was working in the Apple II division. This was after the Apple III project was closed down, so the engineers from that department became Apple II engineers. A lot of them just gravitated around me. It was fun. And there were some cool people with some cool projects starting up in my building at the time. For instance, just as I got there, on the next floor down from me, they were finishing up the Apple II C computer. This was the small Apple II—a really small one—as small as today's laptops except you had to plug it into a wall. I thought it was just a beautiful computer, my favorite one to this day. I really think it was one of the best projects ever done at Apple.

Well, one of the engineers on that project was this guy Joe Ennis. Joe was the kind of guy I love, the kind who's so enthusiastic and passionate about the products he's working on and where they can go and what he could do with them. He had long hair; he was kind of hippie-looking even though it was already 1985. And he had these ideas—all sorts of great ideas about extending the Apple II into areas far beyond anything even the Macintosh people were talking about.

Like he thought you could have an Apple II programmed to be a complete telephone switchboard. (Today, telephone switchboards are just computer cards you plug into a computer.) He imagined you could store voices digitally—that was so ahead of his time—and he thought you could route them out to other channels digitally. He just had idea after idea after idea about the future of computers. I thought his brain and his ideas were just wonderful.

• ○ •

Now, for a while I'd had this really nice home up in the Santa Cruz Mountains with all this really high-end audio and video equipment. By that time TV sets all had remote controls, and VCRs did, too. I also got into laser discs, so I had a remote control for that, too. Then there was this expensive hi-fi system I had from Bang & Olufsen. It also had a remote. That was rare at a time when no other stereos came with remotes.

I was also, at the time, considering getting a satellite TV. This was so rare; you couldn't even buy them in stores. I lucked into mine through a friend, Chuck Colby, who was building custom dishes for people. But, man, there it was. Another remote control.

So typically I would turn on the TV with one remote control and maybe I'd turn on the hi-fi with another (because I had the speakers routed to the TV), and then I would turn on the satellite and then I'd press a few buttons for the channel I wanted on the satellite and I think I had to turn on my VCR to pass a signal through it—all the signals passed through it to get to the TV the way I had it hooked up. I'm pushing all these buttons on different remote controls and it was just obvious to me.

Here I am, sitting in bed, operating all of this equipment with all of these different remote controls. It was crazy. I wanted one remote control with one button that was programmable to deal with all of the devices. I didn't want a button that turned on a TV and another button that turned on the VCR and another button that turned on the satellite and another button that selected the satellite channels and another button that entered that number.

I wanted one remote. Just one. And I wanted that one main button to be able to do multiple things. I wanted to push it and have it go zip, zip, zip, zip, zip and have all the infrared signals come out of one remote control that turned everything on to the status I wanted.

If I wanted to watch a laser disc, it'd turn on the TV, then select input 3 on the TV, and turn on the laser disc player and start playing, for example.

So it was real clear to me that a single remote control solution was necessary. And I knew I was able to see it before most people, because most people in the U.S. at the time didn't have as many different remote controls as I did. Most people would look at me and say, "What do you mean? I only need two remote controls, one for the VCR and one for the TV."

But I realized that soon people would need more remote controls and it would become a problem, like it had already become for me.

I started talking to a few people about this idea and I got excited because I realized how easy it would be to build. This would actually be an easy project. A little microprocessor can look at the codes coming in, store the data, and then output the same codes when you press the buttons.

And I like to be first, as you know. And I thought, I'm the one to do it. And I really did become the first person in the world to do what is now known as a universal remote control.

• ○ •

Let me go a bit deeper and explain exactly what it was that the remote, as I designed it, was doing.

As I said, it was very important for me to make sure this remote didn't have to have one button corresponding to each button on each corresponding remote control. In that case, I would've had a million buttons—all the ones on the TV remote control, plus all the ones on the VCR remote, plus the ones for the satellite TV remote, and so on.

I wanted a *single* button on my control to sequentially emit many infrared codes corresponding to buttons on another remote control—or even countless other remote controls. I didn't want to, as a consumer, have to press five buttons in a row just to turn things on and turn it to my favorite starting channel—in those days, The Movie Channel. I wanted to press one button one time to do all of that.

That meant that the buttons on my control were like macros. One button could represent a whole sequence of things. (In Word, for instance, you could set up a macro on one key so you could just hit that key—say, CTRL+S—to check spelling on your document, accept all changes, and then save the document again.)

I realized that this is exactly like a program. I would have to write a little program for each button. So I came up with the idea not only to let the consumer decide what a button does but also to reprogram the button to redefine what another button does. I built a programming language into the remote, and I went a step further, adding an ability, referred to by the prefix "meta," that would allow a program on a particular button to write an entirely new program for that very button, for itself.

It was a beautiful language, I was proud of it. As it turned out, it wasn't the easiest way to do what the vast majority of users would want, but it would be very attractive to software geeks like me.

• ○ •

I was still at Apple when I got this idea. And I started telling people about it. People like Joe Ennis. As I said, I loved the way his brain worked. He was always interested in unusual uses for technology. And I told him about my remote control idea and we started talking about it all the time. He really got it.

So I pitched real heavily to Joe the whole idea of, "Let's leave Apple and start this company."

I never felt like I was turning my back on my own company. Never. By this point Apple was a large company, and it wasn't and still isn't the love in my life. The love in my life is starting small companies with small groups of friends. Bringing new ideas out and trying to build them. By then the Apple idea wasn't so new.

At the time, I was heading up a new Apple II that was supposed to be better than anything, called the Apple II X. But shortly after we started, upper Apple management canned it.

Looking back, that was probably a decent decision. After all, they were used to products that sold 20,000 a month, and a high-end product like the Apple II X, because it would be so expensive, probably wouldn't sell more than 2,000 a month. So, like I said, they canned it.

Another Apple II product was actually born out of the Apple II

X: the Apple II GS. The joke was that it stood for Granny Smith, a type of apple, but it actually stood for graphics and sound. And that was a great project. With graphics—real graphics in 24-bit color that worked with computer monitors instead of TVs—and sound—real sound, not just chirps—suddenly you could do really interesting things. Like games and software for kids, who really would need that level of production to be engaged.

I was so happy to see that we got a project that all of a sudden brought the Apple II into where it really needed to be. There were some morale problems in my group as a result of the people in the Apple II group feeling undervalued compared with the Macintosh group. (The Mac was in development.)

And I was ready for something new.

Very quickly after I started talking to Joe, and also to my assistant Laura Roebuck, I decided I was going to go ahead and do it—start a company to build the remote control. They both wanted to do it. And I was so lucky to get Laura—she'd just had a baby and wanted to work part-time, and Apple didn't have part-time positions.

Anyway, it was such a simple idea; I really didn't need a bunch more engineers than Joe and me. (Things are different now, of course. A venture capitalist would make you hire twenty right away!) But this was in February of 1985.

• ○ •

The first thing I did was to call my boss's boss, Wayne Rosing in the Apple II division, and tell him I was leaving to start a remote control company. You know, I had a job and had to tell someone, "I'm leaving. I'm leaving to start a company."

I didn't call Steve or Mike Markkula or anyone on the board. I had a job in engineering, and I felt like I just had to tell someone I reported to so they would know.

I sat them down and sketched out my idea and described it just like I've described it to you. I told them I was doing a remote control that would be a single remote control that would work with all of the consumer electronics someone had. It was going to be one remote with one button, very simple. It would not compete with anything Apple did.

They gave me a release very quickly, saying they'd seen my design and there was nothing competitive about it. The letter also wished me well.

I left within about a week, but I did stay on the payroll as an Apple employee. I am to this day. I just have the absolute lowest salary a full-time employee can have. I still represent Apple at computer clubs this way.

Steve probably heard I was leaving the same day almost everyone in the world heard it—instantly—the day a piece came out in the *Wall Street Journal*. But the piece got it all wrong.

The reporter called me the very day I was leaving, the day I was packing up, and said, "I understand you're starting a new company?" So the rumor was out. I told him yeah, and he asked me what it was all about. And I told him.

He asked me, "Are there any things that you aren't happy about at Apple?" And I told him the truth. I told him yes, and then I stood up for the people I was working with who were offended by the lack of respect they received.

At the time I was leaving, the people in the Apple II group were being treated as very unimportant by the rest of the company. This despite the fact that the Apple II was by far the largest-selling product in our company for ages, and would be for years to come. It had only just recently been overtaken as number one in the world by the IBM PC, which had connections in the business world that we didn't have.

If you worked in the Apple II division, you couldn't get the money you needed or the parts you needed in the same way you could if you worked in, say, the new Macintosh division. I thought that wasn't fair.

It boiled down to certain kinds of expenses, what kinds of components you were allowed to buy from other companies, how much money you were allocated to work on projects, despite having such a hugely successful computer in the world. Like I said, a lot of things were being trimmed way down.

Also, there were limitations on the Apple II in terms of taking advantage of new advances in technology. We'd hear, "No, Apple II will stay the Apple II, and we're not going to let it move into newer, more advanced areas." Things like that.

So I made some comments like this, and then the reporter asked, "So that's the reason you're leaving?"

And I said, point-blank, "Oh no, that's not the reason. I'm leaving because I want to do this remote control."

But the *Wall Street Journal* printed the article suggesting I was mad at Apple and that was the reason I was leaving. It was wrong, very wrong, because I went out of my way to tell the reporter not to get it confused. Maybe it was more interesting to shape the story the way they did. They just left out a couple of words, the words "That's not why I'm leaving," and that was the same as implying that that was the reason I was leaving.

Oh my god. I have to think it was an accident, but let me tell you. It's been picked up by every book and every bit of history ever since. It's just wrong. I mean, they asked specifically, "Is that the reason you're leaving?" And I went out of my way to say "No." But it didn't make it into print like that. Everyone in the world ended up thinking I left because I was mad at Apple or something.

The only reason I left my day-to-day-job at Apple is that I was enthusiastic about the idea of doing this new neat project that had never been done before. I saw that remote controls were going to be more important in people's lives as satellite TVs and other devices came in. Remember, there was no store you could go down to yet to buy a satellite TV. You had to be in a select group of people to know how to even buy a home-built receiver for that.

If I hadn't had the remote control idea, I would have stayed right where I was. But this was such a cool idea. And we got moving pretty quickly.

● ○ ●

Our first thoughts were where to locate. I lived on Summit Road in the Santa Cruz Mountains. Up there at the Summit were two restaurants, the Summit Inn and the Cloud 9. I knew that the Cloud 9 was closing, so I suggested it as a site. How cool would that be?

Joe Ennis picked up on the name Cloud 9, too. We had the lawyers who incorporated us check it out, and they found that Cloud 9 was taken. I can't remember which of us came up with CL 9. It may have been that I saw it on a license plate, but it's hard to remember. At any rate, we settled on CL 9, which was still a great name.

Maybe two weeks after that, we got an office in this older part of Los Gatos, the town where I lived. It was right up against the Santa Cruz Mountains on the last little corner with a few shopping places. The space was small—maybe around 900 square feet—and it was right above a Swensen's ice cream place. And that's where Joe, Laura, and I moved in.

It was great. It felt just like the early Apple days, so exciting. We were building something no one else had thought of yet. Who had ever thought of playing your remote control into a device that would learn its code? That had never happened. I mean, today it's more obvious because we have universal remotes and things, but not back then.

The first thing we did was to start meeting with representatives of components that might apply: infrared sensors; infrared transmitters; microprocessors. We started looking over the data sheets and the books and figuring out what microprocessor we'd use. We started making some choices and got together an idea that was more in our heads than on paper, but it wasn't like a finished design you could actually breadboard and wire together and build something from. This process was exactly like what I did with the Apple II.

There were a couple of areas that were tougher. One problem we had to tackle was how do you receive infrared signals in the remote? We didn't have that much expertise in this area. I didn't, and Joe wasn't so sound on how you build a sensor for infrared. So we actually hired a consulting firm in Sunnyvale to help us basically read an infrared signal. If you placed your own remote control right next to our receiver, the signal coming out of yours was a very strong signal.

In the same way that the closer you get to a lightbulb the brighter it is, so it is with a remote control. The consultants designed an intricate circuit with an awful lot of parts and filters. And I said, "If you're close and it's powerful, then why can't you just detect it with a lot simpler circuitry?" Just go straight to a photo transistor. You know me. I like to do things with the simplest possible circuitry. You don't need all these special amplifiers that need power all the time. Just go straight to the photo transistor, which is a transistor that senses light instead of electronic signals.

And that idea actually worked out.

They had to put in a couple of little parts and capacitors to filter it just right to avoid the signal bouncing around in a weird way. And they came up with a very good circuit that worked reliably. You could play your remote control into our little receiver device and it would capture the signal very accurately. It could determine how many microseconds the infrared signal was on and how many it was off.

Then it could trace the signal and make a time recording of it, the signal from your remote control.

• ○ •

The time also came for us to come up with a plastics design for the remote. Very early, just after we moved into the second building on Alberto Way, we started going around to a few design companies to see if they would show us some samples, or some ideas we could look at.

One of those companies was Frog Design, which had done the Macintosh. We called them up and they said, "Sure, we do third-party development for people other than Apple."

They said they'd take anyone who walked in the door and talk to them, design for them. We told them what we wanted, and they did it up in a few models. A couple of them were a little too fancy-looking for my taste. I wanted the most normal-looking design, just totally straightforward, where every button is sort of square, a real symmetrical design.

I wanted it to look like an everyperson product, not something that looks like it's from outer space, you know what I mean. And we liked some of the other products they came up with to fit that description.

But in the end, they dropped us.

It turned out Steve Jobs was over at Frog for some reason and saw a CL 9 prototype. From what I heard, he threw it against a wall and put it in a box and said, "Send it to him." As if Apple owned it. The Frog guy told me that Steve told him they couldn't do any work for us because Apple "owned" Frog. Not true, and everyone knew it. But Frog told us they felt uncomfortable doing it without Apple's permission—Apple was a big customer—so they weren't going to do it.

Well, I wasn't going to argue. I don't truly know what the real story was, but I thought, Good, fine. We'll go somewhere else. And we did go somewhere else.

● ○ ●

Of course, I had to choose a microprocessor for the device. I ended up choosing two processors. So the remote later went down in history as the first remote control with a dual processor!

Anyway, thinking about the two microprocessors and working

with Joe, I decided it might be nice to have one microprocessor for small tasks like reading the keyboard and keeping time, and another to do the heavy-duty work. The larger processor I used was an updated version of the old MOS 6502 I'd used for the Apple I. The other was a smaller, cheaper processor. I think we paid 50 cents apiece for it in quantity. It was a 4-bit processor—meaning, remember, it could process only 4 bits of data at a time. That was all we needed for these smaller tasks.

However, a little processor like that is hard to write a program for. Man, was it hard to control. It was almost as hard as programming the state machine in the floppy disk. Nothing was built into the hardware, and when you don't have the hardware resources, you have to take advantage of what you do have inside the chip. And you wind up with weird instructions that do things in weird ways. That's because the chip didn't already have built into it well-thought-out instructions a human could easily understand and use. That was to keep the cost to a minimum.

But the program on the 4-bit microprocessor wound up doing two basic things: keeping the time of day, monitoring the keyboard, running the LCD display, and enabling power to some of the rest of the circuit, and it also communicated with the bigger, 8-bit microprocessor, telling it what keys had been pressed and receiving data to display on the screen.

We sat down and sketched out on paper where we wanted the lines of letters, numbers, and a few special words to pop up on our LCD. And we found a company that would make us an LCD. We gave them our layouts, and they eventually brought us back LCDs with a bunch of connection pins. And that LCD would actually connect to the same 4-bit microprocessor chip that was reading the keyboard.

Now, the real guts of our product—memorizing all these different infrared codes and repeating them when you pressed buttons—was going to be done by the second, more powerful microprocessor. Because of the updated version of the 6502, I thought, Great. I am so familiar with this! It had a very beautiful architecture inside. The way it was structured to be, with very few transistors inside doing a lot of work, it was just so good and it did the right job.

The Apple II had my little development system that I wrote myself, and I could type instructions in quickly and test them out. What if I could have that for this microprocessor? So we actually designed our board in such a way that you would be able to hook up through a serial port so that we could connect a terminal or computer directly to it. That would enable you to type and see data on the screen, although the remote control was really the computer. (It was like a little cousin of the Apple II.)

What terminal? Well, I decided the Apple II C would be a great terminal. There were programs that could make it behave like a terminal that talked to other computers.

Remember how I told you that in the Apple II I had added this mini-assembler that let me type in things like LDA for loading the A register, or #35, which meant 00110101, the binary language of 1s and 0s that computers can understand? That program and many other development tools were built into the Apple II, but would really be useful in the remote control as well.

I had a friend I'd worked with at Apple, John Arkley. He was a consultant, and he offered to convert the debugging and other code I'd written for this new 6502 microprocessor. We paid him and he did it.

And it was great. I would hook a little Apple II C into our breadboard—our wired prototypes—and type away and do the debugging. It's like I had a new little Apple II inside of the remote control. It had all the fun of an Apple II.

And when we finished designing it, this product was great. We were all just blown away by how great these tools turned out.

So then we had a manufacturing issue. Who was going to manufacture the device? And suddenly an old friend of mine showed up from my childhood days with the Electronics Kids. Remember my neighbor Bill Werner? He was the one who did all the toilet-papering of the houses with me and got all that phone cord to create the house-to-house intercom system in our neighborhood.

By high school, though, Bill had kind of gone in a bad direction. Not like me. He got bad grades, got a motorcycle, got in trouble for burglarizing an electronics store, got into some bad stuff. But now he'd turned his life around, and we ended up hiring him—he had worked at the Silicon Valley manufacturing firm Selectron. And we hired his wife, Penny, too, to do some secretarial work. So our team was building.

Selectron was the kind of company we needed. It did manufacturing, like I said, and that was the one thing we had left—figuring out how to build this device in mass quantities.

• ○ •

Meanwhile I got a call one day from a venture capitalist in England. You see, years before, in the early days of Apple before we went public, he'd called me up and offered to buy some of my stock at a low price, and I'd said yes. But he hadn't bought it.

Well, he called at a slightly later date and asked again if I would sell him the Apple stock at that price. I'm not sure what the offer was, but it was low. By this time Apple stock was easily worth ten times whatever he was offering, even though it wasn't yet public. He said, "You promised to sell me some at this price. Will you?"

So I kept my word. His venture capital company made a ton of money on the London market, a ton of money.

Now, at CL 9, I told him all about this new company I was starting, and he said, "Can I visit you?" I told him sure. He showed up. I remember thinking, Man, this guy is really staid. Just very formal—so reserved in his language and manner. He was English, okay. I guess he was stuffy compared to us, and you can imagine how loose we were.

Anyway, I described to him what we were doing, and he immediately said he wanted to invest. I told him I wasn't taking any money, that I was financing it all. But he actually begged me.

Well, when people beg me and say they want to be a part of something, I always give in.

After his investment came in, I suddenly had another big investment from the big Silicon Valley venture firm New Enterprise Associates (NEA), which had also done 3Com, Adaptec, and Silicon Graphics. This guy from England had brought his friends in, you see. So all of a sudden we had two or three million dollars.

So we pulled that off in a few months, and we began to realize we were going to need a bigger place to set up shop. I called an old friend of mine from Commodore, Sam Bernstein, a guy who'd written articles for newspapers. He was sort of a reporter. And I always liked the way he thought and the way he organized his thinking. So I asked him to come on board—this was early on—as president. We got along splendidly.

● ○ ●

We ended up keeping CL 9 in business for about three years, maybe a little more. There are still people out there who talk about how amazing our product was. I don't regret doing it for a second. I ended up selling the company to someone, but they couldn't raise money and closed it down.

But at the time, I had other challenges to think about. I had two small children at home (Jesse and Sara). So it was hard making sure I had enough time to devote to them.

I mean, after the 4-bit microprocessor project was done, it was time to do the 8-bit. And I set out to do it and was just having a lot of difficulty getting started on that job. I had my kids I was giving a lot of attention to. And my relationship with Candi was starting to get rocky. We were fighting. We weren't getting along at all. We had fights about how to raise the children, especially. And we were talking separation.

Well, I had an idea to just take off and hang out in a hotel room somewhere beautiful for a week. I planned to just disappear from the world and go to Hawaii and write the code.

So I went to Hawaii, the Hyatt on Kaanapali Beach, and I set up my little Apple II C so I could start typing the new program in. (Someone was watching the kids.) I thought solitude would help me finish the project. At least I hoped so.

But what happened was, I didn't do a single thing that entire week. I literally sat there looking out my window and watching whales every day; I got used to the hotel schedule. I swear, about ten times a day somebody would come into the room to restock the minibar, change the sheets and towels, check this, check that. All day there were these major interruptions. I hated that.

So after that week of doing nothing, I thought I should stay another week. I found out I could keep that same room that I loved for another week.

Well, guess what? I wound up staying there for four weeks and not doing one single bit of code. I did nothing there, absolutely nothing. I just enjoyed being there. While I was there the *Challenger* space shuttle disaster happened—it was January 28, 1986—and that was really extremely upsetting to me. But whatever the reason, I did nothing.

At first I thought this was okay. Many times in the past, as I've described to you, my head is thinking about a problem ahead—it's all in my head—and by the time I sit down to write things down, the code, I can write it really quickly and productively. I can do a lot in a short time because I've figured it all out beforehand. So I expected that to happen and it didn't.

It was then that I thought, You know what? There are a lot of engineers in the world and I've got kids. I think I'd rather just hire somebody to do this part of the code. It was like I had sort of reached my limit of being able to mentally—with the 4-bit microprocessor—put myself through this kind of design effort.

So we hired another programmer to do that job on the 8-bit microprocessor. I wanted to spend more time with my children.

I stayed at CL 9 for another year, but that was really when my life changed once again.

Giving It Away

I didn't start Apple so that I would get more money than I would ever need to live on. I never planned in my life to seek great wealth. And I'd always been inspired by stories of those who gave in order to do good things in life.

So I felt this was the right thing to do. And it felt good. I was around people on the boards of the museums and the ballet who were more inclined to social activity. They were less about humor and jokes, less than I was, anyway. But they were good people who believed in what they were doing, and I believed in them.

The first project I funded was the Children's Discovery Museum of San Jose. I funded it entirely for many years, eventually to the tune of a few million.

Then I helped start The Tech of Silicon Valley, a computer museum. I also did the initial financing for the San Jose Cleveland Ballet, now known as the Ballet of Silicon Valley. Why ballet? Again, it was the people. They were great and I had confidence in them.

I also contributed to an expansion of the Center for the Performing Arts in San Jose, which benefited both the ballet and the orchestra. This was a donation that would directly benefit the city of San Jose. How neat to donate to a city.

And though I didn't expect it, in 1988 San Jose's mayor, Tom McEnery, called me to say they were going to name a street after me! In fact, it would be the same street the Children's Discovery Museum would be on. The name of the street is Woz

Way. And it's one of the proudest things in my life—to have a street named after me! Not a dumb name, but a cool name. It would be a bummer to have a dumb-sounding street named after you.

Chapter 19

The Mad Hatter

I think there's a time in everyone's life when you look back and ask yourself, What else could I have been? What else could I have done? With me there's just no question about the answer, none at all.

If I couldn't have been an engineer, I would've been a teacher. Not a high school teacher, not a college teacher. A fifth-grade teacher. I specifically wanted to be a fifth-grade teacher ever since I was in fifth grade.

This was something I wanted to do since so early in life. Who knows where these things come from? Probably because my fourth- and fifth-grade teacher, Miss Skrak, was so good to me and I liked her so much. I felt she had helped me so much in life by encouraging me. And I believed, truly believed, that education was important.

I remember my father telling me way back then that it was education that would lift me up to where I wanted to go in life, that it could lift people up in values. I remember how he said that the world was kind of screwed up at the time—there was the Cold War between the USSR and the United States and all that. And he said that with education, the newer generation could learn from the mistakes of their parents and do a better job.

I felt these were really mighty goals in life: looking consciously at the sort of person you want to be, the sort of life you want to live, the sort of society you want to help build.

But by the time I was in high school and college, I'd kind of forgotten about my goals of working in education. There were times when it glimmered back at me. This girl at Berkeley, Holly, the first girl I kissed, well, a relative of her roommate brought round to our dorm a baby, four months old. And Holly, who was interested in child psychology, started doing all kinds of little games with the baby, trying to test where the baby was in its own head. Like she'd move a pencil and see if the baby's eyes would follow it, that sort of thing. I remember how that just struck me that day, this notion of cognitive development. How shocking it was to me to suddenly realize that the mind really develops in identifiable stages. Almost like logic in a computer, it's predictable. It was like logic, the thing I was into at the time, an intriguing kind of process—a game with rules.

That made me really remember my desire to be a teacher, and for the rest of my life I was always paying a lot of attention to children wherever I went. Infants, babies, younger children, older children. I'd try to relate to them, to smile, to tell them jokes, to be kind of part of their company. I'd been brought up with the idea that there were "bad people" who might hurt children or kidnap them, so I decided I would be a "good guy" any kid who met me could rely on.

• ○ •

Some people just love being around children, others don't as much. I remember one summer when I was working at HP, Steve Jobs told me he really needed a job for some extra money. I drove him down to see the job listings over at De Anza Community College, and we found this job listing for people to stand in Westgate Mall for a week dressed in *Alice in Wonderland* costumes. They needed an Alice, a White Rabbit, and a Mad Hatter. I was so intrigued. I drove Steve down to the guy who was interviewing people and telling them what it was like. Basically you put on these costumes, he said, and carry some helium balloons and you stand around. You can't talk to the children, but they'll all be around looking at you, he said.

"Can I do it, too?" I asked. I loved the idea. So basically, they hired Steve, his girlfriend Chris Ann, and me as the *Alice in Wonderland* characters. We took turns in the costumes with some other people because, even after a twenty-minute stretch, these costumes got terribly hot and sweaty inside. You could hardly breathe. So sometimes I would be the White Rabbit and Steve would be the Mad Hatter, and sometimes it would be the other way around.

It was kind of funny because you had really limited mobility in those big costumes. I remember I went out as the Mad Hatter once, and all of a sudden about ten kids started grabbing me by my arms and my sleeves and spinning me around. For fun. They were laughing! And I couldn't say anything to stop them, because there were a lot of kids doing it and I wasn't allowed to talk. They could have toppled me! I was lucky they didn't.

I thought this job was so fun I even cut back my engineering hours and took an hourly minimum wage for that week so I could spend more time doing it. I loved looking at the kids' faces when they saw us. I just loved it.

We'd take lunch breaks in our regular clothes and eat at this little restaurant in the mall. One day this little kid—this tiny little kid—points at my tennis shoes and says, "Hey, he's the Mad Hatter!" I told him, "Hey, be quiet!" Ha. That was a very fun week. So fun.

But Steve didn't enjoy it as much as I did. I remember years and years later, I was commenting to him how much fun that *Alice in Wonderland* mall job was, and he said, "No, it was lousy. We hardly got paid anything for it." So he had bad memories of it, but

I just had the best memories of it. I guess I thought everyone was like me and would like doing something like that with kids.

● ○ ●

I loved being a parent, too. It was great. I didn't read books on parenting; I didn't want to read about any structured rules. I wanted to relate to and communicate with the child. Because if you can talk to them, then they'll talk to you about most of the things in their life. I wanted to expose them to creative thinking, I wanted to show them that you don't have to narrow and restrict your thinking the way so many people do. I never once tried to impress even my own values in life on any one of my kids.

I wanted to be like my dad. I remember his conversations with me; he would always point out all sides of an issue. I would know what he thought about it, but he would let me come to my own decisions, which very often turned out to be like his. He was a very, very good teacher. So I intended to be that way, too.

Candi and I had three children. The first was Jesse, who was born the night before the US Festival that Labor Day weekend in 1982. Then Sara came two years later. And Gary was born in 1987, after Candi and I had already divorced. So that was hard.

● ○ ●

With Jesse, when he just a few months old I had the most fun with him doing what I called these "flying tours." I would hold him so that his belly was over my palm and he could see everything from the correct perspective. (I got the idea from Candi's brother, Peter Clark, who told me that if you hold a baby on its back, it's always seeing everything differently than grown-ups do.) But the other way, the baby could see the world like we do. It was just logical.

So I used to hold baby Jesse that way, and all of a sudden I could see his eyes would look to the left or the right a little. Then his head would move in one direction and stay there, and I'd realize, Oh, okay, he's looking at the window shade. So what I did was

I'd take him over to it. It was only fair. I'd let him touch it—I'd move his hands against it—and when he was done, he'd turn his head again, like maybe back toward his mom, and we'd zoom back to her.

So we started getting in the habit of doing this. He'd be lying on my palm, looking at the big TV, and I'd take him to it. Or to the shelf, which had a top and an edge he could feel. So he started getting around the world this way, and he'd always come back to home base at the end.

Jesse got more and more confident. We'd start from home base and then go room by room through the entire house. He'd explore. I could feel his muscles tense in a certain way I could interpret as "Lift me up a little more" or "Let's go a little lower." Sometimes, when he got a little bigger, he would wave his arms and his feet like he was a mad swimmer, and that meant "Go as fast as you can." So we had this great form of communication between us, and this was all before he was even eight months old. I was no longer just looking at the movements his head made; I'd feel his muscles tensing to tell me which way to go. I used to tell people this, and they didn't believe me. So I'd tell them, "Okay, I'll close my eyes. Drop something." And then Jesse would just tense his muscles and lead me right down to it. It really surprised people.

I would try this with other babies—these flying tours—and I found out that after about twenty minutes, I could do it with them, too. All babies were the same! All babies gave the same muscle signals. I loved that I had figured out a way to let Jesse choose what to explore, before he could even crawl or walk, without having to be totally dependent on someone else.

When Jesse got bigger and too heavy for the flying tours, I got into these little Honda scooters. I had the little 80 and 120 cubic centimeter scooters. They're real small, like a bike with a little motor in it.

Up there in the Santa Cruz Mountains where we lived, there were a lot of little windy roads and very few cars. So I could put Jesse on the scooter and we could just go everywhere. I'd let him decide if we would go left or right, and I'd describe things we saw and then let him touch them—we'd say the words "leaf," or "water," or "tree." He chose every single turn we made. Eventually—over a period of a couple of years—he could get into his favorite routes. I remember these as such wonderful, wonderful days.

● ○ ●

By 1988 I was a full-time dad. I was finished with CL 9. By then we had also had our second child, a girl this time, Sara. Sara and Candi became really bonded, as bonded as Jesse and I were.

But Candi and I still weren't getting along. By this time we were already heading for divorce. A critical point happened the night after a concert at the Shoreline Amphitheater. We had a tradition with Jesse that the front passenger seat was the "story seat" and whoever got to sit there would get a story I would make up from the driver's seat. Now, I'm not a writer, and don't ask me how I did it, but I could come up with the most amazing stories. Science fiction stories, usually, and they would go on and on.

But one night Candi and I got into this fight. She felt like she'd drunk too much to drive, and she wanted me to drive. That was fine with me. But she wanted to sit in the story seat, the front passenger seat. Jesse objected, because he wanted to hear a story. And I begged him, begged him, to please sit in the back and I would still tell a story. But he wouldn't get in the backseat. And Candi and I got in the hugest fight because of that. Very shortly after that, it was divorce time.

● ○ ●

So now, suddenly, I was in a new house of my own in Los Gatos. The kids spent one week at my house and one week with Candi. I didn't have any business going on, CL 9 wasn't going on, so I could focus all my energy on the kids.

It was at about this time that I redirected my philanthropic activities from museums and ballet to schools in Los Gatos. This was about 1989, and computers in schools were starting to become the big talked-about thing. There were going to be computer "haves" and computer "have-nots." So I started providing computers to schools—setting up computer labs with dozens of computers in them as gifts to the schools and the kids.

Eventually I worked out a deal with my local elementary school, the one that Jesse was by then attending. It was the Lexington Elementary School in the Santa Cruz Mountains. It sure was an unusual environment for a school. Not like the ones that are all flat and spread out. It looked rustic, out in the middle of nature with the mountains, the trees, and the Lexington Reservoir nearby. This school was also neat because it only had one classroom for every grade. It was a small school.

So I got to know a lot of people there, especially the school moms, who really are the ones who do so much of the stuff. I couldn't really bring myself to do the home school club—that was the PTA-style group they had—I couldn't make the time. But with the computers, I thought I could make myself useful to the kids and the school in other ways.

Around this same time, I started teaching Jesse about computers. He was in the fourth grade by this time. He would go into his room—he had his own computer with a keyboard—and he was this little kid sitting in front of it. He would just type away all day long. At first he couldn't type very well. He would hunt and peck. But very quickly he learned how to cut and paste text from one page to another so he wouldn't have to retype it.

By the end of fourth grade, his computer skills had evolved so quickly. Sometime during that year, he was actually answering questions I had—like if I was having trouble finding out where something was in the system, he would tell me what menu to look in. I showed him how to do spreadsheets and do calculations so he could do his math homework from school with it. He could set it up and do it all on the spreadsheet so the teachers wouldn't see the formula, just the answer. But, of course, I told him he had to do it by hand first, before doing it on the computer. He had to have one handwritten one done, to show me he knew how to do it, and then he would turn in these really nice printouts.

Believe me, there was no other kid in fourth grade who was turning in a spreadsheet and printout for his math homework assignments.

And Jesse just loved doing it. He always stuck by the rule of having to do the homework the real way first—before you do it on the computer. But he loved any homework he could do with his computer. Like typing reports. He loved that.

That year, one of Jesse's schoolmates, Elena, was having trouble in school. I'd known her since she was born. Her mom called and told me that her grades were going down; she wasn't achieving, just having a really hard time. I cared a lot about Elena. So I decided I would go over to her house and we would sit down together. I would take her through ideas to put in reports she would write. We would try to put in comedy—just to make it fun for her. And I'd show her how you do it on the computer.

That became her motivation, doing it on the computer. It was something special, and she really got into it. All her grades in school started going up. Her parents gave me all this credit. She loved doing any homework she could do on the computer; she was a smiling girl and doing well in school. She grew into a woman who is today an incredibly great speaker as well as an actress.

So then I started thinking. If this was so successful with Elena—taking her from basically flunking out of school to A's and B's—what if I could do that with other kids? Why not give it a try? But I was a little scared. Can I teach a group of kids? What's involved? I really did want to teach them normal things—math, reading, writing, history—but how was I going to be able to do that? I don't have a teaching credential or anything.

So I thought, That's it. I'm going to be a teacher. I'll teach a computer class. The next year was the fifth grade. I took six kids out of Jesse's fifth-grade class and put them in computer class. And we started out the class by unscrewing the computers to look at the parts, and I taught them Base 2—1s and 0s, how numbers were represented in computer language. We didn't carry the Base 2 stuff very far throughout the year; I thought I was going to teach them how computers work. It's something easy for a fifth grader to learn; you don't need higher-level math. And we did that.

But the primary goal was to teach them how to make their homework look good. The state of computers back then was such that this only got about one-third of class time attention. Back then, computers were more unreliable, and more subject to software and hardware bugs. On any given day, a hard disk might stop working. Or a battery might go bad. A buggy program might corrupt some files.

Back then, maintaining a computer was a difficult task. So another third of the class involved maintaining the computers. Installing new software and hardware, identifying hardware problems, identifying and fixing software problems of all types. Finally we spent a lot of time on online and network things. Every single year, from the very first class on, I bought AOL accounts for all the students.

It was important that they learn to communicate with people far away, and in a way that had never been done before. The two things my students did the most were to download fun software like games and freeware utilities and visit chat rooms. I encouraged them to go as far as they could in chat rooms. They found it amusing to pretend to be other people, to pretend to be older than they were. Even though it might take them two minutes to type a short sentence, the girls would claim to be nineteen years old. The boys were always honest.

Some of the girls would get too excited and scream to the rest of their class that they were making a date with another nineteen-year-old! Yeah, right. The thing I always noticed was that the other "nineteen-year-old" was also typing a sentence every two minutes. None of them could type when they started my class, but they sure started learning.

And the things I learned in my ten years as a teacher, well, they're just too numerous to count. I felt this was the most important time in my life.

Chapter 20

Rules to Live By

Maybe you're wondering why I haven't written a memoir before this. People kept asking me to. There are a lot of reasons I didn't. I was busy—too busy. A couple of times I even tried to start working on it, but my plans always fell through. I just didn't have the time.

This time is different. At this point in my life—I'm fifty-five as I write this—I think it's time to set the record straight. So much of the information out there about me is wrong. I've come to hate books about Apple and its history so much because of that. For instance, there are stories that I dropped out of college (I didn't) or that I was thrown out of the University of Colorado (I wasn't), that Steve and I were high school classmates (we were several years apart in school) and that Steve and I engineered those first computers together (I did them alone).

Of course I understand that inaccuracies and rumors happen when you're in the public eye. And I even have a good insider's perspective as to how they happen. A perfect example of this, which I mentioned before, is when I was leaving Apple to start CL 9, my remote control company, in the late 1980s. The *Wall Street Journal* reporter called me and asked me directly if I was leaving because I was unhappy at Apple, and I told him directly that, no, I wasn't leaving because I was unhappy at Apple. Though I mentioned there were a few problems with morale in my view, I explicitly told him the only reason I was leaving was that I wanted to start a new company. Not because of any problems. And in fact, technically, I wasn't leaving at all.

To this day, I'm an Apple employee—I still have my Apple Employee ID card—and I receive a very low salary. And I continue to represent Apple at events and at speeches.

But the article the paper printed was wrong in two key places: It said I left Apple, and it said I left because I was disgruntled. Both untrue!

But you know what? Both errors went down as history. I mean, pick up almost any book on Apple's history and you'll probably read that wrong version of my story. Everything else major newspapers or early books got wrong about me went down as history, too.

So that's what's been bothering me—the fact that no one has gotten the story straight about how I built the first computers at Apple and how I designed them, and what happened afterward. So I hope this book sets the record straight, finally.

And there's another reason I've written this book, though I didn't realize it until I was well into it. I'd like to give advice, for what it's worth, to kids out there who are like I was. Kids who feel they're outside the norm. Kids who feel it in themselves to design things, invent things, engineer things. Change the way people do things.

I've learned a lot of lessons over the years, and not all of them involved how to handle ex-wives. Ha. In fact, none of them did.

No, my advice has to do with what you do when you find yourself sitting there with ideas in your head and a desire to build them. But you're young. You have no money. All you have is the stuff in your brain. And you think it's good stuff, those ideas you have in your brain. Those ideas are what drive you, they're all you think about.

But there's a big difference between just thinking about inventing something and doing it. So how do you do it? How do you actually set about changing the world?

• ○ •

Well, first you need to believe in yourself. Don't waver. There will be people—and I'm talking about the vast majority of people, practically everybody you'll ever meet—who just think in black-and-white terms. Most people see things the way the media sees them or the way their friends see them, and they think if they're right, everyone else is wrong. So a new idea—a revolutionary new product or product feature—won't be understandable to most people because they see things so black and white. Maybe they don't get it because they can't imagine it, or maybe they don't get it because someone else has already told them what's useful or good, and what they heard doesn't include your idea.

Don't let these people bring you down. Remember that they're just taking the point of view that matches whatever the popular cultural view of the moment is. They only know what they're exposed to. It's a type of prejudice, actually, a type of prejudice that is absolutely against the spirit of invention.

But the world isn't black and white. It's gray scale. *As an inventor, you have to see things in gray scale.* You need to be open. You can't follow the crowd. Forget the crowd. And you need the kind of objectivity that makes you forget everything you've heard, clear the table, and do a factual study like a scientist would. You don't want to jump to conclusions, take a position too quickly, and then search for as much material as you can to support your side. Who wants to waste time supporting a bad idea? It's not worth it, that way of being stuck in your ego. You don't want to just come up with any excuse to support your way.

Engineers have an easier time than most people seeing and accepting the gray-scale nature of the world. That's because they already live in a gray-scale world, knowing what it is to have a hunch or a vision about what can be, even though it doesn't exist yet. Plus, they're able to calculate solutions that have partial values—in between all and none.

The only way to come up with something new—something world-changing—is to think outside of the constraints everyone else has. You have to think outside of the artificial limits everyone else has already set. You have to live in the gray-scale world, not the black-and-white one, if you're going to come up with something no one has thought of before.

● ○ ●

Most inventors and engineers I've met are like me—they're shy and they live in their heads. They're almost like artists. In fact, the very best of them *are* artists. *And artists work best alone*—best outside of corporate environments, best where they can control an invention's design without a lot of other people designing it for marketing or some other committee. I don't believe anything really revolutionary has ever been invented by committee. Because the committee would never agree on it!

Why do I say engineers are like artists? Engineers often strive to do things more perfectly than even they think is possible. Every tiny part or line of code has to have a reason, and the approach has to be direct, short, and fast. We build small software and hardware components and group them into larger ones. We know how to route electrons through resistors and transistors to make logic gates. We combine a few gates to make a register. We combine many registers to make an even larger one. We combine logic gates to make adders, and we combine adders to create others that can be used to create an entire computer. We write tiny bits of code to turn things on and off. We build upon and build upon and build upon, just like a painter would with colors on a paintbrush or a composer would with musical notes. And it's this reach for perfection—this striving to put everything together so perfectly, in a way no one has done before—that makes an engineer or anyone else a true artist.

Most people don't think of an engineer as an artist, probably, because people tend to associate engineers just with the things we create. But those things wouldn't work, they wouldn't be elegant or beautiful or anything else, without the engineer carefully thinking it out—thinking how to create the best possible end result with the fewest number of components. That's sophistication.

In my entire life I've only seen about one in twenty engineers who really exemplify that artistic perfection. So it's pretty rare to make your engineering an art, but that's how it should be.

I was very touched recently by a scene in the movie *Walk the Line*. In it, a producer tells Johnny Cash to play a song the way he would if that one song could save the whole world.

That line summed up a lot of what I look for when I talk about art in engineering or in anything.

● ○ ●

If you're that rare engineer who's an inventor and also an artist, I'm going to give you some advice that might be hard to take. That advice is: *Work alone.*

When you're working for a large, structured company, there's much less leeway to turn clever ideas into revolutionary new products or product features by yourself. Money is, unfortunately, a god in our society, and those who finance your efforts are businesspeople with lots of experience at organizing contracts that define who owns what and what you can do on your own.

But you probably have little business experience, know-how, or acumen, and it'll be hard to protect your work or deal with all that corporate nonsense. I mean, those who provide the funding and tools and environment are often perceived as taking the credit for inventions. If you're a young inventor who wants to change the world, a corporate environment is the wrong place for you.

You're going to be best able to design revolutionary products and features if you're working on your own. Not on a committee. Not on a team. That means you're probably going to have to do what I did. Do your projects as moonlighting, with limited money and limited resources. But man, it'll be worth it in the end. It'll be worth it if this is really, truly what you want to do—invent things. If you want to invent things that can change the world, and not just work at a corporation working on other people's inventions, you're going to have to work on your own projects.

When you're working as your own boss, making decisions about what you're going to build and how you're going to go about it, making trade-offs as to features and qualities, it becomes a part of you. Like a child you love and want to support. You have huge motivation to create the best possible inventions—and you care about them with a passion you could never feel about an invention someone else ordered you to come up with.

And if you don't enjoy working on stuff for yourself—with your own money and your own resources, after work if you have to—then you definitely shouldn't be doing it!

• ○ •

It's so easy to doubt yourself, and it's especially easy to doubt yourself when what you're working on is at odds with everyone else in the world who thinks they know the right way to do things. Sometimes you can't prove whether you're right or wrong. Only time can tell that. But if you believe in your own power to objectively reason, that's a key to happiness. And a key to confidence. Another key I found to happiness was to realize that I didn't have to disagree with someone and let it get all intense. If you believe in your own power to reason, you can just relax. You don't have to feel the pressure to set out and convince anyone. So don't sweat it! You have to trust your own designs, your own intuition, and your own understanding of what your invention needs to be.

• ○ •

If you could easily predict the future, inventing things would be a lot easier! Predicting the future is difficult even if you're involved with products that are guiding computers, the way we were at Apple.

When I was at Apple in the 1970s and 1980s, we would always try to look ahead and see where things were going. It was actually easy to see a year or two ahead, because we were the ones building the products and had all these contacts at other companies. But beyond that, it was tough to see. The only thing we could absolutely rely upon had to do with Moore's Law—the now-famous rule in electronics (named for Intel founder Gordon Moore) that says that every eighteen months you can pack twice the number of transistors on a chip.

That meant computers could keep getting smaller and cheaper. We saw that. But we had a hard time imagining what kinds of applications could take advantage of all this power. We didn't expect high-speed modems. We didn't expect computers to have large amounts of hard-disk storage built in. We didn't see the Internet growing out of the ARPANET and becoming accessible to everyone. Or digital cameras. We didn't see any of that. We really could only see what was right in front of us, a year or two out, max.

But there was one exception. Right around 1980, Steve and a bunch of us from Apple got to tour the Xerox Palo Alto Research Center (PARC) facility, which is one of Xerox's research and development labs.

Inside, for the first time ever, we saw real video displays—computer monitors—and they were showing something entirely new. They were showing the first graphical user interface (GUI)—an interface that lets you interact with icons and menus to control a program.

Up to this point, everything had been text-based. That's going to sound odd to all the people who don't remember it, but that's how everything worked back then. A computer user had to actually type in text commands—long, complicated ones—to make something happen.

But this experimental Xerox computer had windows popping up all over the place. And they were using this funny-looking device everyone now knows as a mouse, clicking on words and small pictures, the icons, to make things happen.

The minute I saw this interface, I knew it was the future. There wasn't a doubt in my mind. It was like a one-way door to the future—and once you went through it, you could never turn back. It was such a huge improvement in using computers. The GUI meant you could get a computer to do the same things it could normally do, but with much less physical and mental effort. It meant that nontechnical people could do some pretty powerful things with computers without having to sit there and learn how to type in long commands. Also, it let several different programs run in separate windows at the same time. That was powerful!

A few years later, Apple designed the Lisa computer, and later the Macintosh, around this concept. And Microsoft did it a couple years after that with Microsoft Windows. And now, more than twenty-five years after we saw that experimental computer in the Xerox PARC lab, all computers work like this.

It's so rare to be able to see the future like that. I can't promise it'll happen to you. But when you see it, you know it. If this ever happens to you, leap at the chance to get involved. Trust your instincts. It isn't often that the future lets you in like that.

• ○ •

It's funny. In some ways, Apple is the bane of my life. That's because I'm hounded by people all the time—it's as if my whole life is constantly being directed by Apple's worldwide fame. But there was a time in the late and mid-1990s when it looked as if

Apple was in trouble. At least that's what all the media was reporting. That was shocking to me. Like most things in the world, the perception was pushed by the mass media and people's psychology. People would read things saying Apple was in trouble and the whole situation would just feed on itself. After reading stories like that, people were afraid to buy Apple products. I mean, at the time there were a lot of people going to Apple-using companies and schools and demanding that they switch over from their Macs to the new PCs. They were worried Macs weren't going to be around anymore. I was stunned by what was happening to Apple.

During the time Apple was supposedly going under, Gil Amelio was the CEO. He realized that the answer was to tighten up, start making more accurate amounts of product according to what we were going to sell, tighten our belt and restore profitability. But there was another problem. Macs running the operating system at the time, Mac OS 7, were crashing a lot. The sense that Macs running this operating system were weak and unreliable was a widely held belief throughout the Mac community: among the users, the executives, the employees—everyone. So one of the other things Apple decided was that it was going to need a new operating system.

At the time, this was an issue that meant a whole lot to me. I felt that Apple didn't need a new operating system. I felt that the current one was great—it was invulnerable to hackers and viruses, for one thing. I ran a major network in my home, and I never even once needed a firewall. I was as aware as everyone else of the Macs crashing, but I felt that fixing the current operating system would be a far better solution than finding a whole new one. And then one night, by accident, I figured out what the problem was. It was thanks to my son Jesse, who always likes to think different and not use the mainstream products that are out there. He downloaded a web browser called iCab and was using it instead of Internet Explorer (IE). Because he was using it, I gave it a try. And I fell in love with it! That first day I used iCab instead of IE, I had no crashes. Not a single one. Hmm. That night in bed, I lay there and wondered what the heck was up. And the next day my Mac didn't crash. I went two weeks before I had to restart the system, and that was a record!

From then on I realized that for the most part I had no crashes at all, and the only thing I'd changed about my system was I'd stopped using IE. I realized that by this time, almost everyone who had a Mac was running IE. That's why there were so many crashes, in my opinion. And it turned out that the reason neither Apple nor anyone else believed me was that the error in IE causing the crashes didn't just happen when you had IE open on your screen, it could happen anytime your computer was running. So it wasn't easy for them to see that it was IE, and not the system, causing the crashes.

As soon as I figured this out, I informed Apple at every possible level. I told every Apple employee and executive I knew. But no one would listen. What's funny is, at the time I did have a few friends who said their Macs never crashed. I figured they were either babying their computers and not really using them, turning them off every night, or lying. But now I asked them what browser they were using, and all my friends who claimed their Macs never crashed said they were using Netscape, which was another browser on the market at the time. I started going online to email lists and asking people what browser they were using. And yep, everyone who didn't have crashes was using Netscape.

I could never convince Apple. This was such a big lament for me at the time. I couldn't convince anyone that it wasn't the Mac OS that was at fault.

Then one day Gil Amelio told me that Apple—in addition to avoiding excess production and inventory and keeping expenses down—was going to buy a new operating system. They were going to buy the operating system from NeXT, which was the company Steve Jobs started after he left Apple.

Gil called me and said, "Steve, I'm letting you know that we're doing a deal with NeXT for $400 million." Wow, was I stunned! I never expected that. And I knew this meant Steve Jobs was coming back, which I'd also never expected! I knew that many people at Apple felt Steve had been disloyal by leaving Apple in 1985. (Steve resigned after a power struggle with the board. They stripped Steve of most of his responsibilities and Steve quit. It's a misconception in Silicon Valley that he was fired. He quit. And that made him look disloyal.)

It turned out that Steve, who just came back as an adviser at first, was exactly what Apple needed. I mean, a company like Apple largely depends on strong passions and the commitment of its customers. Apple became very passionate when its whole success and survival was questioned. The threat to its whole existence was so extreme! But Steve was able to stand up there on a stage and talk about Apple and really restore the loyalty that people had all along. Apple needed marketing leadership and charisma to get people excited again, and that's what Steve Jobs brought when he came back.

It's funny, because the products people credit with bringing Apple back to life—the iPods and the iMacs—all of them were in the design phase back when Apple was in trouble. Their main designer, Jonathan Ives, was already working on them. But the way Steve presented those new products was amazing. He made sure the press leaks were cut down, too, so when these new products came out—the colorful iMacs and, of course, the digital music iPods—they seemed to be totally new and surprising.

To be honest, I was never all that crazy for the iMacs. I had my doubts about its one-piece design. I didn't care about its colors and I didn't think its looks were all that good. It turned out that I just wasn't the right customer for it. Boy, it turned out to be the perfect product for schools—a low-cost, one-piece Macintosh.

And then there was the iPod. Now, you have to understand that, for me, portable music has always been important. Ever since my first transistor radio, I always had music I could carry with me. I was always the one to have the first portable tape players, the first portable CD players. I was the first person I knew with a minidisc player. And during my trips to Japan, where you always see products way ahead of their time and whatever is currently available here, I saw small players that could store music on memory chips. Essentially these devices stored music on little cards with RAM, the same kinds of cards your digital camera stores photos on. I would always buy whatever cool thing I could find there.

So when the iPod came out, I was excited. It was on the expensive side—it had a little disk drive built in—but it turned out that was the way to do it. Steve was always good at that. He really is great at looking at new technologies and choosing the right ones, the ones that will succeed.

The engineer in me wants to use and test a product before judging it. I compared my first iPod to my then-favorite, with no moving parts, the Diamond Rio 500. There's something pure about having no moving parts other than electrons. But the Diamond Rio took about a thousand dollars in memory cards to store the music I wanted for a plane flight. I also compared it to my Sony MiniDisc player, which I carried on every trip. With the MiniDisc, it was cheap to record your own music. Just putting these machines side by side, I couldn't say the iPod was superior. But after using the iPod on one plane flight, something about it felt natural and intuitive. It felt so right, and I knew I'd never go back to the other players. Now I can see that the iPod has changed the world. There's no doubt about it. I think it was the first special thing to happen to music since the Sony Walkman (portable music player) came out. And the iPod had something even bigger going for it. Unlike other MP3 players that were coming out at the time, it had its own software that Apple designed (iTunes) and it treated your computer as the center of things. The computer, your main computer, is where all the music can really be stored. The iPod is really a satellite. And that turned out to be the perfect way to do things.

It was exactly the right paradigm. And wow, it makes so much sense that Apple was the one to come up with it. After all, Apple's whole history is making both the hardware and the software, with the result that the two work better together. That's why Apple computers historically worked better than IBM-compatible PCs, where any company could make the hardware and someone else would make the software. So with the iPod, Apple made iTunes the software and iPod the hardware. They work together as one. Amazing! It's only because Apple supplied both sides of the equation—the hardware and the software—that it was able to create a product as great as this.

I'm proud now. I'm especially proud not just because Apple turned around, but because it turned around in a way so in line with our early values. Those values were about excellence in product design—so excellent that people would drool over the idea of having that product. Those values were about an emotional feeling—a feeling of fun. Like the way we decided to have color on the Apple II in the early days, back when nobody thought it would happen. I'm so proud that Apple has gotten back to the important things.

•　○　•

If you're as lucky as I've been, then you'll get to live in a time when you're young just as a revolution is about to take off. Just like Henry Ford was there for the automotive industry, I was there to see and build the first personal computers.

Back in the mid-1990s when I was teaching school, I thought one time to myself, Wow, I wish I could be twelve now, look at the things I could do with what's out there now.

But then I realized I was lucky. I got to see the before, the during, and the after of some of those changes in life. I got to be one of those few people who could effect some of those changes.

Excellence came to me from not having much money, and also from having good building skills but not having done these products before.

I hope you'll be as lucky as I am. The world needs inventors—great ones. You can be one. If you love what you do and are willing to do what it takes, it's within your reach. And it'll be worth every minute you spend alone at night, thinking and thinking about what it is you want to design or build. It'll be worth it, I promise.

Glossary

adapter See expansion card.

American Radio Relay League The ARRL is the national membership association for amateur radio operators. According to the ARRL's official website, http://www.arrl.org, the U.S. started licensing amateur radio operators in 1912.

analog Before digital technology, electronic transmission was strictly analog—that is, electrical signals were created, stored, and manipulated in terms of waves and their frequency and amplitudes. TV, telephones, and radios traditionally use analog technology. That's beginning to change now. An analog signal can be represented as a series of sine waves. The term originated because the modulation of the carrier wave is analogous to the fluctuations of the human voice or other sound that is being transmitted. See **sine wave**.

AND gate See **logic gate**.

assembler A program that converts basic computer instructions into a pattern of 0s and 1s that a computer processor can understand. The result is often called "assembler" or "assembly" language.

assembler language In a computer's assembler language, a language statement generally corresponds to a single instruction. In higher-level languages, like C or Pascal, a language statement can result in multiple instructions. See **assembler**.

atom The smallest particle that can combine with other atoms to form physical elements.

BASIC A simple and popular computer programming language. Originally designed by IBM engineers John Kemeny and Thomas Kurtz in 1963,

BASIC is well known for being easy to learn and widely available for most types of computers.

bit Short for binary digit, this is the smallest unit of data in a computer. It carries a single value, 0 or 1. Eight bits equals a byte. Thirty-two bits is called a "word." See byte.

board See motherboard.

Boolean algebra See also logic gate. The term "Boolean" is used to describe a type of logic pioneered by early nineteenth-century English mathematician George Boole. It is used to describe a common type of searching on websites where the terms "and" or "or" are used to narrow or expand results. For example, you might search for all websites containing the words Steve AND Wozniak, or choose to search for websites that have either the words Steve OR Wozniak, which would broaden your results considerably. In Boolean algebra, AND and OR are called "operators."

Electromagnetically, Boolean algebra can be used to describe whether circuit states or memory locations are 1 (On, Charged, or True) or 0 (Off, Not Charged, or False). Engineers can design computers that use an AND gate and an OR gate operation to obtain a result that can be used for the next step in a computational task. To do this, an engineer would have to understand the following basic Boolean algebraic rules:

$$0 \text{ AND } 0 = 0 \quad 1 \text{ AND } 0 = 0 \quad 1 \text{ AND } 1 = 1$$
$$0 \text{ OR } 0 = 0 \quad 0 \text{ OR } 1 = 1 \quad 1 \text{ OR } 1 = 1$$

bus The transmission path of signals in a computer or on a network. Every device connected to the computer along this path, or bus, can potentially receive or generate signals. Devices connected to the computer via expansion slots communicate with the computer via a special expansion bus.

byte A unit of data equal to eight bits. Usually represented in multiples rounded off from the powers of two. For instance, a megabyte (a million bytes) is actually worth 2 to the twentieth power—1,048,576. According to most accounts, IBM engineer Dr. Werner Buchholz invented the term in 1956. See bit.

character A printable on-screen symbol that typically depicts text, a numeral, or a punctuation mark. In computers, there are a limited number of symbols you can use as a character. The reigning standard is called the "ASCII set" (pronounced ASK-KEE), from the American Standards Committee.

chip Short for microchip, this term refers to the amazingly complex and tiny modules that contain logic circuitry that perform functions or act as memory for a computer. Most typically, a chip is manufactured from a silicon wafer and then etched with circuits and other devices in a clean, controlled environment. Chips are sometimes also referred to as "ICs," or integrated circuits.

chip set A group of integrated circuits (microchips) that can be combined to perform a single function. They are usually sold in a unit—that is, a set.

compiler A special program that takes statements written in a certain computer language and translates them into machine language that a computer processor can understand.

CPU Short for central processing unit, this is the chip or, previously, the set of chips that contained all the logic circuitry in a computer responsible for running computer program instructions. These days, it is more common to call a CPU a "processor" or a "microprocessor."

current Measured in amperes (amps, or A), current is the flow of electrons or other electrical charge carriers. It can either be direct (DC), flowing in the same direction at all points in time, or alternating (AC). The number of AC signals, in which the flow of electrons changes frequency periodically, is measured in cycles per second (hertz) and is called its frequency. See **frequency**.

debug The process of locating and fixing (or bypassing) bugs and other errors in computer program code or on a computer hardware device. The term "debugging" refers to a procedure that begins with naming a problem, isolating its source, and fixing the problem at its source. This is a necessary procedure in the building and design of any computer software or hardware program.

digital A term describing electronics that creates, stores, and manipulates data as defined in only one of two possible states—1 or 0 (On or Off). Each one of these state digits is called a "bit," and a string of eight bits together is called a "byte." See **bit; byte**.

diode An electronic device that restricts current flow to one direction only.

diskette A removable storage medium for personal computers. Until the early 1990s, most personal computers used a "floppy" format, 5.25-inch flexible magnetic disks set inside plastic envelopes. Most personal computers these days use a smaller, rigid 3.5-inch diskette format.

DRAM Dynamic random-access memory (DRAM) is today the most common kind of memory chip available for computers. The term "random access" refers to a CPU's ability to rapidly find data (in the form of 1s and 0s) stored on computer memory chips—and do so directly. Before DRAM, CPUs had to access the data in memory sequentially, by starting at the beginning of the stored data and proceeding forward. The term "dynamic" means the memory chip does not have to be continually refreshed electrically to retain its information.

dynamic random-access memory See DRAM.

EEPROM Short for electrically erasable programmable read-only memory, this is a type of read-only memory that can be erased and reprogrammed with new data for a limited number of uses, typically by applying high electrical voltage to the chip. See **EPROM**; **PROM**.

electron A negatively charged subatomic particle. In electrical conductors, electronic current is the result of moving electrons from atom to atom—that is, from negative to positive poles. In semiconductor materials, current also results from moving electrons.

electronic gate See logic gate.

ENIAC The Electronic Numerical Integrator And Computer was one of the first true computers in the world. The U.S. Army completed it in 1946—its purpose was to calculate ballistic firing tables for the Ballistics Research Laboratory. The ENIAC (pronounced EENIE-ACK) was built at the University of Pennsylvania by researchers J. Presper Eckert and John William Mauchly.

EPROM Short for erasable programmable read-only memory, this is a type of programmable read-only memory chip with contents that can be erased and reused. Old data is erased if it is exposed to an especially intense ultraviolet light. See **EEPROM**; **PROM**.

expansion card Also simply called a "card," "board," or "adapter," these circuit boards typically bring increased functionality to a computer. A user plugs an expansion card into one of the computer's expansion slots, effectively adding circuitry to the computer. See **motherboard**; **slot**.

expansion slot Also called a "slot," this is a connector that allows the addition of expansion boards (or cards), circuit boards that bring more capability to a computer. For instance, a user might plug in an expansion card to add a high-end data plotter or scanner to a computer. These days, all desktop computers come with expansion slots that allow you to increase functionality in this way.

floppy See diskette.

FORTRAN Short for FORmula TRANslation, this computer language was designed especially for use by mathematicians, engineers, and scientists. These days, such scientific users typically instead use the C programming language.

frequency Measured in hertz (Hz), frequency is the number of complete cycles per second. For instance, a current measured at 60 cycles per second would be rendered 60 Hz. Megahertz (MHz) and gigahertz (GHz) represent millions and billions of cycles per second, respectively.

gigabyte A gigabyte is an amount of computer data roughly equal to a billion bytes—that is, 2 to the thirtieth power, or 1,073,741,824. See bit; byte; kilobyte.

hard disk drive Also referred to as "hard drive," "disk drive," and "hard disk," this refers to a permanent storage device used by computers. These days, computers can store billions of bytes (gigabytes) of data on their built-in hard disks. If you could see one inside, a hard disk is actually like a mini stack of disks, not unlike the music albums that preceded CDs. They have concentric tracks on their disks, with stored data located throughout the track. The drive typically has two heads, one on each side of each disk, reading data from or writing data to a disk. If you are saving a letter you wrote on a word processor, you are saving it to a hard disk.

hertz A unit of frequency equal to a cycle per second. Named for the German physicist Heinrich Hertz.

hexadecimal A Base 16 system commonly used by today's digital computers, which work with binary digits (1 and 0) and bytes (eight 1s and 0s, or bits) of information at a time. Two hexadecimal digits can represent a byte, as follows:

Binary	Decimal	Hexadecimal	Binary	Decimal	Hexadecimal
0	0	0	1001	9	9
1	1	1	1010	10	A
10	2	2	1011	11	B
11	3	3	1100	12	C
100	4	4	1101	13	D
101	5	5	1110	14	E
110	6	6	1111	15	F
111	7	7	10000	16	10
1000	8	8	10001	17	11

infinite loop Often also called an "endless loop," this is a piece of coding that accidentally or by design repeats indefinitely.

instruction This is a key term in computer technology. It is an order created by a computer program delivered to a computer processor. Each instruction, at its most basic level, is just an order for the computer to do something (like "add" or "subtract") with the 1s and 0s that make up computer data. See **assembler language; register.**

interrupt This refers to a signal that comes from a device attached to a computer—or from a program running on that computer—that causes the CPU system software to stop and pay attention to what should be done next. Almost all computers today use interrupts. That is, they run whatever program they're running instruction by instruction until they are "interrupted" by a device or another program. For instance, if you hit the G key while a program is running, the system will pause, notice that the keyboard has interrupted it, and run the program that will display "G" on-screen.

kilobyte A unit of computer storage equal to approximately 1,000 bytes of data—more precisely, 2 to the tenth power, or 1,024 bytes.

logic gate A single computer circuit that has several points of input but only one point of output. It is an elementary building block of a circuit. Most logic gates have two inputs and one output.

At any given moment, every terminal is in one of the two conditions—low (0) or high (1)—defined by the voltage level. The state, 0 or 1, changes often as data is processed. For example, the AND gate is called that because if 0 is false and 1 is true, the gate acts the same way as the standard AND operator in Boolean algebra.

With an OR gate, the output is true (or 1) if either or both of the inputs are true (or 1). If both inputs are false (0), then the output is false (0).

The XOR (exclusive-OR) gate acts in the same way as the logical "either/or." The output is "true" if either, but not both, of the inputs is "true." The output is "false" if both inputs are "false" or if both inputs are "true."

A logical inverter, sometimes called a NOT gate to differentiate it from other types of electronic inverter devices, has only one input. It reverses the logic state.

The NAND gate operates as an AND gate followed by a NOT gate. It acts in the manner of the logical operation "and" followed by negation. The output is "false" if both inputs are "true." Otherwise, the output is "true."

The NOR gate is a combination OR gate followed by an inverter. Its output is "true" if both inputs are "false." Otherwise, the output is "false."

The XNOR (exclusive-NOR) gate is a combination XOR gate followed by an inverter. Its output is "true" if the inputs are the same, and "false" if the inputs are different.

Using combinations of logic gates, complex operations can be performed. In theory, there is no limit to the number of gates that can be arrayed in a single device. But in practice, there is a limit to the number of gates that can be packed into a given physical space. Arrays of logic gates are found in digital integrated circuits (ICs). As IC technology improves, the physical space it takes up becomes smaller and smaller. That means faster chips in smaller packages—and increasing computer power at decreasing prices. See **Moore's Law**.

machine code The basic-level language that a computer can understand, this refers to a stream of binary digits—0s and 1s—or bits. See **bit**; **byte**.

memory The electronic holding place for instructions and data that your computer needs to reach quickly. Typically referred to as "RAM" (short for random-access memory), memory is typically located on a set of microchips located physically close to the computer processor. When you turn a computer off, all information held in RAM disappears.

Moore's Law Intel founder Gordon Moore in 1964 made the following now-famous observation: that due to improvements in manufacturing, every eighteen months engineers would be able to double the number of transistors on a chip. Moore's Law has held true to this day.

motherboard The physical layout inside a computer that contains its basic circuitry and components. The motherboard most typically contains the CPU, the main system memory, the basic input/output system (BIOS), a group of expansion slots, and additional interconnection circuitry. Also sometimes referred to as the "main board" and the "system board."

NOR gate See **logic gate**.

OR gate See **logic gate**.

oscilloscope A laboratory instrument commonly used to display and analyze the waveform of electronic signals. On a screen, the device draws a graph of voltage over time.

processor The logic circuitry in a computer that responds to a computer instruction. Generally people use the term "processor" to refer to a computer's central processing unit (CPU). Another common term for the CPU is "microprocessor." See **CPU**.

PROM Short for programmable read-only memory, this is a type of computer chip with data that can only be changed with a special machine. Such a machine, often called a "PROM programmer," actually blows a fuse on the chip—hence the term "burning a PROM." See **EEPROM**; **EPROM**.

RAM Short for random-access memory, this is the type of memory chip a computer uses for short-term storage and calculation. This kind of "memory" is not to be confused with the permanent storage a hard disk or CD-ROM drive provides. RAM chips lose their contents whenever you power down the computer. See **memory**.

register In a computer processor, a register is a holding place for any kind of data, including a storage address, individual characters, or a computer instruction. For example, a computer instruction might command that the contents of two registers be added together. A register is typically large enough to hold a 32-bit instruction, though there are smaller registers, such as half-registers, in some computer designs.

resistance Denoted by the representation R, this is the opposition a given substance offers to the flow of current. Measured in ohms.

resistor An electronic component that controls the flow of current in a circuit by resisting, or turning away, electricity. Typically, resistors are mounted on a printed circuit board or built into a chip.

ROM Built into every computer, ROM, short for read-only memory, is computer memory that contains data that can only be read. It is designed to store data permanently, and not be erased or modified by a user. A ROM chip contains the program that allows a computer to be restarted and still remember its basic settings every time. Unlike the computer's RAM (random-access memory), the data on this chip stays intact even when you turn the power to the machine off. The ROM is typically powered by a small long-life battery. See **EEPROM**; **EPROM**; **PROM**; **RAM**.

signal Most simply, this is an electric current or field used to carry data from one place to another. A direct current (DC) signal that can be switched on and off is a simple form of carrying information—it's how the early telegraph signals worked. A more complicated signal consists of an alternating current (AC) to carry more than one stream of data at a time.

sine wave The most familiar alternative-current waveform, varying with time. A waveform is a pictorial representation of how alternating current (AC) varies over time.

slot See expansion slot.

storage Refers to the place in a computer where data is held in electro-magnetic or optical form for access by a computer processor. The term "primary storage" generally refers to the place in memory where data is held; the term "secondary storage" generally refers to permanent data holding on hard disks, tapes, and other storage media.

transistor A tiny device for regulating electronic signals. Invented by three scientists at Bell Laboratories in 1947, this was a key invention that enabled computers and computerized devices. Before transistors, vacuum tubes were in use—but they quickly became obsolete after the transistor was widely available for the purpose of regulating current (voltage). Transistors act as incredibly tiny and effective switches for electronic signals. See **vacuum tube**.

transistor circuit See **transistor**.

vacuum tube Also known as an "electron tube," a vacuum tube was once commonly used to amplify electronic signals. It is now mostly obsolete, having been replaced in electronics by the transistor. See **transistor**.

Acknowledgments

First, I must thank my parents for helping me find my own values and for assisting my education.

This book could not have happened without believers in the publishing industry. John Brockman did a splendid job in finding our publisher, W. W. Norton. We lucked out to get the legendary nonfiction editor Angela von der Lippe on this book. Her true interest was part of what I needed to get this project done. Countless others had important roles as well.

More thanks than I can ever give should go to Gina Smith, who had the drive to create this book and who met with me on countless occasions to put it all together. Just having a schedule and a purpose and prodding made all the difference. We would get together and speak stories into recorders, and go over and over the paragraphs to get the right sound. Thanks also to Michele Earl for a lucky and unusual encounter that led to my meeting Gina.

I have to thank those responsible for my successes in life. To Miss Skrak for seeing so much in me. To Mr. McCollum for finding so much valuable education beyond the school he worked for. To Steve Jobs for wanting to do Great and Big things. To Randy Wiggington, Chris Espinoza, Dan Sokol, Bill Fernandez, and the Homebrew Computer Club members for the whole appreciation of a computer for people. To all my HP friends, including Stan Mintz and Peter Dickinson, for a great environment in which an engineer could develop. Most of all, thanks to Allen Baum, who was involved in some way in so many of the big steps in my computer life. And for his parents who appreciated jokes and humor and had such good values in life. My memory of them still brings tears.

I must thank my first wife, Alice, without whom Apple would never have happened for me; Candi, my second wife, for the most wonderful creations of Jesse, Sara, and Gary; and my third wife, Suzanne, for Hard Rock Cafes and bungee jumping and for being so wonderful and decent.

Friends who made this possible for me, digging up needed photos and reminding me of stories, included Laura and Dan and Alex. Sharon was the most loyal in all cases, always looking out for me and making sure needed things got done.

● ○ ●

Gina thanks her friend Michele Earl for introducing her to Steve at a rock concert. Within a week of our meeting, the *iWoz* book proposal was in to our phenomenal agent, John Brockman.

Gina thanks the exceptional team at Norton, including editor Angela von der Lippe, her assistant, Lydia Fitzpatrick, and all the others who helped along the way. Thanks also to Keith Blate and David Street, Steve Wozniak fans and editors who spent much time reading the earliest drafts of this book.

Gina also wants to thank her wildly supportive family and friends, without whom this book could not have been completed: Tops on the list are her ever-patient husband, Henry, and their small son, Eric. Special thanks go to her beautiful and intrepid late mother, Emilia Sladjana Djuran Ferguson, for teaching her that, in America, it always pays not to be afraid to talk to the big shots! And to her father, David A. Malby of Riverdale, New York, Gina owes the highest thanks for his support, reading and writing suggestions, and encouragement through the years. Thanks also to Gina's half-sister, Isabella, her husband, Roger, and Gina's much-loved nieces, Victoria and Alexandra. Thanks also to Maria Lopez and Gina's in-laws Lisa and Henry Schaefer for their babysitting support during this enormous project. And finally, Gina is forever grateful to those who have stood beside her the longest: Sister Laura Saucedo and Brother Keith Prewitt. Love and peace to you all.

●   ○   ●

Steve and Gina both thank the two restaurants they dominated weekly while doing fifty-six two-hour interviews. The first half of the book was completed at Pearl's, in the West Portal District of San Francisco. The second was completed at The Hick'ry Pit in Campbell, California, where we especially thank our waitress Racquel and her boss, Brian, for bending the rules for us every now and then.

●   ○   ●

Thank you, readers. We hope you enjoy Steve's adventure as much as he enjoyed telling it and Gina enjoyed hearing it!